THE JEWISH RELIGION

IN THE

SOVIET UNION

THE JEWISH RELIGION
IN THE
SOVIET UNION

By

Joshua Rothenberg

KTAV PUBLISHING HOUSE, INC. · NEW YORK

PHILIP W. LOWN GRADUATE CENTER
FOR CONTEMPORARY JEWISH STUDIES,
BRANDEIS UNIVERSITY.
WALTHAM, MASSACHUSETTS

© Copyright 1971, Philip W. Lown Graduate Center
for Contemporary Jewish Studies
Brandeis University

SBN 87068-156-7

LIBRARY OF CONGRESS CATALOG CARD NUMBER: 75-149602

MANUFACTURED IN THE UNITED STATES OF AMERICA

To the memory
of my mother, Yehudis and my wife's
parents, Yosef and Bella Ost, ז״ל *,*
who perished in the Holocaust.

The Philip W. Lown Graduate Center for
Contemporary Jewish Studies

INSTITUTE FOR EAST EUROPEAN JEWISH STUDIES
BRANDEIS UNIVERSITY

Previously Published and Announced

1. Erich Goldhagen, editor—*Ethnic Minorities in the Soviet Union*, Frederick A. Praeger, 1968.

2. Joshua Rothenberg—*An Annotated Bibliography of Writings on Judaism Published in the Soviet Union, 1960–1965*, Brandeis University, 1969.

3. Yehoshua Gilboa—*Black Years of Soviet Jewry*, Little, Brown, 1971.

4. Elias Schulman—*A History of Jewish Education in the Soviet Union (1918–1948)*, Ktav and Brandeis University, 1971.

CONTENTS

This book is the result of a research project undertaken by the author while he was a Senior Research Associate of the Institute of East European Jewish Studies of the Philip W. Lown School of Near Eastern and Judaic Studies of Brandeis University. The book was published with the cooperation and support of the Graduate Center for Contemporary Jewish Studies at Brandeis University.

Introduction

FOR HUNDREDS OF YEARS, the Jews living in the territories now included in the Soviet Union enjoyed a national and religious semi-autonomy, organized principally within the framework of the *Kehilah* (Jewish community council). Although the Tsarist regime discriminated against the Jews, and severely restricted their rights of residence, it did not interfere too deeply in the religious and cultural affairs of the Jewish community. This situation allowed the Jewish community of Tsarist Russia to develop a meaningful Jewish life and Jewish culture in spite of discrimination and persecution.

Religion and religious concepts permeated all walks of life. Indeed, the "religious" observances were indistinguishable from the "Jewish" customs and the Jewish way of life. Jews considered themselves, and were considered by others, not only as a separate religious community but also as a different historical and national entity, although till the end of the nineteenth century the understanding of the concept of a Jewish nationality was rather vague, more felt than defined and articulated. The new political and social movements within the Jewish community, primarily Zionism and socialism, weakened the all-embracing hold of the Jewish religion and the religious establishment on Jewish life, but by no means destroyed it. Indeed, the new movements even tried to adapt the old religious institutions to their own secular purposes.

At present, the Jews are recognized in the Soviet Union as one of the many nationalities in the Union. In the Soviet census of 1959, 2,268,000 persons declared themselves to be of "Jewish nationality." Religion, on the other hand, is considered a private matter of individual concern, and inquiry about religious affiliation, even of those who are members of religious associations, is not permitted. The number of Jews by religion, as distinguished from Jews by nationality, cannot therefore be known.

1

Since all Jewish "religious believers," with negligible exceptions, are members of the Jewish nationality, and membership in the Jewish religious group is not made public, a situation is being created where any action or policy of the regime concerning either of these groups affects all Soviet Jews. An attack on "Judaists" (followers of the Jewish religious group) will be hardly distinguishable from one on "Jews." There is no way a Soviet citizen can ascertain to which group his Jewish neighbor belongs short of spying on his conduct at home or on his attendance at a synagogue.

Because there is at present a suppression of secular Jewish channels for the expression of Jewish identity in the Soviet Union, a sublimation of Jewish "national" feelings into religious channels, holidays, and symbols is apparent, as is evidenced in the participation of nonreligious Jews—among them many young Jews—in synagogue observances. In a situation where suppression of the Jewish religion is not balanced by the simultaneous existence and support of a meaningful secular Jewish culture, such suppression inevitably takes the form of a gradual destruction of the only existing form of Jewishness in the Soviet Union.

In the Soviet Union today, the "Jewish establishment" in the form of synagogues and clergy represents only a tiny part of a powerful wellspring of Jewish consciousness. In addition to the large numbers of religious, observant Jews, there are many thousands of nonobservant Jews for whom Jewish religious literature, particularly the Bible, and Jewish tradition, remain an integral part of their Jewish identity.

The intertwining of these two elements in Jewry, the religious and secular, is not only characteristic of the Soviet Union, but also of Jewish communities in other countries, particularly in Israel, where a strict separation of the religious Jewish element from the nonreligious is nearly impossible. Whether eating matzohs on Passover or lighting Hanukah candles is for a particular Jew a religious commandment or a national custom cannot be satisfactorily ascertained.

In discussing the Jewish religion in the Soviet Union one must, therefore, be constantly aware of the particular interrelationship of the various elements in Judaism, a problem with which innumerable Jewish thinkers—for example, Ahad Ha'am, Dubnow, Yehezkel Kaufman, and Mordecai Kaplan—have wrestled incessantly. In the Soviet Union, as well as in other countries, the problem emerges both in philosophical terms and in practical application.

This study was prepared in the years 1966–1968, while the author was Senior Research Associate of the Institute of East European Jewish Studies at Brandeis University. The principal emphasis of the study was focused on the period immediately preceding the time when this work began. For a proper understanding of the topics which are discussed, each chapter includes a brief historical review of pertinent problems as they have developed since the Bolsheviks seized power in November of 1917; in some cases the historical review goes back to a period before that date.

Official Soviet sources of information concerning particular religious cults, institutions, and activities are very scarce, and that information which is available is biased. It conveys the position of the regime on religious matters, however, and points out contradictions in its position. But oftentimes the Soviet press inadvertently divulges valuable information concerning a particular event or act of the authorities. In addition, wide use was made of reports by journalists and other writers who visited the Soviet Union at various times and later published their findings and impressions in the press or in books, and by written material smuggled out of the Soviet Union and later published. The lack of free access to information and to primary sources of research, which is one of the sad realities of a totalitarian regime, has in some cases forced the inquirer to qualify his findings in this generally unexplored area of study. The author considers the present text only as a contribution towards an ultimate history of the Jewish religion during the first half-century of Soviet rule.

The legal aspects of religion are discussed in greater detail, both because this is still an unexplored field and because the Soviet authorities have on the whole kept this information from most of their citizens as well as the outside world. The legal aspect of religion is of importance both for the sake of factual information and to demonstrate how these laws are continually violated by the regime which promulgated them.

Repetition which occurs in several chapters of the book is either unavoidable, as topics and problems are often intertwined, or intentional in order that the reader who is interested only in a particular chapter of this treatise will not have to seek out additional information in other parts of the book.

The English transliteration of Russian, Hebrew, and Yiddish words follows the rules accepted by the Library of Congress with some exceptions in words in which a different transliteration has been widely accepted, such as Simchas (instead of Simkhas) Torah, Yevrei (instead of Evrei), and so on. Yiddish words of Hebrew origin, including the names of Jewish holidays and rites, are transliterated according to the pronunciation used by Jews in the Soviet Union, i.e., the Ashkenazic pronunciation.

I wish to express my thanks to those who, in one way or another, helped publish this work: To Professor Erich Goldhagen, former Director of the Institute of East European Jewish Studies of the Philip W. Lown Graduate Center of Contemporary Jewish Studies, Brandeis University, who conceived the idea of this research project; to Dean Leon A. Jick, Director of the Philip W. Lown Graduate Center, without whose efforts this book would not have been published; to Professor Andrew Blane of Lehman College and Dr. William Korey, Director of B'nai B'rith International Council, for their valuable suggestions and observations on several chapters of this volume; to Professor Emanuel Goldsmith of Brandeis University for his useful suggestions and remarks; to Mrs. Anne Falkof and Mrs. Annette Slocombe who spent many hours typing up the manuscript; and to all those who contributed information, made suggestions and encouraged the author in the completion of his work.

CHAPTER 1

The Laws on Religion[*]

According to Marxian theory, a legal system is simply an expression of the class structure of a given historical period in a given country; it serves the needs of the ruling class of the moment. Accordingly, the legal system of the Soviet Union was tailored to the needs of the proletariat—the ruling class. It follows that all legislation in the area of religion, cults, and religious observance was also intended to meet the needs of the regime and the new society it was building.

Almost every Soviet handbook dealing with antireligious work is divided into three parts, in the following order: 1) excerpts from the writings of Marx, Engels, and Lenin (as well as those of the current leader); 2) pronouncements and resolutions of the Communist Party on religious matters; and 3) relevant governmental legislation.

Understandably the writings of the theoreticians of communism serve as the ideological basis for both the Party and the government. In religion, as in literature and other areas, Marxian theory as such tends to be modified by the local Russian experience and interpretation. These differences notwithstanding, the normative influence of the theoreticians on legislation has been very great indeed, and for a full understanding of the legal framework one must be familiar with their work.[1]

As soon as the Bolsheviks seized power in 1917, they began to implement their policies pertaining to religion. This was done through the dual agencies of power, the Communist Party and the Soviet government. It is virtually impossible to give a brief and accurate characterization of the relationship between the two; formally only

---

[*] This chapter is, with revisions and additions, excerpted from my essay "The Legal Status of Religion," in the anthology *Aspects of Religion in the Soviet Union: 1917–1967* (University of Chicago Press, 1970). Several case studies not included in the original essay were added to this chapter.

government legislation has legal validity, although Party pronouncements usually formulate general policy and indicate the nature of the
legislation to be enacted. Practically speaking there is little contradiction between the two and both are binding at all levels.

The first official act of the Soviet government touching religion
was the "Declaration of the Rights of the Peoples of Russia" *(Dek-
laratsiia Prav Narodov Rossii)* of November 2, 1917,[2] abolishing all
national-religious privileges and restrictions. The declaration was
aimed mainly at the Russian Orthodox Church, which had been the
state church of the Russian Empire. It abolished the preeminent
position occupied by the Orthodox Church and equalized the legal
status of all religious cults in the Soviet Union.

Towards the end of 1917, several legislative acts directly concerning religion were announced. For instance, on December 11,
1917, an ordinance *(postanovlenie)* over Lenin's signature was issued
ordering all religious organizations to transfer their "schools, seminaries, academies, lower, intermediate, and higher schools and institutions of the religious bodies" to the People's Commissariat of
Education.[3] A few days earlier a decree had been issued that
nationalized all land, including that of the Church.[4] (Religious educational institutions and monastic lands were extensive.)

The *fundamental legal act* concerning religious life was issued
January 23, 1918, in the form of a Decree of the Council of People's
Commissars. The Decree, in its final form,[5] was entitled "On the
Separation of Church from State and School from Church."[6] It
granted to every citizen the right to profess any religion or no
religion. Any indication of religious affiliation or nonaffiliation in
official documents was barred (paragraph three). The teaching of
"religious dogmas" was prohibited in all state schools and in all private
educational institutions where general subjects were taught. Citizens
were free to study and teach religion only privately (paragraph nine).
The churches and other religious associations were denied the right
to own property and did not enjoy the rights of a legal entity.

This Decree of January 23, 1918, served as the guide for religious
policy for many years. The deprivation of property rights, the loss of
the status of legal entities, and the prohibition of religious instruction in schools were all carefully enforced and seriously curtailed

church activities as they had existed up to that time. Two paragraphs of the total of thirteen proved to be especially significant in later years, primarily because they permitted considerable latitude in interpretation.

Paragraph five of the Decree states that "the free performance of religious observances is guaranteed insofar as they do not disturb public order and are not accompanied by encroachments upon the rights of other citizens." This vague clause provided almost unlimited opportunity for restricting the exercise of the right to religious observances, in and outside houses of prayer.

Paragraph thirteen reads:

> All property of the church in Russia and of religious associations is declared to be the property of the people. Buildings and objects earmarked for religious observances may be given for the free use of the respective religious associations by special decision of the local or central state authorities.[7]

The state thereby became the owner not only of the buildings belonging to religious groups, but also of all objects belonging to them as well. The cults were thus in the position of having to lease their property from the state.

There were ambiguities and contradictions in the policy toward religion followed by the Party at this time. This can be explained in terms of the events of the period. The Civil War was at its height, and the anti-Bolshevik forces made good use among believers of the communist attitudes towards religion. There was considerable hostility toward the new regime on the part of large segments of the clergy and faithful of the Orthodox Church, and to a lesser degree, of the other minority religions. The regime's need for maximum popular support gave rise to a checkered pattern of stern measures and concessions; the interpretation of the decrees changed with the time and the place.

The Constitution of the RSFSR (Russian Soviet Federated Socialist Republic), adopted by the Fifth Congress of Soviets on July 10, 1918, included elements of this ambiguity. On the one hand article sixty-five-g relegated members of the clergy to the category of third-class citizens along with "capitalists, merchants, former members of the police, criminals and imbeciles." They could not hold public office, and even the right to vote was denied them. (This restriction gave rise to other limitations in the area of food rations, housing, etc.). On the other hand, article thirteen stated: "To secure true freedom of conscience for the workingman, the church is separated from the state and the school from the church, and *freedom of religious and antireligious propaganda is recognized as the right of every citizen.*" [8] (Emphasis is added.) In the "Stalin" Constitution of 1936 this formula was altered to retain the right to profess a religion, but not to propagate it.

It took seven months to prepare a detailed "Ordinance-Instruction" to carry out the Decree of January 23, 1918. On August 24, 1918, the People's Commissariat of Justice issued the "Ordinance for Carrying out the Decree on the Separation of Church from State and School from Church." [9] This Ordinance-Instruction enumerated the churches and cults that were included in the provisions of the Decree. (*Churches:* Russian Orthodox, Old-believers, Georgian, Catholic, and Protestant churches of all denominations. *Creeds:* Judaism, Mohammedanism, and Buddhism. It was also to be applied to other cults and beliefs not mentioned specifically.)

The main provisions of the Instruction were as follows: the property of all religious cults was to be turned over to the local soviets; all funds were to be confiscated; an inventory of the property was to be submitted, and the property could then be given to the worshipers for free use provided that a group of twenty *(dvadtsat)* persons would assume the responsibility for the property and its upkeep. [10] The *dvadtsatka* was charged with making all repairs and paying all expenses necessary to maintain the property. In case of "abuses and embezzlement" the property was to be returned to the local soviet.

With these detailed instructions in hand, local authorities began to implement the Decree of January 23. In many areas the disestablishment was accomplished with excessive zeal with the result that on January 3, 1919, a circular letter was issued which pointed out the "mistakes" made by many in the interpretation and application of the instruction. This "Circular on the Problem of the Separation of Church and State," from the Eighth Department of the People's Commissariat of Justice, began as follows: "Recent reports received from various places reveal that not all local officials correctly understand the tasks of the Soviet authorities concerning the separation of church and state." [11] From the admonitions of this Circular it is clear what excesses had been committed. For example, it said that a house of prayer was to be closed only if a group of twenty could not be found to assume responsibility for it, or if the local soviet, because of the need for suitable quarters for public use and "satisfying the demands of the working masses," should decide to close it. Ridicule and humiliation of clergymen should be avoided; similarly, unseemly forced labor, such as cleaning streets, was not to be administered to clergymen, since such punishments were apt to anger believers and cause them to regard the clergyman as a martyr. It was also said to be inadmissible to prohibit ministers of the cult from giving sermons on religious topics in their houses of prayer.

The program of the Communist Party adopted at the Eighth Congress in March 1919, stated, in paragraph thirteen, that the Party was not satisfied to let matters rest with the separation of church from state and school from church, measures that "even the bourgeois democracies have included in their programs, although they have not realized them." It spoke of the need for well-planned scientific antireligious propaganda, disseminated with all due regard to avoid offending the feelings of believers as this would only lead to an increase of religious fanaticism.[12] A resolution adopted at the Congress, while warning against counterrevolutionary propaganda in the guise of religious preaching, was nonetheless very explicit about restrictions of religious freedom or the use of force, saying that those who violated these precepts should be severely punished.[13]

The Tenth Party Congress (March 1921) charged the Committee for Political Education *(Glavpolitprosvet)* of the Commissariat of Education with organizing and conducting antireligious propaganda on a massive scale.[14] The Central Committee of the Party subsequently issued an Ordinance, "On the organization of antireligious propaganda and on the violation of paragraph thirteen of the program." [15] In addition to refusing Party membership to anyone fulfilling any religious function, it called upon all Party members to participate actively in antireligious activities.

The end of the period of War Communism and the inauguration of the New Economic Policy saw a further elaboration of the element of caution. In 1922 the Party issued "Directives of the Central

Committee of the Communist Party to the Soviet and Party Organs on the Question of the Attitude toward Sects and Policy in Relation to Religious Groups in General." [16] This document stresses the need to be "especially' thoughtful in carrying out all kinds of measures that touch upon the religious views of the broad masses of the peasantry" while at the same time being careful not to neglect their scientific antireligious education. Party members were reminded that "the present period is not at all opportune for pressing the antireligious struggle."

Another Party resolution, "On propaganda, the press and agitation," concerned itself mainly with the state of antireligious work among the national minorities. [17] This resolution, passed by the Twelfth Party Congress in 1923, said that the New Economic Policy had fostered the growth of bourgeois and clerical-national sentiments among the minorities. Thus vigor was detected in such movements as Pan-Islamism, Pan-Turkism, and Zionism, as well as Catholic activity among Poles and Baptist influence on Latvians and Estonians. The resolution called upon the Communists among these minorities to organize antireligious programs aimed at them.

As the 1920s drew to a close, the regime felt that it had sufficiently consolidated its position so that it could proceed to the implementation of new programs. The five-year plans were designed to achieve a purely socialist economy. In the area of religion, too, the often hesitant and ambiguous policies of the 1920s were replaced by more forceful and aggressive measures. Likewise, the increased importance accorded to matters of religion and religious cults was emphasized by the establishment, on April 8, 1929, of a Standing Committee on Affairs of Cult, attached to the Presidium of the All-Union Central Executive Committee (headed by Smidovich).

This adjustment of religious policy was mainly enunciated by two documents. They were the "Law on Religious Associations" *(O Religioznykh Obedineniiakh)* of April 8, 1929, [18] and the "Instructions of the People's Commissariat of the Interior" of October 1, 1929, entitled "On the Rights and Obligations of Religious Associations" *(O Pravakh i Obiazannostiiyakh Religioznykh Obedinenii),* which clarifies and supplements the April law. [19]

The two documents which had regulated religious life in the country prior to 1929 (the Decree of January 23, 1918, and the Ordinance-

Instruction issued later that same year) had not provided for many aspects of religious activity, which left some area in which believers could maneuver. It was decided that the new directives had to be more inclusive and more detailed. The two acts of 1929 are still in force and still define most of the rights and duties of Soviet citizens in religious matters; they still define the status, rights, and responsibilities of recognized religious cults and religious organizations. Consequently, it is necessary to discuss these measures in some detail.

According to the provisions of these enactments, citizens have the right to form and to belong to two kinds of religious organizations. Members of a cult, denomination, sect, or doctrine who are eighteen years .of age and over may form *religious societies* or *groups of believers.*

Registration: A religious society or a group of believers must submit an application for registration and a list of its founders. Within one month the registration agencies must register the group or inform the petitioners of the denial of registration.

Collections and expenditures of funds: Members of a religious society or group may collect voluntary donations in the prayer building. Voluntary donations may take place outside the prayer building only among persons who are members of the given religious association (unless special permission has been granted). Religious associations may not establish compulsory membership fees or introduce membership cards. The funds collected may be spent only in connection with the maintenance of religious property, the performance of religious rites, the remuneration of clergymen, singers, and watchmen, and the activities of executive bodies of religious societies or groups. Any kind of religious property, whether donated or purchased from voluntary donations, shall be included in the inventory of religious property and be placed on record with the civil authorities; it thus becomes state property and a part of the existing lease agreement.

Executive Bodies: These bodies are elected by open ballot at general assemblies of the members. A religious society elects an executive body of three members, a group of believers elects one representative. The registration agencies have the right to remove individual members from the executive bodies. Religious conferences and conventions may elect their own executive bodies for the execution of their decisions. All transactions concerning the management and use of religious property must be made exclusively by the individual members of the executive bodies, and not by the executive body itself since the executive bodies do not enjoy the rights of legal entities. They may not acquire property by purchase, or rent premises for prayer meetings, or conclude any kind of contracts or transactions.

Meetings and Conventions: Prayer meetings in prayer buildings or in buildings especially adapted for this purpose and considered satisfactory as to technical and sanitary conditions, may be arranged without notification or permission of the authorities. Prayer meetings in premises which are not especially adapted for this purpose (e.g., private homes or apartments) may be arranged, but permission for each separate meeting must be obtained; a religious society or group may notify the authorities in advance of a series of prayer meetings to be held within a period of no more than one year. *Believers who have not formed a society or group must notify authorities regarding each prayer meeting separately* (paragraph twenty-two of the Instruction). An application must be filed and written permission obtained for general assemblies of religious societies or groups.

Processions and ceremonies: Religious rites and ceremonies or the display of objects of a cult in public institutions and enterprises is prohibited, with the exception of religious rites for dangerously ill persons in isolated rooms of hospitals and the performance of religious rites and ceremonies in cemeteries and crematoria. Any kind of religious ceremony may be performed *within the family home or apartment without the permission or notification of the authorities.* Permission is not required for religious processions around the prayer building if they are an integral part of the religious service. Permission is not required for religious services connected with a funeral.

Reporting: A list of the executive bodies and auditing committees shall be submitted to the registration agencies within seven days of the request to organize a group or society, together with data on the clergy, preachers, etc. A religious society must submit a list of all its members according to an established form.

Surveillance: The activities of the religious societies and groups are subject to the surveillance of the committees for religious matters. These committees, as well as other authorities "whose duty it is to safeguard the revolutionary order and safety," may send their representatives to each assembly or meeting of a religious society or group for the purpose of "watching over order and safety." Routine inspections of religious societies or groups may be performed at any time by the committees for religious matters.

Liquidation: A religious society or group may be liquidated by a decision of the general assembly of the society or group. In the event of the disclosure of deviations from the rules established for the association, the registration agency shall demand the correction of the defects. If the religious society or group refuses to correct the defects or if it violates the laws under which it operates, the city or district committee for religious matters may ask the Committee for Religious Affairs of the Council of Ministers to liquidate the society or group. A decision to liquidate a society or group may be appealed before the Council of Ministers within two weeks from the date of the delivery of the decision. The liquidation is suspended until the decision on the appeal is handed down. The contract of lease of religious property may be annulled by a decision of the committee for religious affairs of the Council of Ministers at the request of the respective city or district committee. The contract may be annulled if the religious society or group has not observed the orders of the authorities (on reregistration, renovations, etc.), as well as when the prayer building is needed for state or public use. (Paragraph sixty-four of the Instruction.)

Certain additional comments must be made and conclusions drawn in this discussion of the two legislative acts of 1929. Religious societies are those associations that number "not less than twenty members." Religious groups or groups of believers are those that number less than twenty. (As noted, the group of twenty or *dvadtsatka* is widely recognized as the basic unit of organized religious life in the Soviet Union.)

It is clear that the Law made provision for two types of registered religious organizations. However, there is ample evidence to demonstrate that the right to establish a group of believers has seldom been granted, and the provision which makes it possible is currently a dead letter. In a "Summary of Information Relating to the USSR" submitted to the United Nations by the Soviet government, the portion dealing with conditions under which religious associations may be formed says nothing about groups of less than twenty members.[20]

It is reasonable to assume that two other provisions of the Instruction are either not widely known or believers are not allowed to take advantage of them. Paragraph twenty-two states that "believers who have not formed a society or group must notify authorities regarding each separate prayer meeting." This implies *the right of a nonregistered group to exist and to hold religious services.* Paragraph thirty-four permits "the performance of religious ceremonies, such as prayers, requiem masses, baptisms, the bringing in of icons and the like" in the home or apartment of believers *without the permission* or notification of the authorities. There are no specific restrictions as to the number of persons allowed to participate in such rites. Despite this provision, prayer meetings in homes have been subject to disciplinary action and are usually held clandestinely for this reason.[21]

Although the Law emphasizes that religious societies do not enjoy the rights of legal entities, some of its provisions seem to contradict this. For example, prayer houses and objects of the cult are obtained under contract not by individuals but by the whole group. This contractual capacity would seem to endow the group with quasi-legal status. (Admittedly, all other legal acts are executed by the individual members of the executive bodies.)

Cases that have come before Soviet courts illustrate the problems involved in these matters. As an example, the case of *Yarolan v. the Iranian Jewish Synagogue* may be cited. On January 15, 1938, the People's Court of the Kirov District in Tbilisi found against the Iranian Jewish Synagogue and awarded the plaintiff, Sarkis Yarolan, three hundred rubles for injuries sustained while making *matzohs,* as well as eighty rubles a month until he attained his majority. The president of the Supreme Court of the USSR found that the case had to be thrown out because the synagogue, as a religious association, had no rights as a juridical person under the laws in force and could not therefore be a defendant. He directed that in rehearing the case specific individuals, members of the executive organ of the given religious association, had to be brought as defendants.[22]

The Law and Instruction of 1929 are so phrased as to enable the authorities to curtail or halt the activities of a religious association which are normally permitted whenever they deem it expedient. To begin with, it must be noted that in the Soviet Union the judiciary has often been directly or indirectly, in varying degrees, subordinated to the agencies of the Party and the state. At several points the country has experienced almost complete disruption of legal procedure. The atmosphere of uncertainty about law in general which this has engendered has frequently led to wide divergencies in the interpretation of statutes and, occasionally, to their being completely disregarded.

The closing of prayer houses when the local authorities deem it necessary to put the building in question to other use, pursuant to the needs of the state, has often been employed. The law grants the religious association the right to lease or build a new building, but this, too, is dependent upon the selfsame discretion of the authorities. Many buildings have been condemned as unsafe and the Law states (paragraph forty-nine) "that the decision of the technical committee stated in the examination document is binding and subject to execution." No appeal is possible in such a case. In the event of a fire which renders a prayer house unusable, it is up to the authorities to decide whether to use the insurance payments for the restoration of the building or for the "social and cultural needs of the community."

Any member of a *dvadtsatka* (in Soviet parlance, a "religious activist") can withdraw from the association at any time. Since such a withdrawal always leaves the number of responsible members at less than twenty, the contract or lease can be annulled. If new members volunteer to replace those who have withdrawn, registration must be accomplished all over again and a new contract drawn. If the authorities are determined to harass the members of the *dvadtsatka* they have several means of doing so at their disposal: Job placement and advancement, assignment of living quarters, educational facilities available to the members, children, and so forth are but a few of these. In addition, other provisions of the Law may be invoked, such as paragraph twenty-nine-d, which imposes on the signing members the responsibility for compensating the state for any damage done to the religious property occupied. The threat of exorbitant indemnities for real or imagined damage has been effective in obtaining the withdrawal of members of the twenty.

Finally, paragraph fourteen of the Law and paragraph thirteen of the Instruction give the authorities the right to remove individual members from the executive board of an association.

In August 1929, the Council of People's Commissars of the USSR ordered the introduction of the continuous work week (the day of rest falling on various days of the week). Ostensibly, the change was to result in more efficient production. However, the All-Union Trade Union Council exposed another view, in voicing the hope that "this measure will inevitably lead to fundamental changes in the old tradition of life . . . and facilitate a more successful struggle against religion and other survivals of the old way of life." [23] The observance of the religious day of rest and of religious holidays was made even more difficult by the Decree of November 15, 1932, by which one day's unauthorized absence from work *(progul)* could be punishable by the deprivation of the right to ration cards and to the use of housing facilities of the enterprise concerned. [24]

The famous resolution of the Sixteenth Party Congress (1930), in section six, contained some important lines pertaining to "some completely inadmissable distortions of the Party line in the sphere of the struggle against religious prejudices." Foremost among these distortions was the "administrative closing of churches without the acquiescence of the overwhelming majority of the villagers, which usually leads to the strengthening of religious prejudices." Section seven prescribed the abandonment of such practices, "fictitiously disguised as the public and voluntary wish of the population." Henceforth the decisions of village meetings concerning the closing of churches was to be confirmed by the regional Executive Committee of Soviets. [25]

The Constitution of the Russian Republic (RSFSR) had contained the provision (article four) on the separation of church from state and school from church. It stated that "freedom of religious and antireligious propaganda is recognized for all citizens." [26] Similar provisions had been included in the constitutions of the other republics. The Fourteenth Congress of Soviets (May 1929) amended this provision. The wording "freedom of religious and antireligious propaganda is recognized for all citizens" was changed to "freedom of religious worship and freedom of antireligious propaganda are recognized for all citizens." The new text was later included in the "Stalin Constitution" of 1936, in article 124. [27] The use of the word "freedom" both for religious and antireligious activities was meant to create the impression that the state is "neutral" in the question of religion. Of course, this was not the case, as freedom of antireligious propaganda was sanctioned and religious propaganda had been made illegal. The proposition that atheists are granted the right to conduct antireligious propaganda while depriving believers of the same right is the fundamental fact of the condition of religious associations in the Soviet Union. On the other hand, a reprieve was granted to the clergy in one area. Article 135 of the new Constitution granted the right to vote and to be elected to all citizens of the Soviet Union, including members of the clergy. It thus disposed of the category of *lishentsy* (citizens deprived of rights) that had been established by the Constitution which was adopted by the Fifth Congress of the Soviets on July 10, 1918.

The outbreak of Soviet-German hostilities in June 1941 substantially altered the situation of all religious organizations. The Russian Orthodox Church achieved something of a preeminent position among the churches, reminiscent of its prerevolutionary status. However, these altered circumstances were in no way reflected in new or altered legislation. The Journal of the Moscow Patriarchate published the particulars of the concessions granted the Orthodox Church, but the only official government announcement of any change was that of the decision to establish a separate Council for the Affairs of the Russian Orthodox Church under the Council of Ministers. A similar announcement was made later concerning the establishment of a separate Council for all other religious cults. The government did not admit that the Orthodox Church was receiving preferential treatment; indeed, it stated emphatically that "the creation of the Council for the Affairs of the Russian Orthodox Church bears testimony to the equality of all religions in the Union of Soviet Socialist Republics." [28]

The duties and responsibilities of the two Councils were outlined as follows:

> The Council for the Affairs of Religious Cults and the Council for the Affairs of the Russian Orthodox Church shall be responsible for liaison between the government of the USSR and the leaders of religious associations (of the corresponding cults) on questions affecting those cults and requiring action by the government of the USSR.
>
> The Council for the Affairs of Religious Cults and the Council for the Affairs of the Russian Orthodox Church shall:

a) carry out the preliminary examination of questions raised by ecclesiastical boards or leaders of religious communities (cults) requiring action by the government of the USSR;

b) draft laws and regulations on questions relating to religious cults, instructions and directives, and submit them to the government of the USSR for considerat⋅ ᴜ;

c) supervise the application in correct form and in due time throughout the territories of the USSR, of government laws and regulations relating to religious cults;

d) submit conclusions on questions relating to religious cults to the government of the USSR;

e) provide for the general registration of churches and houses of worship.

Representatives of the Council for the Affairs of Religious Cults and the Council for the Affairs of the Russian Orthodox Church of the Council of Ministers of the USSR shall be attached to the Council of Ministers of the Union and Autonomous Republics and the Regional Executive Committees.[29]

Wartime conditions, coupled with the aforementioned changes in governmental policies, resulted in a marked increase in religious observance during this period. Apparently the extent of this revival was both unexpected and a matter of some concern to the authorities. As early as 1944, the Party felt constrained to reiterate its fundamental attitude toward religion and to call for the renewal and strengthening of "antireligious work through all means of scientific enlightenment, by asking all media of communication—the spoken word, printed materials, the radio, and films." [30]

Several other official pronouncements of the early postwar period also seem to stem in part from the Party's concern at the extent of religious observance thirty years after the Revolution. On July 7, 1954, the Party issued an important ordinance on the subject entitled "On the Great Deficiencies in Scientific-Atheistic Propaganda and the Means of Improving It." [31] Decrying the widespread neglect of an exceedingly important area of ideological work, the Ordinance told how religious organizations had "increased their activities and adroitly adjusted to contemporary conditions." Specific measures to be taken were outlined and the government agencies obliged to take concrete action were indicated, among them the Ministry of Culture; the ministry was to organize lectures and courses of instruction in atheism in all schools and institutions of higher education (another example of the administrative powers of the Party). Indeed, all courses were to be "saturated with atheistic content."

As in previous campaigns the initial document was followed in a few months' time by another, correcting "misinterpretations" of the first. On November 10, 1954, the Central Committee issued another ordinance: "On the Mistakes in the Conduct of Scientific-Atheistic Propaganda Among the Population."[32]

It is clear that Party concern over the extent of "religious survivals" throughout the fifties and sixties stemmed largely from its surprise at the way in which religion sprang back during the war. As late as 1964, L. Ilichev asserted in his article "The Formation of a Scientific World Outlook and Atheistic Education"[33] that the increased influence of the churches, especially of the "western sects" (i.e., Baptists), was a result of the policy shift of 1943–1944, when "the church strengthened its position as a consequence of . . . a retreat from the Leninist legislation on religion, allowing the churches unwarranted relief from taxes and supplying them with construction materials and greater freedom in managing their activities."

Passing from Party pronouncements to legislation, one must first examine the Criminal Code of the RSFSR, which was adopted by the Supreme Soviet of that republic on July 25, 1962. It includes several articles related to religious matters, analogues of which appear in the codes of all the other Soviet republics.[34] Article 142 states that violations of the laws on the separation of church from state and school from church shall be punishable by corrective work for a period of up to one year or a fine of up to fifty rubles. (In March 1966 this article was amended to provide harsher punishment.) Article 143 provides punishment for interference with religious observances. Such interference is punishable "unless the observances disturb public order and are accompanied by infringement upon the rights of citizens." Article 227 of the Code makes punishable "infringements upon the person and the rights of citizens under the appearance of performing religious rites." The article defines such offences as "the organization or leading of a group, the activities of which, under the appearance of preaching religious dogmas or performing religious rites, are connected with inflicting harm on the health of the citizens, or with other encroachments upon the person or rights of citizens, or with inciting citizens to refuse to participate in civic activities or to perform their civic duties, or with drawing minors into such a group." Such activities shall be punishable by confinement for a period of up to five years, or deportation for such a period, with or without confiscation of property. Punishment is lighter for those who merely promote such activities, or in cases where the public danger is less. This article aims principally at members of sects whose beliefs entail self-mutilation (e.g., the *Skoptsy*) or withdrawal from society (e.g., the Old Believers). However, it can be applied against almost any group; both circumcision and baptism by immersion have been construed as being harmful to health. In theory even refusal to take part in atheistic activities, such as courses of instruction in schools, can be interpreted as refusing to participate in civic activities.

In addition to the foregoing articles which deal explicitly with religious matters, there are others which can be invoked against religious activity as well. Article seventy of the Code prescribes stiff punishment for "incitement or propaganda for the purpose of undermining or weakening the Soviet Government," for the "dissemination, for the same purpose, of slanderous fabrications discrediting the Soviet political and social order, or the dissemination, for the same purpose, of literature containing any such material." [35]

In July 1964, the authoritative organ, *Sovetskoe Gosudarstvo i Pravo* (Soviet State and Law), Vol. 7, published an article by Y. T. Milko, which was indicative of new legal trends on religious affairs. The title of the article is significant: "Scientific-Atheistic Propaganda and the Juridical Struggle Against Crimes of Churchmen and Sectarians." [36] This article is equivalent to an authoritative legal interpretation because of the journal in which it appeared. Milko began by stating that the Soviet government not only refrains from interfering in the life of religious groups, but "actively defends this freedom and accords it the protection of law." Similarly, it is not religion or clergymen that the government is fighting but rather their infractions of the law: "The determination of the offense should be based not on the fact that the guilty party belongs to a religious association but on the substance of his criminal activity." Special attention was given to article seventy (on anti-Soviet propaganda) which, in his opinion, was too seldom applied to religious offenses. It ought to be applied not only to those who use unregistered religious groups to commit crimes such as taking advantage of the religious prejudices of believers; [37]

the same treatment should be given to members of legal or registered groups. He stated that leaders of the latter have preyed upon their members "to promote anti-Soviet ideologies." "Anti-Soviet ideology" could thus include almost any sort of religious belief, since communist ideology inherently opposed religious ideology. On the question of what constitutes anti-Soviet ideological activities, the author said this must be decided by the courts in each particular case.

In addition to encouraging greater use of article seventy, Milko also adduced examples of offenses which could be cited as infractions of article 227. Prohibition of attendance at movies and other cultural activities, as well as the prohibition of racial or religious intermarriage, while not done with the purpose of weakening the government, are nonetheless fostered by religious fanaticism and thereby violate this article. Milko gives examples of what constitutes "doing harm to the health of a believer": ". . . zealous prayer or long fasts, or refusal to receive medical help, and the results of making sacrifices in expiation of sin."

The edict of the Presidium of the Supreme Soviet of the RSFSR, "Strengthening the Fight Against Persons Avoiding Socially Useful Work" (May 4, 1961) is not specifically aimed at clergymen and religious believers. It can easily be applied, however, to members of religious cults and ministers of religion whose work is, by Soviet definition, not socially useful. Pauline B. Taylor aptly describes the decree (known as the antiparasite law) as "a multi-purpose control that embraces prostitutes and poets, as well as monks and mullahs." [38] Any person who leads a "parasitic way of life" can be forcibly resettled in specially designated areas for a period of from two to five years, or he can be assigned to hard labor for that period. This can be accomplished either by court order or by the decision of the collective of workers of any area, subject to final approval by the local soviet.[39] While it has not been widely applied (the case of the poet Yosif Brodsky is one well-known example of such action), it clearly could be invoked to place most clergymen outside the law at any time.

The antiparasite law was amended in 1965, partly because it was amiguous, but primarily because Soviet jurists felt that it undermined the prestige of the cours (by creating, in effect, additional courts) and the validity of the Criminal Code by its very ambiguity. The amendment was passed by the Presidium of the Supreme Soviet of the RSFSR in September, 1965.[40]

In June 1963, a plenary session of the Party's Central Committee described as the duty of all Party members a "stubborn fight against religious survivals" and "the development of scientific-atheistic work." [41] Shortly thereafter the Ideological Commission of the Central Committee of the Party issued a lengthy and important document entitled "On Measures to Strengthen Atheistic Education of the People." The Central Committee adopted the document and instructed the lower echelons of the Party to take appropriate action.[42]

With regard to the enforcement of existing legislation, the Commission said: "in order to restrict the unlawful activities of the clergy and believers (individuals and groups), control must be increased to shield children and adolescents from the influence of clergymen, as well as insuring that parents do not force their children to practice religion."

Of all the measures requested by the Ideological Commission the most dangerous for believers was the call for increased control in shielding children from the religious influences of parents and clergymen. The provision is very ambiguous; it is not clear, for example, what "forcing" children to practice religion means, or who shall control parents and others in this regard. Several incidents of children being taken from their parents have been reported in the Soviet press.

Administration and Supervision of the Laws on Religion

Soviet materials on the administration of the laws on religion are not as readily available as those pertaining to other branches of the legal structure. Most of the information included here has been deduced from indirect Soviet sources, such as references in books, articles in magazines, and so forth.

Two agencies are directly responsible for the administration and supervision of organized religious life: the councils for the affairs of religious cults at the Council of Ministers, which are empowered to act directly or through their local representatives; and the local soviets. (In January 1966, the merger of the two councils into one body responsible for the affairs of both the Russian Orthodox and all other religious groups was announced in *Pravda*.) Local soviets exert their control over religious life in the capacity of the highest administrative body at the local level, but also directly through their specially designated committees or sections for religious affairs.

According to the Law and the Instruction of 1929, the Committee (later Section) for Religious Matters of the city or county soviet *(gorsovet* or *raisovet)* is the agency at which the registration of local religious associations is performed (paragraph forty-two of the Instruction). The religious sections of the soviets act as the lessors in contracts leasing religious property.

These sections, according to the provisions of the law, in addition to registering all religious associations, exercise control (in conjunction with the representatives of the Council for Religious Cults) over the activities of the congregations, over their elected bodies and their clergymen. Religious associations must submit to these sections lists of their members, information about their clergymen, financial accounts, and reports about almost anything that is taking place in the organization.

The instruction issued later by the Commissariat of the Interior elucidated the procedure concerning provisions that were not clear. According to the Instruction, the prerogatives of the Council on religious matters were the following:

a) Granting permission for all-Union and RSFSR religious conventions and conferences.

b) Inspection of executive bodies of religious conventions and conferences.

c) At the request of the local committee on religious matters the Council decides upon the liquidation of a religious society or group. (The decision may be appealed to the Council of Ministers itself.)

d) At the request of the local committee on religious matters the Council decides upon the annulment of a contract leasing prayer buildings and religious property (which is *not* identical with liquidation of a religious association, as is generally assumed).

The Council on Affairs of Religious Cults has evolved into the most authoritative agency concerned with the administration of legislation, overshadowing the local soviets. The Council has its deputies at the local levels of administration who are responsible for exercising control at the lower level. Y. T. Milko, in the aforementioned article in *Sovetskoe Gosudarstvo i Pravo,* stated that "control over the observation of legislation on religious cults is entrusted to the executive committees of the local organs of authority [soviets]: the two Councils for religious matters at the Council of Ministers and also their representatives in the localities." In what manner the religious sections of the local soviets and the deputies of the Council complement each other and cooperate is not completely clear.

The representative of the Soviet Union at the Commission on Human Rights of the United Nations remarked in 1959 in his report that the Councils "have representatives in regions, territories and republics to maintain liaison between state agencies and local religious organizations, to carry out the registration of religious communities and the official transfer of church buildings, both to existing and to newly organized religious communities."[43]

The report seems to indicate that the local representatives of the Council have assumed some prerogative previously held by the local Soviets, such as the registration of religious communities and the transfer of prayer buildings.

Charges have recently been leveled at representatives of the Council to the effect that they have renounced their prerogative of being the "liaison between state agencies and religious organizations" and have assumed instead the functions of principal supervisors of local religious organizations. Moreover, they have been accused of acting contrary to existing Soviet laws on religious matters, giving oral and phone orders which they are unwilling to confirm in writing, thus instituting a new kind of "oral legislation" or legislation by telephone.[44]

Several other Soviet agencies of control are in some other way connected with religious matters, through their subordinate departments and through the militia. The militia has wide powers for the maintenance of public order and has the authority to impose fines by administrative decision, to detain, and to conduct preliminary investigations in many types of suspected crime.[45] Religious associations are always under the surveillance of the local militia.

The local militia functions in close cooperation with the local executive committees of the soviet. Whether the local militia acts, in religious matters, as the agent of the Ministry of Public Order, of the local soviet, or of both, is not certain. A fair assumption is that it acts in the double capacity.

In religious matters the Communist Party assumes not only the commanding authority it exercises in economic and administrative matters, but the additional role of interpreter of communist ideology and of protector against ideological enemies.

For every *gorsovet* (city soviet) there is a *gorkom* (city Party committee), and to every *obsovet* (district soviet) there is the powerful *obkom* (district committee of the Party). Attempts have often been made to define the lines of demarcation between the authority and powers of the agencies of the soviet government and of the Communist Party at the lower levels of command. The accepted assumption is that the Party apparatus had the responsibility of *supervising and controlling* the state apparatus.

In reality, the areas of activity and the responsibilities of the two authorities are ill-defined and constantly overlapping. The Russian word *kontrol* means more than the English word "control," also connoting "checking" and "correcting."

It is safe to assume that the "control" of the lower Party organs in matters of religion is even more pronounced than in the economic field, because of the more immediate ideological involvement. It is also a logical assumption that the closing of a house of prayer is not done without the knowledge and approval of the local Party committee, which decides whether it is safe and expedient to do so.

The security police (from 1917 to 1921 the *Cheka;* from 1921 to 1923 the GPU; from 1923 to 1934 the OGPU; and later the NKVD, MVD, MGB, and KGB) has special departments or sections to deal with religious affairs, both on central and local levels.

It has been widely reported that the executive bodies of religious associations and seminaries are infiltrated by secret agents and informers. As religion and religious cults are considered to harbor actual or potential enemies of the regime, it would be logical for the guardians of state security to keep a watchful eye on them.

General supervision of the implementation of existing legislation is vested in the State procurator, now a very important office in the Soviet Union. The authority and power of the *prokuror* has increased constantly since the beginning of the post-Stalin period. It is the procurator's responsibility to see that the laws on religious matters, like all other laws, are correctly implemented and the offenders prosecuted.[46]

The Commissariat of Jusice has also been closely associated with the implementation of religious laws. It issued the Instruction for carrying out the Decree of Separation of the Church from the State (August 24, 1918) and the Instruction to the Law on Religious Associations of 1929.

Several ministries have jurisdiction over particular matters relating to religion; most important is the Ministry (formerly Commissariat) of Public Education, which has issued circulars and instructions on the problems and the legal aspects of religious instruction for children. One of these circulars (Circular of the Commissariat of Public Education, March 3, 1919) even contradicted the basic law of January 23, 1918, by insisting that "teaching religious doctrines to persons younger than eighteen years is not permissible." (The law said that such instruction is permissible when given privately.) The Commissariats (later Ministries) of Education of the republics have issued various, often contradictory, instructions and orders.

By way of conclusion, it is a fair assumption to say that decisions on religious matters of limited importance would be made by four agencies:

1. The local representative (plenipotentiary) of the Council for the Affairs of Religious Cults.
2. The local executive committee of the soviet and its religious section.
3. The local Party Committee.
4. The local security agencies (militia and/or a representative of the KGB).

Generally, the local Party Committee would be the coordinator and arbiter when there is a difference of opinion. (The individuals who represent the above agencies are, as a rule, all members of the Party.)

In more important matters—decisions pertaining to the closing of important holy places, the holding of religious conferences, etc.—the district committee of the Party (obkom) would voice its opinion and the matter would then be handled centrally by the Council of Ministers of the USSR.

On questions of *highest policy* in religious matters, the Central Committee of the Communist Party and its Ideological Commission are the organs to decide and issue authoritative instructions and opinions, later to be implemented by the administration.

Conclusions

The general tendency in Soviet legislation on religious matters has been to *increase* restrictions and controls over organized religious life in the country. The comparatively liberal decree of January 1918, still in force, has been superseded in fact in some of its more lenient provisions by later legislation, especially by that of 1929. The Constitution of 1936 replaced *freedom to propagate* religious beliefs by *freedom to practice* religion. The articles of the Criminal Code of 1960 and the amendments of 1962 pertaining to religious matters are stricter and more inclusive than the corresponding articles in the previous codes. For example, the edict of 1961 against persons avoiding socially useful work was a legal innovation which is potentially dangerous for the clergy. Periodically there have been amendments and more liberal interpretations of the law, but in general these have not altered the essential severity of legislation.

Soviet policy in regard to religion has not necessarily followed legislation, and has not always been synchronized with changes in legislation. Short liberal intervals in the generally restrictive policy were not accompanied by corresponding legislative enactments. This was even true of the great detente in antireligious policies during the "Fatherland War." The existing legal framework has not prevented the Soviet regime from using the law alternately for relaxation and restriction.

Soviet legislation and the administration and observance of existing laws have always been the weakest links in the state's chain of functions. The laws were often violated, their very existence unknown to most citizens, and their validity problematic. At present, however, the equitable application of the law and general esteem for legality seem to be on the increase.

Obviously, the separation of church and state in the Soviet Union differs from the same phenomenon in many other countries by virtue of the fact that the Soviet regime has a professed desire to erase religious beliefs from the consciousness of the Soviet people.

Although official documents of the Party were usually careful to delineate the division of authority between state and Party, from time to time this division has been all but lost. The peculiar status of the Party was officially recognized in the 1936 Constitution in paragraph 126 where it is stated that the Communist Party "represents the directing core of all organizations of the toilers, both voluntary and state." This "directing core of all organizations" clearly stated in its program that it is not neutral in the controversy between church and state. The Party retains ultimate control over both legislation and the administration of the law.

Soviet legislation in general and legislation on religion in particular has always been characterized by a wealth of ambiguities which lend themselves to widely divergent interpretations. There is reason to believe that in some cases the ambiguities are intentional, aimed at permitting both central and local authorities to maneuver to their best advantage.

Existing Soviet legislation, discriminatory and restrictive though it is, would still suffice to permit believers to practice their religion— with some limitations—provided the administrative authorities would not use the powers at their disposal to make the law stricter than it is. We have seen, for example, that the laws of 1929 permitted even very small groups of persons to register and conduct prayer services. Nonetheless, small groups, even of recognized religions, are frequently denied this right in practice and forced to lead an illegal life in regard to their religion.

The greatest single area of potential interpretation of the law to the disadvantage of believers seems to be vested in the Criminal Code and legislation covering offences under administrative jurisdiction.

The greater concern for legality noted of late has its roots in several factors. For example, undue repression has often led to uncontrollable underground religious organizations. Also, there is an emerging public opinion at home which occasionally finds the harsh restrictions on religious believers unjust. Finally, the exigencies of the struggle within the communist bloc may impel the Soviets to restrain their anti-religious programs; foreign communists have often reacted un-favorably to harsh measures in this area, preferring purely legal procedures and educational approaches.

There is, perhaps, little hope for any genuine tolerance for religion, given the Party's understanding of the nature and content of its ideology in this area, but at least one can hope for an increase of respect for the legal process.

CASE HISTORIES

For a better understanding of how the law works (or does not work) in actual life situations, we have chosen several cases which were reported by the Soviet press. Although the procedures and tactics described in these accounts are not typical for every locality and each republic of the Soviet Union, it can be said that they were typical for the *overall* approach in the administration of the laws pertaining to religious life. In the framework of a policy to diminish as much as possible the influence of religion and the number of religious institutions in the country, Soviet methods and tactics do change considerably from time to time and from place to place.

In order to perceive the particular aura of each case we thought it best to reprint *in toto* articles that have been published in the Soviet press, and to make them the basis of our discussion.

Of necessity, our discussions are based on the presentation of one side of the argument, the Soviet authorities', as related by the Soviet press. The other side, which is accused of various offences against Soviet society and law, cannot, unfortunately, be heard. In spite of this obvious limitation there is sufficient material in the articles and letters cited below for some relevant conclusions.

Case No. 1

Smolensk religious Jews endeavor to obtain a House of Prayer.

Around the "Minyan"

Pensioner Zalman Yevseevich Aronov has two daughters, Frida and Tsiva. Oh, what good girls they are! Clever, educated. Only recently they were diligent pupils and now they teach. And they are not just teachers. They instruct in secondary schools, read lectures, educate the growing generation in the Communist spirit.

Tsiva went further than Frida. She joined the Party, married Effim Georgevich Lifts, a teacher at Secondary School No. 22, who also carries the Party membership card in his pocket. Tsiva obviously progressed, but the father cannot complain about Frida either.

Zalman Yevseevich delights in his daughters; then goes to the "minyan." There he meets his friends Movsha Vulfovich Bruk, Yankel Leibovich Gorbachev, Abram Izrailevich Tseitlin. There Torah scrolls, prayer books and prayer shawls are to be found.

Zalman Yevseevich once accomplished good deeds for our society. He still remembers them. But he fell ill. He was affected with a disease, the name of which cannot be found in any medical encyclopaedia. His ailment is religious fanaticism. This disease had led him to bad actions.

Yevseevich and his friends are not simple believers. They are diligent religious activists, the heads of the "minyan." Zalman Yevseevich also acts as slaughterer. Only three rubles are paid per chicken but this is still profitable for a man without income, apart from keeping him occupied.

The community leaders divide all functions among themselves. Thus Yankel Leibovich Gorbachev served, for a long time, both as community treasurer and head of the "burial office." He also robbed the believers, pocketing their donations and, within a short period, became "the richest man in Smolensk," as stated by the believers themselves. It is not difficult to guess which of the three above functions this extortioner regarded as fundamental.

The believers lost their trust in Gorbachev (believers are also capable of not believing!) and at the meeting of the community board dismissed him from the post of treasurer. But a holy place does not remain vacant. It was occupied by Leib Yankelevich Kaplan and Solomon Mendelevich Gvozdikov who soon also appropriated Yankel Leibovich's third function. According to the believers, the community has not yet had an administration which did not engage in robbery.

The "minyan" is an illegal organization, but as the proverb goes "you cannot hide an awl in a sack." Oh! what an awl! On the surface what is wrong if men gather on Saturdays at pensioner Mendel Yevseevich Khesin's house? There are many houses in Smolensk and many people go in and out of them. Should doors be locked?

But the inhabitants of Metallistov Street, on which Khesin's house stands, became indignant. Honest Soviet people do not like secret gatherings. They began, so to say, to give signals and the more so, drinking bouts being frequently organized in that house.

The active members of the religious community then decided to obtain permission for the opening of a synagogue. On collecting 17,000 rubles from the believers, they purchased a house and registered it officially under the name of a certain Gitlin. But this Gitlin was a "practical" man. He was not interested in the least in religious traditions; what interested him was money. He resold the house for a higher price, then left for an unknown destination.

Gitlin's trick had a crushing effect on the community leaders, who did not regain their wits for a long time. But the idea of their own synagogue gave them no peace. A collection on a larger scale was organized again last year, 37,000 rubles amassed and another house in Smolensk purchased.

The community leaders did not hurry to perform all the necessary purchase formalities. Who knows these believers? And what will happen if a new fictitious owner will follow in Gitlin's footsteps? They scanned each other suspiciously looking for a suitable candidate, conferred secretly and conjointly. Their choice finally fell on Haim Volkovich Roitberg. And do you think that was just incidental? No, Haim Volkovich Roitberg is a trustworthy man! He has two communists in the family; a daughter and a son-in-law. Can such a man disappoint them?

The decision reached, implementation followed. But, lo, unexpectedly—justice steps in. The building is confiscated and handed over to the State. This blow fell like thunder from a blue sky. Here is a legitimate question: what do Haim Volkovich and his son-in-law Gurfinkel need a house for? They own a cosy communal apartment which they do not plan to vacate. Thus, another illegal transaction for a synagogue turned out a complete fiasco.

In the meantime, the "minyan" continued its existence. It was no longer held in Khesin's house, but in Samuil Isaevich Shteingard's apartment in House No. 14, Pervyi Krasnyi Pereulok.

Here something happened which the community heads still cannot remember without excitement. The illegal "minyan" was visited last year by the Israeli diplomatic representative Shermon and his spouse, who left Zionist literature and Israeli chocolates for distribution.

Oh! How these religious leaders delighted in these chocolates. They were almost declared holy. How could our Soviet chocolates compete with the Israeli product?

Abram Yakovlevich Merson, the old rascal from Kharkov, also honoured the "minyan" with his presence. This inveterate preacher of obscurantism held a speech which brought tears to the eyes of Aronov and his friends.

Merson is a universal pluralist. Though receiving a government pension, he travels simultaneously to various towns in the Soviet and receives private orders for photographic enlargements. Though a family man, with a wife in Kharkov, he has an affair with a woman in Smolensk, and do you think in Smolensk only? What can such a man preach apart from obscurantism?

Such are Zalman Yevseevich Aronov's friends at the "minyan," the same Zalman Yevseevich who has two daughters and a son-in-law teaching in secondary schools.

But is he the only one to be such a lucky father? Monus Tsemakhovich Freidin, for instance, has a daughter, Sarah Freidina-Lenskaia, who works as a doctor in Children's Hospital No. 1, and is married to Vladimir Markovich Lensky, a party member and an interrogator at the oblast procurator's office. On Saturdays, when the son-in-law goes to his office, the father-in-law proceeds to the "minyan."

The active member of the religious community, Haim Leibovich Yenin, lives with his daughter Raissa—a teacher at the working youth school—and his son Yerukhim—an engineer in the sovnarkhoz. As to Vladimir Solomonovich Averbach, his son is the director of the Zadneprovsk market.

We have shown you how several fathers successfully combine the practice of religious rites with dishonest transactions around the "minyan." And where are their children, particularly those with party membership cards in their pockets?

No! It seems that Zalman Yevseevich does not delight in vain in his two daughters. What educated girls! They act as though they do not notice where and why their father goes on Saturdays.

A. Beregov.
[*Rabochii Put,* Smolensk, September 13, 1959; translation from Russian in *Jews in Eastern Europe,* London, April 1960]

Let us analyze briefly what indeed happened in this case according to the newspaper "feuilleton." A group of religious Jews in Smolensk, a large town in the RSFSR, had held religious services in a private home of one of the members of the group. The Smolensk group was entitled to be registered, if they numbered less than twenty members, as a "group of believers" (paragraph three of the "Law on Religious Associations" of 1929), or if they numbered more than twenty members as a "religious society" (paragraphs three and five of the above law), whether they had a prayer building or not.

The group decided to obtain permission to open a synagogue. A "religious society" may receive from the local soviet, under a contract, special prayer buildings free of charge. A "group of believers" may use for prayer buildings "other premises left to them by private persons or local soviets on lease" by paragraph ten of the law. So the group had two possibilities under the law: to ask the authorities to lease them a place of prayer (under a contract, free of charge, if they numbered more than twenty members), or to find *themselves* a place to worship.

If "special prayer buildings" (i.e., former houses of prayer) are not available in a certain locality, or the authorities are not willing to relinquish any of them, as may have been the case in Smolensk where many synagogues had been taken over by the local authorities for other uses, the only alternative was to secure a place of worship by building a new prayer house or by buying a house that could be converted into a prayer house. Acquisition and construction of new prayer buildings is allowed by the cited law (paragraph forty-five). However, Soviet law does not grant the status of legal entity to religious associations (paragraph three). Even transactions for the management and use of religious property may be made only by *individual citizens* who are members of the executive body (paragraph eleven). These restrictions explain why the Smolensk group had to buy a building for a house through a private person.

The Smolensk group must have been quite numerous, and the determination to have a place of worship very strong ("the idea of their own synagogue gave them no peace," the article says). The group was able to collect 17,000 rubles in the first instance and 37,000 rubles in the second—the latter quite a substantial amount of money, equal to about 100 average monthly salaries.

The property transaction, whether done by an individual or as a representative of the religious group, was clearly legal—it is legal in the Soviet Union for a private person to buy a small house from another private person—yet "justice steps in," says the newspaper, and "the building is confiscated and handed over to the State." Thirty-seven thousand rubles collected from private citizens, workers, employees, and pensioners was confiscated by the government.

There was no legal basis for the confiscation of the money. Even if the Soviet authorities did consider the transaction not in conformity with the law, confiscating money donated by private persons instead of returning it to the donors, was sheer robbery.

There is nothing in Soviet law that would make possession of a "religious building" a prerequisite for the registration of a "religious group" or "religious society." The Soviet authorities seem to have required the possession of a "special prayer building" to register a religious association, and at the same time left no possibility to acquire such a building.

The following case is distinguished by the fact that the synagogue and its leaders are not accused of any offenses against the law or of unlawful activities.

Case No. 2

The closing of a synagogue because believers "can pray at home."

We Will Sweep Away the Survivals of the Past.
Is a Synagogue Needed in Buinaksk?

Assisted by the great Russian nation and the brotherly Dagestan peoples, the small eleven-thousand-strong Tat people has, in the years of the Soviet regime, made an enormous step forward in its economic and cultural evolution.

The Tat kolkhozes' Derhent wine-growers are far-famed in Dagestan. Several foremost men from these kolkhozes were the first in Dagestan to receive the honored title of Socialist Labor Hero. There are also quite a few Tats in the front rank in Buinaksk enterprises.

The Tats have representatives among the Dagestan scientists, instructors in higher educational institutions, engineers, physicians and teachers.

Though small in number, the Tat people have their own literature, writers and poets.

In other words, the Tat people gives its modest contribution to the building of communism and is full of gratitude to its own Communist party and its elder brothers in the family of Soviet nations.

At the same time, we still find in the small family of the Tat people, backward elements, carriers of harmful survivals of the past, who hamper our progress.

One of these factors is the existence of a synagogue in Buinaksk. Though it is frequented by a few dozens of aged people only, the mere fact of its existence brings great harm.

All harmful survivals and rites such as circumcision, old marriage customs, ceremonies and many other things are inspired and supported by the synagogue, which contributes to their preservation and revival, similarly to the mosque and Moslem Spiritual Board in Buinaksk.

It may consequently be said with certainty and without exaggeration that the synagogue brings harm to the subsequent Communist education of the Tat youth, the building of communism and the subsequent evolution of the Tats.

Time has therefore come for Tat public opinion to raise the question of the synagogue closure. This does not mean, of course, that we ignore the religious feelings of the believers. They can perform their necessary religious rituals without hindrance, in their homes, without a synagogue, just like believers in the Lower Dzhengutal and in other auls do.

[*Kommunist*, Buinaksk, Dagestan SSR, July 7, 1960; translated in *Jews and the Jewish People*, Vol. 1, No. 2, p. 1]

The Tats, a Jewish tribe called also "Mountain Jews," numbering some 20,000, live in the Caucasian mountains, mostly in the Dagestan Autonomous Republic of the RSFSR.

The call to close the only synagogue in the Dagestan ASSR was based not on charges of "machinations and speculation" or pro-Israeli sympathies, but on the newspaper's statement that the "mere fact of its existence brings great harm." The harm consisted of: (a) "inspiring and supporting" religious rites; (b) "bringing harm to Communist education of the youth and to the building of communism."

Clearly there is no basis in the law for closing a synagogue under these charges. Performing religious rites is an inherent part of the functions of religious cults and is explicitly allowed by existing Soviet legislation.

By the basic tenets of communist theory, communist and religious ideologies are inherently alien to each other, and consequently the existence of any religious cult or house of prayer would "bring harm to Communist education." Under this reasoning all religious cults and all houses of prayer in the Soviet Union should be subject to liquidation by administrative measures. The only alternative left to believers, according to the newspaper, would be to perform religious rituals at home. This is, of course, not what Soviet law says about "religious associations," their rights and allowed activities.

The synagogue in Buinaksk was consequently closed (see *Jews in Eastern Europe*, December 1965, p. 25).

Notes

1. References to religion are to be found in various works of Marx, Engels, Kautsky, Plekhanov, Lenin, and other Marxist writers. The reader will find some references pertinent to this study in the following works: Karl Marx, *Kritik der Hegelschen Rechtsphilosophie: Frühe Schriften* (Critique of the Hegelian Philosophy of Law: Early Writings) (Stuttgart, 1962, p. 488); Karl Marx, *Das Kommunistische Manifest* (The Communist Manifesto) (Vienna, 1921, p. 41); Lenin, *Sochineniia* (Works) (4th ed., Moscow, 1947, Vol. 10, pp. 65–9: "Sotsializm i Religiia" (Socialism and Religion), Vol. 15, pp. 371–81; "Ob Otnoshenii Rabochei Partii k Religii" (On the Attitude of the Working Class to Socialism), *ibid.*, pp. 382–90; "Klassy i Partii v Ikh Otnoshenii k Religii i Tserkvi" (Classes and Parties in Their Attitudes to Religion and Church), *ibid.*, pp. 382–90.

2. F. Garkavenko, ed., *O Religii i Tserkvi: Sbornik Dokumentov* (Moscow, 1965, pp. 95, 119).

3. *Ibid.*, p. 119.

4. *Ibid.*

5. The preparation and publication of the Decree of January 23, 1918, has an interesting history. In fact it was printed two days earlier, January 21, in the government daily *Izvestia* under a quite different, and characteristic name: "On the Fredom of Conscience, the Church and Religious Associations." This text had traces of "revolutionary romanticism." It was Lenin who changed the title of the published Decree from "On Freedom of Conscience, etc." to "On Separation of Church from State, etc." The basic tenet of the decree was, in Lenin's opinion, not freedom of conscience but the separation of the Church from the state on the terms outlined in the Decree. A facsimile of the first text of the Decree with an added handwritten note by Lenin is reprinted in the publication of the Soviet Academy of Science, *Voprosy Istorii Religii i Ateizma* (Moscow, 1958, p. 16) hereafter VIRA.

6. In Russian: *"Ob otdelenii tserkvi ot gosudarstva i shkoly ot tserkvi"* (in *Sobranie Uzakonenii i Raspriazhenii Prabochevo i Krestianskovo Pravitelstva*, No. 18, January 26, 1918; reprinted in *Garkavenko, op. cit.*, p. 96).

7. Paragraph nine of the Decree.

8. *Istoriia Sovetskoi Konstitutsii v Dokumentakh, 1917–1956* (Moscow, 1957, p. 145, 155).

9. VIRA, Vol. 5, 1958, p. 11. According to VIRA, *ibid.*, this Instruction was in force until 1929 when a new one was introduced.

10. This was the first time that the *dvadtsatka* or "group of twenty," the basic unit of religious associations, was introduced. Still in use today, the group's functions and responsibilities have been elaborated in greater detail over the years.

11. In Russian: *Tsirkular po Voprosu ob Otdelenii Tserkvi ot Gosudarstva* (in *VIRA, op. cit.*, No. 5, 1958, p. 34, where the date of the Circular is given as January 3, 1919; also in Garkavenko, *op. cit.*, p. 100, where the date is given as December, 1918).

12. *KPSS v Rezolutsiiakh* (Moscow, 1954, Vol. 1, reprinted in Garkavenko, *op. cit.*, p. 56).

13. Garkavenko, *op. cit.*, p. 56–7. In Russian: *O politicheskoi propagande i kulturno—prosvetitelnoi rabote v derevne* (On political propaganda and cultural-enlightening work in the villages).

14. *Glavny politiko-prosvetitelny komitet narkomprosa RSFSR* was in existence from 1920 to 1930.

15. In Russian: *O postanovke antireligioznoi propagandy i o narushenii punkta 13 programmy* (in *Izvestiia TSK RKP (b)*, No. 33, Moscow, 1921, pp. 32–3; reprinted in Garkavenko, *op. cit.*, pp. 57–60).

16. In Russian: *Direktivy TSK RKP sovetskim i partiinim organam po voprosu ob otnoshenii k sektam i politiki v otnoshenii religionznykh grup voobshche* (in *Spravochnik Partiinovo Rabotnika,* Moscow, 1922, 93–4; reprinted in Garkavenko, *op. cit.,* pp. 61–3).

17. In Russian: *O propagande, pechati i agitatsii* (In *KPSS v Rezoliutsiakh, op. cit.,* Vol. 1, 741–2). See also Garkavenko, *op. cit.,* pp. 63–4.

18. Edict (*Postanovlenie*) of the All-Russian Central Executive Committee of the Soviets and the Council of People's Commissars (in *Sobranie Uzakonenii . . .,* No. 35, 1929, text No. 353; amendments in No. 8, 1932, text No. 41 II, p. 6).

19. N. Orleanskii, *Zakon o Religioznykh Obedineniiakh RSFSR* (Law on Religious Societies of the RSFSR) (Moscow, 1930, pp. 26–42, reprinted from the *Bulletin of the NKVD of RSFSR,* No. 37, 1929.)

20. "Study of Discrimination in the Matter of Religious Rights and Practices," (*Conference Room Paper No. 35,* January 30, 1959, United Nations Commission on Human Rights, Subcommission on the Prevention of Discrimination and the Protection of Minorities). This is a summary of information related to the Union of Soviet Socialist Republics; special reporter Areot Krishnaswami.

21. In the early years of Soviet rule several "test cases" in this area resulted in the decision to uphold the Separation Decree. In each case the Fifth Division of the Commissariat of Justice declared that Soviet citizens may conduct their prayer meetings in their own homes without hindrance, provided they have submitted to the authorities information on the time and place of such meetings. For details of these decisions see P. V. Gidulianov, *Otdelenie Tserkvi ot Gosuderstva* (The Separation of Church and State) (Moscow, 1924, p. 10).

22. *Sovetskaia Iustitsiia* (Soviet Justice), No. 15–6, 1939, p. 70, as quoted in John N. Hazard and Morris L. Weisberg, *Cases and Readings on Soviet Law* (New York, 1950, pp. 137–8).

23. The seven-day week was adopted again in 1941.

24. *SSSR: Sobranie Zakanov* (USSR: Collections of Laws) No. 475, 1932.

25. *Pravda,* March 15, 1930.

26. V. Gsovsky, "The Legal Status of the Church in Soviet Russia" (in *Fordham Law Review,* Vol. 8, No. 1, 1939, pp. 1–28). See also *The Church and State Under Communism,* a special study prepared by the Law Library of Congress, 1964, pp. 1–2.

27. *Konstitutsiia Soiuza Sovetskikh Sotsialisticheskikh Respublik* (Constitution of the Union of Soviet Socialist Republics) (Moscow, 1959, p. 26). Article 124 of the Constitution states: "In order to secure for citizens freedom of conscience, the church in the Soviet Union is separated from the state and the school from the church. Freedom of religious worship and freedom of antireligious propaganda are recognized for all citizens."

28. U.N. Commission on Human Rights, *op. cit.,* p. 18.

29. *Ibid.,* extract from Order No. 628 concerning religious councils, confirmed by the Council of People's Commissars of the USSR on May 29, 1944.

30. *Sputnik Agitatora* (The Agitator's Companion) (1944, No. 19–20; pp. 28–9; reprinted in Garkavenko, *op. cit.,* pp. 69–71). "Ordinance ob Organizatsii Nauchno-Prosvetitelnoi Propagandy" (On the Organization of Scientific-Educational Propaganda).

31. Reprinted in Garkavenko, *op. cit.,* pp. 71–7.

32. *Pravda,* November 11, 1954; reprinted in Garkavenko, *op. cit.,* pp. 77–82.

33. L. Ilichev, "Formirovaniie Nauchnogo Mirovozzreniia i Ateisticheskoe Vospitanie" (in *Kommunist,* No. 1, 1964).

34. *Ugolovnoe Zakonodatelstvo Soiuza SSR i Soiuznykh Respublik* (Penal Code of the Soviet Union and the Union Republics) (Moscow, 1963, pp. 123, 142). See also Harold J. Berman, *Soviet Criminal Law and Procedure: the RSFSR Code*

(Cambridge, Mass., 1966, p. 141ff., and *Church and State Under Communism,* p. 39).

35. *Ugolovnoe Zakonodatelstvo,* p. 108.

36. Y. T. Milko, "Nauchno-Ateisticheskaia Propaganda i Ugolovno-Pravovaia Borba s Prestupleniami Tserkovnikov i Sektantov" (Scientific-Atheistic Propaganda and the Legal Struggle with Crimes of Church Members and Sectarians) (in *Sovetskoe Gosudarstvo i Pravo,* Vol. 7, 1964, pp. 67–75).

37. *Ibid.,* p. 65.

38. Pauline B. Taylor, "Sectarians in Soviet Courts" (in *The Russian Review,* July 1965, p. 286).

39. *Sovetskaia Iustitsiia* (Moscow, 1961, No. 10, p. 25).

40. R. Beerman, "The Anti-parasite Law of the RSFSR Modified," *Soviet Studies,* January, 1966, p. 387.

41. *Plenum Tsentralnovo Komiteta Komunisticheskoi Partii Sovetskovo Soiuza 18–21 Juniia 1963* (Plenum of the Central Committee of the Communist Party of the Soviet Union June 18–21, 1963), Moscow, 1964. Cited in Garkavenko, pp. 84–5.

42. *Partiinaia Zhizn* (Party Life), No. 2, 1964. Reprinted in Garkavenko, pp. 85–92.

43. U.N. Commission on Human Rights, *op. cit.,* p. 17.

44. Letter of two Russian priests to the Chairman of the Presidium of the Supreme Soviet. Text in *Religion in Communist-Dominated Areas* (New York, May 15 and May 31, 1966).

45. Leonard Schapiro, *The Government and Politics in the Soviet Union* (New York, 1965, p. 160); Berman, *op. cit.,* pp. 65–8.

46. In fact, the functions of a *prokuror* (procurator) are more diverse and larger in scope than those of a prosecutor. The office of procurator (the *prokuratura*) in the Soviet Union has become a powerful judicial institution with vast prerogatives. (See, for instance, Harold J. Berman, *Soviet Criminal Law and Procedure— The RSFSR Codes* [Cambridge, 1966, pp. 67, 16–78].)

CHAPTER 2
Synagogues

For centuries, Jewish life in the East European countries revolved around the synagogue. It was the House of Assembly *(Bet Kneset)*, the House of Prayer *(Bet Tefilah)*, and the House of Study *(Bet Midrash)*. Most communal activities and institutions, such as the ritual slaughterhouse, the ritual bathhouse, and the hostelry, were, as a rule, centered around the synagogue.

With the advent of Jewish secularism in the nineteenth century, the synagogue lost some of its previous status but it still retained a powerful position, particularly in the smaller towns where most of the Jewish population still lived.

The Bolshevik revolution brought radical changes. In the first four years of Soviet rule, the fight against religion was treated as a necessary but not immediate task. Not until 1921, four years after the Bolsheviks seized power, did they feel strong enough to initiate an organized campaign to close down houses of worship.

The Jewish Communists, the Yevsektsiia, were torn between two opposing attitudes. On the one hand, they were aware of the peculiarities inherent in the position of a minority religion which had been oppressed and debased by the Tsarist regime and by the dominant church. On the other hand, the Jewish Communists felt uncomfortable in admitting the differences in the treatment of religious groups. Therefore, they continually underscored the harmful influences of all religion and all clerics. More often than not they instigated action against Jewish clergy for a particular synagogue whenever a non-Jewish clergyman was arrested or other drastic action was taken against a Christian church.

They felt that not acting against Jewish religious institutions might provoke anti-Semitism. But linking innocent Jewish clergymen and houses of prayer with their non-Jewish activist counterparts alienated the "Jewish masses." Nevertheless, Jewish Communists insisted that such joint action be taken regardless of the Jewish reaction.

Sometimes communist voices were discreetly raised, criticizing this tactic. For instance, the Jewish communist leader, A. Merezhyn, described in *Der Emes* (October 2, 1921) the campaign to take over the Choir Synagogue in Smolensk for "cultural needs," where, wrote Merezhyn, "the Revolutionary Tribunal mixed in. The Tribunal had before it not only the problem of the Choir Synagogue which was accused of handling social security cases and speculation, but the crimes of the Russian Orthodox and Catholic clergymen as well. The Revtribunal considered it politically expedient to combine the trials of all three beliefs in order to get a full picture of the clergy in general." Then Merezhyn subtly adds his criticism that "the Revtribunal should have first discussed this problem with the members of the Bureau [Yevsektsiia]," instead of combining all three trials. "One consequence," reported Merezhyn, was the cessation of the propaganda campaign against the Choir Synagogue which the Jewish Communists had already started, for such propaganda would at this time not achieve the desired results.

In the closing of synagogues, the Jewish Communists had their own set of priorities. First on the list were the so-called "choir synagogues" which were modern and spacious and to which the wealthier Jews belonged. Then would come the systematic reduction of the existing smaller houses of prayer, by emphasizing the pressing needs of the community for the buildings. This would be coupled, in case of compliance, with the promise of leaving other synagogues in peace.

The "pressing needs" were often real. Hundreds of thousands of orphans or abandoned children roamed the countryside and many people were homeless as a result of the destruction of thousands of buildings. There was also an acute shortage of housing for educational and social welfare purposes. Demands that some of the existing prayer houses be converted into emergency housing evoked sympathetic responses even among believers. Soviet officials adroitly used this situation to reduce the numbers of prayer houses so that they would be able to concentrate their efforts at some later date on a diminished number of targets. Periodically, the communist Jewish press reported "successes" in having the larger synagogues closed. In many cases, the Jewish population vigorously opposed these actions as illegal because the closures were not in accordance with the wishes of the worshipers, as the law required. Sometimes the struggle was protracted, when Jewish delegations protested the lawless action before higher authorities. Frequently they succeeded in postponing the closing of the synagogues, but in the end the local officials had their way and a "victory" was proclaimed.

Der Emes of January 19, 1923, rhapsodized: "There is now a holiday among the Jewish workers at Kharkov. They did take over the Choir Synagogue for their cultural needs," and this "victory" came after a long and stubborn fight. The same newspaper reported (April 10, 1924) that the house of prayer in Polotsk was taken over by the Educational Department after several individuals were tried for allegedly storing smuggled alcohol in the building.

In some localities religious Jews resisted the closing of synagogues with force. Notable was the confrontation in 1921 in Vitebsk when worshipers attacked the Jewish communist leaders who had come to effect the closing. When efforts to prevent the closing failed, the worshipers assembled in the yard, donned their prayer shawls and refused to move. Force was used to take over the synagogue. *Der Emes* explained (September 14, 1921) that Vitebsk had seventy-three prayer houses "which are almost always empty." Subsequently, the Jewish Commissariat "invited the representatives of the local illegal *kehilah* functioning legally under the name of the Council of Synagogues and explained that it would not be wrong to give up a few places for Jewish educational institutions." The religious representatives responded that they could not agree to give up houses of prayer, but, cognizant of the critical housing situation, they would be ready to find and furnish quarters where such installations could be set up. *Der Emes* accused the religious leaders of not keeping their promise. Such was the Communists' justification for the strong-arm tactics used in confiscating the Vitebsk synagogue.

It is interesting to note here the reference to the existence of a Council of Synagogues in Vitebsk in 1921. Soviet propagandists maintain that the chief reason Soviet synagogues are not organized into larger bodies is due to the fact that such central bodies never existed. But in fact the religious *kehilahs* were for a time centrally organized, and synagogues in some towns had united, as, for instance, in this case described by the Soviet newspaper.

Der Emes reported (October 13, 1922) another case of violence in the town of Liazne where the Youth Club found a place for its activities in the synagogue. On the first day of Rosh Hashanah, "a band of Jews attacked the synagogue, broke the lock and burst in." One of the youngsters tried to resist and was beaten up. The Kommandant of the town (apparently a non-Jew) attempted to make peace between the warring factions and was in favor of allowing the Jews to pray in the synagogue. The *Roite khevra* (Red gang), continued *Der Emes,* "was unwilling to abide by the decision. One of them, a hothead, fired a shot in order to chase the people away. This enraged the Kommandant. "The Jewish nation won the battle," commented *Der Emes* sarcastically. "They have annexed the synagogue and as a result an investigation by the higher authorities is in progress."

The Soviet regime tried other methods in an attempt to weaken the Jewish religion. One abortive scheme was the attempt to organize an apostatic "Living Synagogue" modeled after the Living Russian Orthodox Church, which introduced drastic innovations into the Church dogmas and ritual and which was fiercely opposed to the established Church. While the Living Church of the Russian Orthodox faith, organized in the 1920s, succeeded initially in shaking the Church to its very foundations, the "Living Synagogue" was soon abandoned by its founders; it was regarded by all Jews, believers and nonbelievers alike, as an absurd parody of Jewish religion. This venture proved, if proof were necessary, that an "opposition" to the existing "Synagogue" was totally unrealistic since—in contrast to the Christian ecclesiastical establishments—Jewish religion was not organized hierarchically and was not actively opposed to the existing regime.

The vicious new antireligious campaign initiated in 1927–1928 was designed to decimate the clergy and to reduce the number of houses of prayer to a bare minimum. This goal the Soviet regime largely achieved. (One illustration of the general condition created by these actions is the case study of the synagogues in Odessa, described at the end of this chapter.)

Hundreds of rabbis, *shohetim* and other clergymen were arrested or deported to far-away provinces. Many lost their health, many more never came back. The tragic chapter of the persecution of Jewish clergymen, and the heroic resistance of the clergymen to their oppressors must be written separately and in much greater detail than is possible here.

The role of the Yevsektsiia, the Jewish sections of the Communist party, in religious persecution and in the arrest of the Jewish clergymen is a dreary episode in the history of Soviet Jewry. The Yevsektsiia has been widely accused of being more harsh to Jewish religion than the Soviet government. It is true that in a number of cases flagrantly illegal acts of the Yevsektsiia were overruled by the higher authorities who sustained appeals from the local Jewish citizens. However, as we gain more historical perspective, we are inclined to conclude that these "excesses" of the Yevsektsiia were either instigated or welcomed by the same authorities who later rescinded them. This seems obvious by the fact that the liquidation of the Yevsektsiia in 1930 did not bring any amelioration of the condition of Soviet Jewry. The harshness in antireligious measures became even more rampant in the years after the liquidation of the Yevsektsiia, most notably in the years from 1930 until 1935.

There was a slight relaxation of antireligious efforts after 1935, but whenever the local authorities saw an opportunity to close a synagogue or even a small house of worship, they eagerly seized it.

With the attack on the Soviet Union by the Germans in 1941, there was a complete halt of the liquidation of houses of prayer of all denominations. The majority of the Jewish population lived in the path overrun by the Nazi hordes who destroyed most of the Jewish houses of prayer along with the Jews they found. When the Soviet forces reoccupied the lost territory, they did not allow the survivors to rebuild their synagogues. Services were held semilegally—in private homes or in the ruins of houses of worship.

It is highly ironic, and one of the unexpected twists of Jewish history, that it was the antireligious Soviet regime which then reinstated the synagogue as the sole expression of Jewish identity in the Soviet Union. During the "Black Years" of 1948–1953, all remaining Jewish secular institutions were closed down. Thus the synagogue became the only existing Jewish institution in the country. Only through the synagogue and the observances there, could Jews, including those who were not religious, express their identification with the Jewish people.

The situation has changed very little since 1959 when feeble manifestations of secular Jewish culture were again permitted; concessions were made principally to satisfy public opinion abroad and to serve as a symbol of equal rights granted to other Soviet nationalities.

Even then, the synagogue still remained the only place, except for occasional Yiddish performances and very rare literary gatherings, where a Jew could meet other Jews and participate with them in Jewish activities. (Similarly, European history notes many cases when churches and religious institutions have become exponents or depositories of *national* strivings of minorities.)

This paradoxical situation and the impact the Soviet synagogues were bound in these circumstances to exert upon even nonreligious Jews is clearly reflected in the report of a Jewish visitor from the United States. According to his own admission he had not attended a synogogue service for "many years," probably not since he joined the Socialist "Bund" some fifty years earlier.[1]

> The young Soviet Jew knows very little about any form of Jewishness. Nevertheless his Jewish feelings are very strong. Seeking to express them, he goes to the synagogue. A strong emotion overtakes you when you enter a synagogue in Russia—a sad mysterious stillness descends upon you. One communicates with another with the help of a prayer or just a sigh. The prayer links the person not only with God and his fellow Jews, but also with Jews the world over.... Young people also attend the synagogue. They stand still. They cannot read the prayers, but in this place they become united, as it were, with other Jews. Perhaps they come here just to meet Jews, to speak to Jews. Where else can they do this?
>
> The atmosphere overwhelmed me, too. It has been many years since my feet crossed the threshold of a synagogue. Yet when I saw the timid, helpless Jews, their anxiety took hold of me and I began to say the prayers along with them. I wanted to become united with them.[2]

Many, perhaps most, Jewish tourists who come to Moscow pay a visit to the large synagogue on Arkhipov Street. Taxi-drivers, hotel managers and guides often express surprise and some misgiving as to why "all" foreign Jewish tourists visit the synagogues, whereas non-Jews do not visit churches, except those which have been converted into museums. They sometimes ask the Jewish visitors what they have in common with a "Soviet synagogue."[3]

The "surprise" of the Moscow taxi-drivers and others clearly characterizes the present significance of the synagogue in the Soviet Union. Admittedly, most Jewish tourists do not visit the synagogue for the purpose of praying but rather because the synagogue is the one remaining visible symbol of Jewishness in the Soviet Union today.

Number of Synagogues

The number of synagogues in the Soviet Union has been a matter of speculation and dispute. The government cannot fail to have full knowledge of all legally constituted synagogues functioning in the Soviet Union, since every religious body is required by law to register with the authorities. But instead of disclosing the figure, Soviet officials have at various times given widely differing numbers. A few quotations from Soviet sources will illustrate the divergences.

The late Rabbi Schlieffer, who seldom expressed an opinion in public contrary to that of the government, reported in an interview given in September 1955 the number of synagogues "to be more than one hundred." [4] M. Voschikov, a member of the Soviet Council for Religious Cults, told Tullia Levi, an Italian reporter in Moscow during the visit of former Italian President Giovanni Grouci, that there were *400 synagogues* in the Soviet Union, serving 500,000 practicing Jews. [5]

In 1959, the Soviet Union informed the United Nations that the number of synagogues in the Soviet Union was 450. [6] Only a short time later, *The Soviet Union Today,* a weekly of the Soviet Embassy in Vienna, stated that "Jewish religious services are being held in one hundred and fifty synagogues." [7] The same number was given by the Moscow Radio in January 1961. But in the spring of that year, Pavel Dogorozhny, vice-chairman of the Council of Religious Cults in the Soviet Union, told Rabbi Rosenberg of Toronto, Canada, that there were one hnndred synagogues in the Soviet Union. [8] Rabbi Judah Leib Levin of the Moscow synagogues was quoted as saying that there were ninety-six synagogues. [9]

The 1965 handbook *USSR—Questions and Answers* contained a paragraph on the Jewish religion: 'Practicing Jews are taking advantage of the full freedom to exercise all their religious rituals. There are ninety-seven synagogues in the Soviet Union." These figures are not only contradictory; they are, as far as we could ascertain, all greater than the actual number.

As stated in the chapter "The Laws on Religion," two principal types of religious associations exist in the Soviet Union, religious societies and groups of believers. The first type occupies synagogues leased to them by the state. The second type is commonly called "legal minyanim." There are also groups called "illegal minyanim," which are unregistered.

As far as could be ascertained, there were sixty-two synagogues in 1966. To the best of our knowledge, all of them belonged to the category of "religious societies," which according to Soviet law must have a certified membership of not more nor less than twenty persons (to form a *dvadtsatka,* from the Russian word *dvadtsat,* meaning twenty). These persons are by law *individually* responsible to the Soviet authorities for the religious property and the conduct of the synagogue.[10]

The most striking fact as shown in the table presented here is the very high proportion of functioning synagogues in the non-European areas. Thus 13, or more than 20 percent of all Soviet synagogues, were located in the Georgian SSR. The Jewish population of Georgia was 51,582 in 1959 or a little over 2 percent of the total Jewish population in the Soviet Union. But there were ten times as many synagogues in proportion to the Jewish population.

Similarly, the Caucasian and the Central Asian Soviet Republics accounted for almost one half (30) of all synagogues in the entire country, whereas the Jewish population accounted for only 10½ percent of the total Jewish population. The preferential treatment accorded to the "Oriental Jews" and its plausible explanation are discussed at greater length in other chapters of this study.

Let it be noted here briefly that the "Oriental" Jewish communities, and particularly the Georgian Jews, not only have more religious freedom than the "western" Jews, but that they are more zealous and determined in defending their religious freedom than the European Jews. The history of the European Jews progressed in a different way. The westernization and secularization of the community had weakened the previous mode of Jewish life to a much larger degree

Table[11]

Synagogues in the Soviet Union
According to areas (1966)

Area	Jewish Population	% of total	Number of Synagogues	% of total number of synagogues
Caucasian republics (Georgian, Azerbaidzhan, Armenian SSRs)	92,810	4.1	19 (of which 13 are Georgian)	31.5
RSFSR	875,307	38.6	17 (Including 3 in Moscow)	27.0
Central Asian Republics (Uzbek, Kazakh, Kirgiz, Tadzhik, Turkmen SSRs)	147,495	6.5	11 (of which 7 in the Uzbek SSR)	18.0
Ukrainian SSR	840,311	37.1	8	13.0
Latvian SSR	36,592	1.6	2	3.0
Lithuanian SSR	25,100	1.1	2	3.0
Belorussian SSR	150,084	6.6	1	1.5
Moldavian SSR	95,107	4.2	1	1.5
Estonian SSR	5,000	0.2	1	1.5
Total	2,267,806	100.0	62	100.0

than in the Oriental Jewish communities; in the eastern Jewish communities, unlike the western, Judaism was still identical with Jewish religion. The religious zeal and determination of the Oriental Jews can be measured by the following act: when the authorities of Kutaisi, Georgia SSR, decreed to close the local synagogue and trucks had already arrived to remove the synagogue property, hundreds of Jews, young and old, threw themselves before the trucks. The authorities finally retreated and gave up their plan to close the synagogue.[12]

Such a display of determination is hardly conceivable in European Russia. Religious Jews would not dare to act in a similar way, and it is questionable whether the authorities would retreat as they did in Kutaisi.

In the European areas of the Soviet Union, the situation is strikingly different. There is only one legally functioning synagogue in the entire Belorussian Republic (in Minsk, the capital) with a Jewish population of 150,000 according to the 1959 census, or three times the size of the Jewish population in Georgia. Several Belorussian towns famous as former centers of Jewish life, such as Vitebsk, Bobruisk, and Gomel, which still have sizable Jewish communities, are totally deprived of legal Jewish houses of prayer.

The Moldavian SSR with a Jewish population of 95,000, the highest percentage of Jews of all Soviet republics (3.3 percent) has only one functioning synagogue, which is in the capital, Kishinev. Most of the territory of the Moldavian SSR (formerly known as Bessarabia) was incorporated into the Soviet Union during World War II. The Jewish community of Bessarabia was known for its deep attachment to the traditional Jewish way of life. The Moldavian SSR which was occupied by the Romanian allies of the German Reich during the war had the highest proportion of Jewish survivors of the Nazi onslaught— 95,000 of its former number of 150,000. It is inconceivable that the existence of only one synagogue is the result of so fast and complete a victory of "scientific materialism" and atheism among the Bessarabian Jews, the majority of whom grew up in pre-Soviet times.

In the western districts of Belorussia and the Ukraine, former territories of Poland which accounted for approximately one third of the area and one third of the Jewish population of prewar Poland, not one Jewish house of prayer is presently functioning.

The district of Zacarpathia (formerly a province of Czecho-slovakia, incorporated into the Soviet Union after World War II) has only one synagogue, despite the fact that the Jewish community here was known before the war as a fortress of ultraorthodox Judaism. (Its foremost exponent was the Rebe of Mukachevo.) Sizable Jewish communities still exist, not only in the town of Khust with its one synagogue but also in the towns of Mukachevo and Uhzgorod, where there are no synagogues.

It would be expected that the number of synagogues in the more recently acquired Soviet territories which were exposed to Soviet influence for a shorter period of time would be proportionally higher than in the older Soviet territories, but the reverse, as we see, is true.

All synagogues in the Soviet Union, large or small, are of equal rank. None has the status of a "central synagogue." Although the Moscow synagogue on Arkhipov Street is frequently described as the Central Synagogue and its Rabbi is often called Chief Rabbi of the Soviet Union, these terms do not reflect their official status. In fact, the Rabbi of the "Central Synagogue" does not even have jurisdiction over the two small synagogues which function in the suburbs of Moscow. If occasionally the Moscow synagogue and its Rabbi do assume a de facto position as representative of the Jewish religion and its institutions in the country, this is due to the fact that the Soviet authorities consider it necessary at certain times, for foreign consumption, to find a spokesman for Soviet religious Jewry.

The Personnel of the Synagogue

Before the advent of Soviet rule, the central synagogue in an average Russian town *(shtot-shul)* would traditionally carry on its payroll only a cantor and a sexton *(shames):* the rabbi would serve the whole Jewish community *(shtot-rov)* and be paid by the Com-munity Council *(kehilah).* Other religious services, such as those calling for additional cantors, readers of the Torah *(Baal Kore)* and *Baal Tokea* (blowing the shofar on the High Holiday), would usually be performed without remuneration by members of the congregation. In the smaller synagogues and houses of prayer very often the only paid employee was the sexton, who would perform in some other religious capacity as well.

Today only larger Soviet synagogues have three paid functionaries—a rabbi, cantor, and sexton. Most synagogues have no paid fulltime employees, limiting their staffs to a parttime sexton and a cantor hired for the High Holidays.

There were about fifteen to twenty rabbis functioning in the Soviet Union in 1966. Finding replacements for deceased or old rabbis is one of the most acute problems of Soviet Jewish religious life. The Moscow Yeshivah, which for a while raised hopes as the institution able to train future members for the Soviet rabbinate, has failed to fulfill expectations.

However, it should be remembered that, in contrast to several other religious cults, Jewish religious law does not consider a formal education in a higher institution of religious learning as an indispensable requisite for ordination of ecclesiastical leadership. A rabbinic certificate (smikha), and certification as an interpreter of religious law (moreh horaah) can be granted by recognized religious authorities, even when the candidate has acquired his knowledge from a private teacher, and in exceptional cases even by self-study. The determining requirements are scope of knowledge and the analytic prowess of the applicant. These conditions may seem to mitigate the problem of replenishing the Jewish clergy. Actually, private study of such demanding scope is possible only in rare cases.

Because of the acute shortage of Jewish clergymen, it is not easy for a congregation to engage a new rabbi. Furthermore, when a suitable candidate is available, he must receive the approval of the Soviet authorities who supervise religious activities (the Plenipotentiary of the Council for the Affairs of the Religious Cults and the Religious Section of the local Soviet). For this reason the congregation finds it more expedient to receive prior approval for the candidate. Reportedly, the name of the candidate is sent beforehand to the central office of the council for religious cults, which keeps a file of registered clergymen, and renders its opinion of the candidate to the local authorities. Only when the candidate receives prior approval from the central authorities is he engaged for the position.

Cantors, for the most part, are men in their fifties and sixties, although several are younger. The cantor is relatively well paid. Larger congregations vie with one another to get the cantor with the best possible voice. Congregations that cannot afford a fulltime cantor make strenuous efforts to obtain the services of a good cantor at least for the High Holidays (Rosh Hashonah and Yom Kippur). Not infrequently Soviet cantors are pensioned opera singers or singers with stage experience. This is confirmed by tourists and by indications from Soviet sources.[13]

A local organization of the trade unions (*Profsoiuz*) existed in the Moscow Synagogue. The statutes of the Soviet Trade Unions allow employees and church servants who are not members of the clergy to be admitted to the trade unions.[14]

On December 11, 1960, *Trud,* the central organ of the Soviet Trade Unions attacked the *Proforg* (Union Organizer) of the Choral Synagogue in Moscow for allowing several "unqualified" employees of the synagogue to join the Trade Union. One of them was the yeshivah teacher, S. Trebnik, the other a janitor who "in reality acts as a cantor and performs funeral services,' and therefore has no right, according to *Trud,* to belong to a Trade Union."[15]

Administration of the Synagogue

The twenty members who sign the lease agreement of the synagogue premises are, as was indicated before, *individually* responsible for the property so leased and for the conduct of affairs at the synagogue. The religious associations should elect, according to the provisions of the Law on Religious Associations of 1929, executive bodies from among their members by open ballot, a religious society an executive body of three members, and a group of believers one representative (paragraph thirteen of the law). In functioning synagogues an executive body of three members must be elected. The general assembly may also elect an auditing committee of not more than three members.[16]

The administration of the synagogue is not only entrusted with the administrative and financial affairs of the synagogue, but must also answer for what the authorities term "anti-Soviet acts and anti-Soviet propaganda in the synagogues." Just what constitutes "anti-Soviet propaganda" is determined by the authorities—in some cases by the central authorities and in other instances by the local authorities—according to the contingencies of the hour. Inquiries about Israel, receipt of a gift from an Israeli or United States tourist, or any contacts with a foreigner may also be interpreted as anti-Soviet acts, depending on the circumstances.

Therefore, foreign visitors who mingle too freely with worshipers are viewed with apprehension by synagogue leaders. Sometimes they are even prevented from speaking to the congregation. Often, the separation of visitors from worshipers is a result of explicit instructions issued by the local authorities; in other cases, it is done by synagogue leaders of their own accord, so as not to antagonize the authorities or endanger the existence of the synagogue.

The journalist B. Z. Goldberg visited the Chernovtsi synagogue in 1966. Upon being greeted by the "young rabbi" of the synagogue, Goldberg was driven away by the beadle *(gabai)*, who nervously shouted at him: "Don't speak, not here. You shouldn't speak here, not here—not even to the Rabbi." Later, one of the worshippers whispered into the ear of Goldberg's wife: "There was trouble *(a tsore)* here, that's why the beadle is so scared." [17]

It is, of course, very difficult for visitors to distinguish between synagogue officials who are in the service of the regime and those who must enforce imposed rules, sometimes rudely, in order to save the only remaining house of prayer from being closed down. [18]

Government Pressures on Synagogues

Soviet authorities exercise control over the synagogues, overtly through the far-reaching impositions explicit in Soviet law, and covertly through men in the synagogue whom they can trust.

The most efficient tool of control is the power of the authorities to approve and remove the religious and lay leadership according to their discretion. For example, the Executive of the Moscow synagogue was reportedly dissolved in 1960 by the organs of State Security (KGB—Kommisarist Gosudarstvennoi Bezopasnosti), which then appointed three new members, Fishlevich, Michalovich, and Olitsky. [19] According to a later report, the three-man Executive was ousted (in 1964) and the KGB again appointed replacements. [20]

Pressures exerted by the regime upon religious and nonreligious activists to renounce religion were very strong. For example, the "powers of persuasion" of one antireligious lecturer, Hanna Rusokovska, reportedly were so compelling that the beadle, the cantor, and three members of the *dvadtsatka* of the Chernovtsi synagogue were prompted, at one and the same time, to express their "convictions on the vanity of religious superstitions." The Soviet press further reported that as the result of the success of her persuasive powers in antireligious propaganda, Hanna Rusokovska had been the recipient of anonymous threatening telephone calls at her home.[21]

Another successful coup of atheist propaganda was reported from Velikii Tokmak (Zaporozhe District, Ukrainian SSR), where Rabbi Z. Drannikov declared from the pulpit that "religion makes the believer blind, deaf, deprived of will and strength."[22]

These are but a few examples of elderly leaders of their congregations who suddenly, just before their synagogue is closed, become "nonbelievers."[23] Public renunciations of religion are not unfamiliar in Jewish history—they were, for instance, frequent at the time of the Holy Inquisition in Spain.

For a synagogue to function legally, it must at all times have the twenty signatures (no more and no less) to the lease agreement accountable to the local soviet. If one of the "twenty" moves out, dies, or retracts his consent, another signatory must be found. It is often not easy to find a new signatory in an atmosphere where professing religious beliefs, let alone being actively engaged in support of a religious institution, reflects heavily on the individual and makes him vulnerable to all kinds of pressure and mistreatment. It is therefore not surprising that most members of the *dvadtsatka* are retired persons on pensions.

Fear of undertaking responsibilities of lay religious leadership has brought about a peculiar development: women sometimes become trustees of the synagogue and members of the *dvadtsatkas*. Even in the most liberal (Reform) western synagogues, one rarely finds a woman member of the Board of Trustees or on the Executive Board of a congregation. Thus the exigencies of life have emancipated women in the exclusively orthodox religious establishments of the Soviet Union. The regime has heralded as one of its greatest achievements the full emancipation of women in the life of the country. It would seem grotesque for Soviet spokesmen to oppose the inclusion of women in the leadership of an institution simply because they belong to the female sex. However, the Ukrainian newspaper *Radianske Slovo* (March 3, 1959) charged a violation of Jewish law occurred in the Drohobych Jewish congregation when "five women, two of them very young, participated in the Synagogue Council." The Drohobych synagogue was later closed by the authorities; (it is not known whether this was done solely because of Soviet indignation at this transgression of Jewish religious law.) Fifty Jewish residents of the town subsequently signed a request to reopen the synagogue, but their request was rejected.[24]

Closing of Synagogues

The legal reasons given by the authorities for closing a synagogue are discussed at greater length in the chapter "The Laws on Religion." They vary from legal and technical grounds to broad accusations of anti-Sovietism or Zionism.

A classical pattern for closing a house of prayer has developed. There are three stages in this pattern. The first stage: letters and articles in the press cite illegal or criminal activities or pro-Israel propaganda in the synagogue. The second stage: requests from readers, including "religious believers," to liquidate the "nest of corruption" and/or the "hotbed of pro-Israel propaganda." The final stage consists of the closing of the synagogue "in compliance with the wishes of the community," sometimes expressed at a "mass meeting."

Other grounds for closing a house of prayer are alleged violations of the laws governing religious associations; or lack of the required twenty members (dvadtsatka); or the requisition of the building for the "rehabilitation of the area," or its condemnation as unfit as a house of prayer.

Infiltration of Informers and Agents

The Soviet regime makes ample use of agents and informers. Their existence is common knowledge in the Soviet Union. Employees of every office and institution take it for granted that at least one, and more often two or more, are "trusties" of the Secret Police.

Houses of worship of other faiths receive much the same treatment. Considered ideological foes, religious institutions are especially vulnerable to suspicion. Students of religion in the Soviet Union have emphasized this disruptive aspect of religious reality in various ways. For instance, Walter Kolarz maintains "one must accept a priori that the Soviet Police infiltrated the church and seminaries. This infiltration undermines the Church."[25]

It must be stressed that internal strife also plays an important part in undermining the position of the synagogue. How much of the strife and mutual mistrust is based on genuine disagreements and human weaknesses, and how much is instigated or inflamed by agents and informers, is impossible to know. Animosities and controversies among various groups were fairly common in East European Jewish communities, but in pre-Soviet times they influenced the position of the Jewish religion in the Jewish community only slightly.

The situation is totally different in the Soviet Union. Being committed to the eradication of religious beliefs among its citizens, the Soviet regime seizes every opportunity to make use of squabbles among the membership or religious leaders to sap the foundations of any synagogue.[26] The writer Elie Wiesel, who twice visited the Moscow synagogue, was painfully aware of the presence of informers around him: "Standing there was the most notorious of the Moscow informers, a short hunchbacked man, wearing a green hat, whose features bore ugly testimony to his vocation. I myself saw him strike a Jew who dared to ask me for a prayer shawl and sidur. It is estimated that "there are at least twenty informers in the Moscow congregation—a number large enough to ensure the perpetration of a constant sense of fear and suspicion among the others."[27] Soviet Jews maintain that while Stalinism and Stalinists have been ousted from most fields of Soviet life, Stalinists still reign supreme in the synagogue.[28]

Religious Jews often describe the KGB-sponsored Executive Committees as *Judenraten*—the Nazi-appointed Jewish administrations of the ghettos.[29] These methods of infiltration are used in respect to all churches and religious cults,[30] but in the case of the Jewish religion they are ruder and more manifest.

Physical Attacks and Hooliganism

Vandalistic attacks on Jewish houses of prayer and cemeteries are infrequent occurrences in the Soviet Union. Proportionately, they are perhaps less frequent than in some nonsocialist countries. However, it should be remembered that in the Soviet system the populace is held in stricter discipline than elsewhere. Riots and any sort of mob action are nipped in the bud and punished most severely. An action which disrupts public order is treated as a potential threat to the regime itself.

The unremitting and vitriolic campaigns against the Jewish religion have had their effect on that part of the Soviet population which was infected with anti-Semitism and was eager to embark on a rampage at the first opportune moment. Notorious was the outbreak in the Moscow suburb Malakhovka in the fall of 1959 which resulted in burning and loss of life.[31]

Several less serious incidents were noted in the same period in Moscow and in the surrounding towns of Pushkino, Perlovka, and Kuntsevo.[32] The incidence of attacks diminished in subsequent years; the Soviet regime was apparently very apprehensive about the existence of clandestine gangs organizing attacks on ethnic population groups.

The Financial Situation of the Synagogue

Funds for the maintenance of synagogues and the salaries of the rabbi, cantor, and other employed personnel are provided by voluntary contributions of the worshipers. Membership fees, assessments, and collections outside the building are unlawful.[33] It stands to reason that *unofficial* assessments are being made, as the regular functioning of any institution working on the basis of an annual budget would otherwise be unthinkable.

Foreign visitors who conversed with synagogue officials and worshipers seldom heard complaints of lack of funds or of financial crises in the synagogue. The general impression of foreign tourists is that financial difficulties do not trouble Soviet synagogues, in contrast to the situation in other countries which have more affluent Jewish communities.[34]

There is reason to assume that financial support of the synagogues comes not only from the worshipers but also from Jews who themselves do not attend synagogues because of the fear of jeopardizing their positions or because they are not religious believers. Some of these Jews see in the synagogues the last bastions of Jewish life which they are anxious to perpetuate.

Contributions by worshipers may take several forms: steady contributions which in fact are equivalent to membership fees; contributions connected with specific occasions or events in the life of the worshipers and their families, such as birthdays, weddings, and funerals; and contributions for some "honors" granted to the worshipers in the synagogue. These types of contributions have been customary for generations among East European Jews.

The selling of seats and the auctioning of honors (the most common that of being called up to the Torah), both time-honored practices in synagogues the world over, became objects of attacks in the Soviet press. The auctions have been described as financial tranactions which, when performed in a house of prayer, are prohibited by Soviet law.

On rare occasions synagogues receive income from the sale of religious articles: religious calendars, memorial *(yarzeit)* candles and the like. In contrast to other religions in the Soviet Union which derive large funds from the sale of devotionalia (especially from the production and sale of candles), the revenue from such a source in synagogues is insignificant. Only when a synagogue is allowed to bake and sell matzohs may part of the profit from the transactions be used for the needs of the synagogue.

Synagogue Buildings and Their Maintenance

Reports by foreign visitors on the state of maintenance and cleanliness of Soviet synagogues vary considerably, depending probably on the place and time the visits were made.

All reports agree, however, that the Leningrad synagogue and the synagogue in Tbilisi, Georgia, both built in Tsarist times, are imposing structures which are well kept. The Moscow synagogue, which was also built in Tsarist times, is spacious but less imposing. According to some visitors, synagogues in large towns, and only the parts of these synagogues which are accessible to foreigners, are kept tidy and clean.

An American journalist who entered the inner rooms of the Bet ha-Midrash (the smaller hall of prayer and study) of the Central Moscow synagogue, described them in the following words: "When I entered the small room I was struck by the poverty and neglect of the place—a picture of gloom. The windows were full of dust, the walls peeling, and torn books were lying around on broken chairs. I had not expected to find such a sight in the headquarters of the largest Jewish community in Europe. The rooms reminded me of the Jewish religious congregation in Harlem which I visited not long ago." [35]

Another foreign visitor reported the following:

The majority of the functioning synagogues are very shabby on the outside. They are located in basements, wooden huts, and houses about to fall apart. From this general rule, one should except the synagogues in Central Asia and the Caucasus, and the great synagogues in Moscow and Leningrad, imposing .edifices created by rich Jews in Tsarist times.[36]

However, a more recent American visitor brought back a different report. "Everywhere the synagogues are kept clean and in good condition," he wrote. "When I visited Moscow, the synagogue was undergoing extensive repairs." [37]

He also visited the synagogue in Tbilisi, "one of the prettiest I have seen in Russia," and he "was astonished" at the great cleanliness of the place. The floor shone with newly applied wax, and the pews and seats looked newly scrubbed.[38]

The interiors of Soviet synagogues are much the same as they were in pre-Soviet times, except for a few modern innovations, such as amplifiers and special lighting arrangements introduced in recent years in the larger synagogues (Leningrad, Moscow, Tashkent).

A new distinguishing mark of the Soviet synagogue is the "Prayer for Peace" in Hebrew and Russian which is prominently displayed on the front walls of the synagogue *(mizrah)*. The prayer reads as follows:

> Father in heaven, bless the government of the USSR, the defenders of peace in the whole world, amen. Father in heaven, strengthen the defenders of peace in the whole world. For the sake of the merits of Aaron, the holy priest, the lover and pursuer of peace, shalt thou grant peace, amen. Almighty, who dwellst in might, thou art peace and thy name is peace, amen. May thy will be bestowed upon us and upon the whole world for the preservation of peace, and let us say, amen.[39]

Charitable Activities

Religious organizations are limited by Soviet law to religious functions only. Charitable activities are not allowed. It can be assumed that *organized* charitable activities do not take place in the Soviet synagogues. However, if one believes the accounts and sarcastic feuilletons in the Soviet press, voluntary collections "for the poor" are made on many occasions, especially on Yom Kippur eve when, following ancient custom, collection plates are placed on a table. Worshipers entering the synagogue make their contributions.

Some glimpses of Soviet life, inadvertently revealed in the Soviet press, indicate that the all-embracing system of Soviet social security and welfare care still leave gaps, either because no system can foresee all cases of human misfortunes, or because of bureaucracy or the ill will of officials in charge of the system. In at least some of these cases the Jewish House of Prayer fills the gap in meeting the time-honored communal responsibility of *tsedakah,* (which is a more comprehensive term than "charity.")

The following item in *Moskovsky Komsomolets,* organ of the Moscow Komsomol organization, shows that the practice of *tsedakah* is not extinct in the Soviet Union: "A short, slightly bent young man steps out from the Moscow synagogue. An invalid of the third category, unemployed, he can't find work or assistance. Some old woman advised him to see the rabbi in the synagogue." [40] The Komsomol newspaper is understandably full of scorn that a young man, an invalid, had to turn for assistance to a rabbi.

There is much evidence, although unofficial, that in the Jewish houses of prayer a person in trouble can turn to his fellow Jews for counsel, assistance, and comfort in time of need.

A Case History: The Odessa Synagogue

The history of the synagogues in Odessa, only one of which remains, is typical of many other Soviet towns, small and large.

Odessa, like Leningrad, is a large port with connections to foreign countries, and before the October revolution was one of the most modern and Europeanized Russian cities. The Jewish community of Odessa was known as one of the most secularized in Russia. Orthodox Jews used to say that the "fires of hell are burning ten miles around the city." Odessa was an important center of the Zionist movement and Hebrew culture.

In spite of its "worldliness," the Jewish community supported a large number of synagogues. With the advent of Soviet rule, they were closed down, one by one, by the authorities. The largest and one of the most beautiful synagogues in the country, the "Broder synagogue," was closed down in 1925 "by the demand of the Jewish workers themselves." Protests were raised and delegations sent to Moscow to rescind the order, but to no avail.[41] Subsequently all other large synagogues and those located in the center of the town were also closed down. Only several small synagogues located in the farthest parts of Odessa remained open.

The Nazis and their Rumanian allies destroyed the Jewish houses of prayer which still remained. B. Z. Goldberg, who visited Odessa shortly after the war, related, "In Odessa I found nothing but a wretched little synagogue, with its members thinking of their dead. Their cemetery had been desecrated, the gravestones broken or removed, and they were collecting funds for the restoration of them." [42]

Slowly and painfully the "wretched little synagogue" has been repaired and restored. Israeli sailors who delivered a large cargo of oranges to that port in December 1951 visited the synagogue and found "twenty worshipers who were afraid to speak to the foreigners." [43]

In the years that followed, a campaign was staged by the authorities against the little lone synagogue in a town with an estimated Jewish population of 118,000.[44] Apparently the local authorities sought to close it. In 1959, the members of the synagogue had been warned that the synagogue was too near a municipal gas station and they would purchase another building on the outskirts of the town. In the present building, they were told, "the congregation was in danger of gas poisoning." [45]

Later, charges were made that the synagogue fosters love for Israel. The local newspaper *Znamia Kommunizma* attacked the Rabbi, Iosif Diment, "who talked for the umpteenth time about the 'Promised Land' and the paradisical life which allegedly awaits all Jews on earth, and that they must all strive to fulfill God's will and go to the 'blessed land of Israel.' Cantor Grinberg intoned the prayer 'God grant us that we should meet next year in Israel.'" [46]

The increased pressure did not, however, hamper the group of devoted worshipers from improving their little house of prayer. A foreign tourist who visited the synagogue in 1963 reported that heating units were installed at considerable cost four months ago.

At approximately this time, two ferociously derisive "feuilletons" appeared in *Znamia Kommunizma,* one on October 27, 1963, and the other on January 24, 1964, with attacks against the Odessa synagogue and the town's Jewish cemetery.[47]

In a feuilleton entitled "From the Living and the Dead," *Znamia Kommunizma* wrote the following: "A gang of extortionists has made a nest for itself in the Third Jewish Cemetery. . . . The income of the Funeral Service Brigade is more than considerable. They are ready to pay any amount of money into the treasury of the Jewish congregation. Last year they readily contributed 2400 rubles. The Rabbi himself, who has descended to Odessa from the height of the capital, doesn't exactly shine with moral purity. In Moscow, there remains his abandoned family—his wife and three children." [48]

The chairman of the synagogue's executive committee allegedly said, "Why do thousands of decent working people really care about the synagogue, and why is it so difficult to find an honest man among the clergy? The clergymen are working just for the money." This was one of the rare occasions when it was acknowledged, albeit indirectly, that thousands of working people do care about a synagogue.

The Odessa newspaper noted also that the cantor of the synagogue was a young man of thirty-eight, a former *kultrabotnik* (worker in the field of culture), and he took this job "because it is more profitable than his former occupation." Additional infractions noted by the newspaper are listed: pews are sold for the price of five to fifteen rubles, "depending on the distance from the ark," collections for the poor are being made in the synagogue, and "two hundred calendars were sold on a holiday with profit."

On May 1, 1964, the *London Jewish Chronicle* published reports that the Odessa authorities had informed the synagogue leaders that the building would have to be demolished to allow for the renovation of the area. This notification came immediately after the synagogue executive committee had requested permission to renovate the synagogue.

Several months later the tenor of the local press changed radically. *Znamia Kommunizma* attacked foreign Jewish tourists who left gifts to the synagogue, and praised the leaders of the congregation who refused to accept the gifts and informed the local representative of the Council for the Affairs of Religious Cults on the "insults to the religious feelings of the congregants and of their indignation." [49]

Underscoring "proper" attitudes of synagogue leadership and worshipers is not ordinarily a prelude to the closing of a synagogue. What made the authorities suddenly incline so favorably towards the leaders of the Odessa synagogue?

Subsequent occurrences hint at a possible explanation. The visit of Israeli diplomats to Odessa had stirred the local Jewish community. Hundreds followed them wherever they went. The Soviet authorities were very much disturbed by the warmth of the reception given the visiting Israeli diplomats, especially at a time when diplomatic relations between Israel and the Soviet Union were strained. Shortly after the Israelis left, a letter by the chairman of the synagogue, Korenfeld, appeared in no less a forum than the central organ of the Soviet government, *Izvestiia*. The letter requested that "suitable measures be taken forbidding the Israeli diplomats, who come to us for the purpose of waging political discussions, to interfere in the affairs of the synagogue." [50]

Then a most unusual statement was published: a political declaration of a religious congregation (which, by law, should restrict its activities to religious matters) against a foreign state. On April 10, 1965, a *Tass* broadcast of Moscow radio's foreign services reported publication of a letter in *Izvestiia* from the religious believers in Odessa regarding the policy of the Israeli government, a letter which the secretaries of the Israel embassy in Moscow refused to accept from the Odessa congregation. The "Odessa religious believers" protested the alleged pro-West German policy of the Israeli government and "expressed the hope that the Israeli government critically review its relations with the Bonn Nazis." [51] The Soviet government had thus used the Odessa synagogue here as a tool in its foreign policy.

The sequence of events, as they developed, suggests very strongly that a "deal" was made between the leaders of the synagogue and the authorities, a *quid pro quo*. First, the congregation requested permission to renovate and possibly to enlarge the synagogue. This was countered by the authorities with a threat to tear down the building altogether. Evidently, the congregation then agreed "to do a job" for the authorities for the price of keeping the synagogue open.

It is not for us, in countries free of antireligious harassment and pressure, to sit in judgment on the course of action the leadership of the only remaining Odessa synagogue took under these circumstances.

Methods of Closing a Synagogue:

1. A campaign in preparation of closing a synagogue

This letter is one of several that have been printed in *Radianska Bukovina* of Chernovtsi, Ukrainian SSR, as part of an intensive press campaign to close the synagogue in Chernovtsi. The synagogue was consequently closed.

Parasites

Splendid are the achievements of the Soviet people. Our local workers also bring their worthy contribution to the great and noble aim of communist construction. We nevertheless find here and there, in secluded corners, spongers, who, crawling like loathsome bugs, poison the fresh air and impair life. The heads of the synagogue on Ruski street, who refuse to be occupied in profitable work for the society, prefer to live a parasitic life under the cover of ritual official-dom, belong to this category of parasites more than anybody else.

We have both heard it on many occasions and know that this synagogue is a convenient harbor for machinations and speculations. Its leaders have hospitably welcomed the Israeli "diplomat," who dared to appear before believers with foul motives. We have been particularly angered by this incident. Whom have Raish, Zilber and Barenboim, the heads of "God's House," invited? The representative of the Ben-Gurion Government, which has come to an agreement with the German militarists. They have forgotten the millions of Jews exterminated by the fascists in the furnaces of the Oswiencim and Maidanek death camps.

And this new "Jerusalem prophet" has, instead of praying, called on us to conceal spies. This will not be permitted: We unanimously demand that he leave our country on account of this kind of utterance! We know one and only one motherland, our great Soviet Union, where Jewish workers build a wonderful life and construct the communist future, hand in hand with the workers of all the other brotherly nations. The Israeli provocateur has not been accidentally expelled from the synagogue by the believers themselves, regardless of the fervent support given him by Raish, Zilber and Barenboim.

We are certain that the synagogue on Ruski street has long ceased to be a prayer home and has become a site for shady machinations, the only aim of which is to extort as much money as possible from people blinded by Judaism. Moreover, anti-Soviet activities are taking place there. Therefore, we demand from the authorities to stop its harmful existence and to close the synagogue.

Inhabitants of Residential District No. 3

E. Kalmanovich, F. Kalmanovich, A. Zolotova, E. Berenshtein, D. Avzciger, L. Vaizner, I. Goldstein, G. Goldin, K. Halperina, V. Leizerman and others—a total of 60 signatures.

[*Radianska Bukovina,* September 9, 1960, as translated in *Jews and the Jewish People* Vol. 1, No. 2, p. 4]

The letter contains all, or most, of the accusations characteristic of a Soviet campaign to close a synagogue. The charges leveled at the campaign were:

a) The heads of the synagogue "refuse to be occupied in profitable work for the society." Services being performed by the clergy are classified as parasitic, i.e., in an unspecified way illegal according to the law that prescribes persecution of persons avoiding socially useful work and leading antisocial parasitic ways of life (Edict of the Presidium of the Supreme Soviet of May 4, 1961). Theoretically, any clergyman can be, according to such classification, accused under this edict.

b) The synagogue is "a convenient harbor for machinations and speculations." The offences are not spelled out in this instance in detail. Similar letters and articles usually contain accusations of black market dealings, stealing of community funds, and illegal dealings.

c) The leaders invited and hospitably welcomed the secretary of the Israeli Embassy in Moscow to the synagogue. In other letters and articles published about the same incident, the diplomat was accused of leaving behind Israeli skullcaps and other presents. He had also read a portion of the Torah in which the story of Rahab in Jericho hiding Jewish spies is told. Whether the portion of the Torah read by the diplomat was the prescribed portion of the Torah reading on this Sabbath, or the diplomat chose another portion to read, is not noted. The reading of this portion of the Torah has been construed as a call "to conceal spies." The presence of the Israeli diplomat with his family, and the hearty welcome given to him, seem to be the central charge. The synagogue has become, in the words of the people who signed the letter, a stage of anti-Soviet activities, the most ominous of all charges.

d) The last indictment is extortion of "as much money as possible from the people blinded by Judaism." How this extortion has been accomplished is not explained.

The Soviet legislature on religious associations states: "In case of a disclosure in the activities of a religious association of deviations from the rules established for such an association, the registration agency shall demand the correction of the defects by the date indicated by the agency" (paragraph sixty-one of Instructions of the People's Commissariat for the Interior of 1929). It would seem that inviting and welcoming the Israeli diplomat would, at most, fall into the category of "deviations from the rules established" and that a correction of the defects, and not the closing of the synagogue, would be the normal procedure. Only when "The religious society or group refuses to correct the defects and also in cases of the disclosure of the violation of the law," the city committee for religious matters (at the local soviet) may ask the committee for religious matters at the Council of Ministers of the Republic to liquidate the society or group (paragraph sixty-one). There is no indication that a warning and a demand to correct defects was given in this case.

The law prescribes a certain procedure to be followed at the closing of a house of prayer and allows an appeal of the decision of closure, in which case the religious society or group may be liquidated only after the confirmation of the decision (paragraphs sixty-one, sixty-two, and sixty-three of the Instructions). This procedure takes a long time. However, the synagogue in Chernovtsi was closed soon after the publication of this letter.

2. The members resign

The following letter is one of several letters and articles requesting the closing of the synagogue in Kishinev, Moldavian SSR.

Every Religion is a Deception of the People

We have, for many years, been members of the local synagogue's "Dvatsatka." We now consider that the time has come to tell all Jewish believers that the synagogue brings nothing to the people but harm. We do not want to cheat workers and ourselves any longer and have consequently come to the conclusion that the existence of the synagogue serves no purpose. Sh. Goldenberg, former Community

Chairman; I. Godyish, former cantor; A. Gandelman, I. Gershkovitch, former community members; Sh. Rabinovich, H. Barenboim, I. Lerner.

[Sovetskaia Moldavia, August 5, 1960, as translated in *Jews and the Jewish People,* Vol. 1, No. 2, p. 1].

One of the several ways of closing a synagogue or other house of prayer is by the resignation of all or most of the twenty members required for the existence of a "religious society" and for the use of a "special prayer building."

According to the existing laws, resignation of *some* members of the society does not automatically involve the dissolution of the society and the closing of the house of prayer. Two separate acts and procedures are often confused. One is the dissolution of the religious society (or group); the other is the annulment of the contract between the local soviet and the group use of the religious building. The law does not prescribe that the two acts follow one another. A religious society can have its contract annulled and still remain in existence without the building. The group may request the use of other facilities or try to build or obtain another building.

When a religious society has been dissolved, another group of twenty members has the right to replace them, to organize themsleves as a religious society, and request a new contract for the use of the same building. If some of the twenty members resign and other members remain, new members may replace the members who have resigned, or they may reorganize themselves into a "group of believers." If there are no persons who wish to use the prayer building for religious purposes, the local soviet must place a notice of this fact on the doors of the prayer building and new applications may be submitted. (See paragraphs thirty-four and thirty-five of the Law of 1929; paragraphs twenty-one, twenty-two, forty-two, forty-nine, and sixty-three of the Instructions to the Law of 1929.)

Notes

1. Zalmen Yefroikin, *A Bazukh in Sovet Rusland* (A Visit to Soviet Russia) (New York, 1962). Mr. Yefroikin was, before his death in 1966, Director of the Educational Department of the American Arbeter Ring (Workmen's Circle), a Jewish fraternal organization with a secularist, pro-socialist orientation.

2. *Ibid.*, p. 102.

3. S. L. Shneiderman, "In der Moskver Groiser Shul" (In the Moscow Great Synagogue) (in *Yidisher Kemfer*, December 29, 1965, p. 5).

4. *American Jewish Year Book* (hereafter *AJYB*), pp. 416–7.

5. In *Voce Republicana* (Republican Voice) of Italy, reported by the Jewish Telegraphic Agency, January 13, 1960.

6. Jewish Telegraphic Agency (hereafter JTA), January 28, 1960.

7. JTA, September 30, 1960, quoted also in the *AJYB*, 1961, p. 287.

8. *AJYB*, 1962: see the chapter "Soviet Union, Religious Life."

9. *USSR*, April 1963.

10. For a detailed discussion on the legal status of the synagogue, on the various types of religious associations and houses of prayer, and on the administrative organs of the synagogue see the chapter "The Laws on Religion" in this book.

11. *Itogi Vsesoiuznovo Spiska Naseleniia SSSR 1959 goda* (Totals of All-Union Population Census of 1959) (Moscow, 1962).

12. This incident is described in Ben-Ami, *Yahadut be-Rusiah ha-Sovetit* (Judaism in Soviet Russia) (Jerusalem, 1961, p. 159).

13. For instance, *Sovetskaia Belorussia* of April 2, 1960, in the feuilleton "Under the Synagogue Vaults," noted that a certain Shimon Shalman, a pensioned artist of the Kiev opera, demanded 8000 rubles, board, and lodging for serving as a cantor for the High Holidays at the Minsk synagogue. Another newspaper, *Zvezda*, asserted (June 6, 1960) that Shalman actually received a very high remuneration (equivalent to eight months of payment for an average worker).

14. Several interpretations, some of them contradictory, were issued on the categories of church employees who may classify as clergymen. An interpretation of the Commissariat of Finance, issued in 1924, did not consider cantors in synagogues and psalm readers and chanters in Christian churches as clergymen (P. V. Gidulianov, *Otdelenie Tserkvi ot Gosudarstva*, Moscow, 1924, p. 158).

15. *Jews and the Jewish People* (hereafter *JJP*).

16. The laws concerning the administration of the synagogues are discussed at greater length in the chapter "The Laws on Religion."

17. B. Z. Goldberg, "Yidn in Chernovitz" (Jews in Chernovtsi) (in *Der Tog*, August 31, 1966).

18. See, for instance, the article of Efraim Auerbach, "Oif der Vogshol" (In the Balance) (*Der Tog*, September 19, 1966).

19. *Yalkut Mogen*, Tel Aviv, August 1960, p. 7.

20. *New York Herald Tribune*, July 10, 1964.

21. D. Koretskii, "Naivishcha Nagoroda" (The Highest Reward) (in *Voiovnichii Ateist*, No. 10, 1962, pp. 36–7, and *Yevrei Yevreiski Narod* (hereafter YYN), No. 10, p. 8).

22. I. Golubovich, ed., *Pravda po Iudeisku Religiiu i Sionizm* (The Truth About the Jewish Religion and Zionism) (Kiev, 1962). The article of former Rabbi Drannikov was published in the collection.

23. Incidentally, the term "believers" (in Yiddish *gloibike*), with which Rabbi Drannikov allegedly addressed his congregation, was not in use by Jews of the older generation; the term, translated from the Russian *veruiushche* is commonly used in Yiddish antireligious propaganda.

24. *Jews in Eastern Europe* (hereafter *JEE*) No. 4, 1960, p. 19.

25. Walter Kolarz, *Religion in the Soviet Union* (New York, 1961, p. 91). Kolarz charts the avenue of infiltration into theological schools: "Every prospective student of a theological school must present a letter of recommendation from his parish priest. In the Soviet Union it is not beyond the power of police to extort such recommendations when needed." It should be added that at the time when the Moscow Yeshivah was functioning, approval of the Soviet authorities was needed for every student admitted.

26. See, for instance, B. Z. Goldberg, "Idn Krign Zich" (Jews Quarrel) (*Der Tog,* August 2, 1966).

27. Elie Wiesel, *Will Soviet Jewry Survive?* (A Commentary Report Reprint, New York, 1967, p. 4).

28. See, for instance, the report of Rabbi Judah Leib Gertner of Caracas, Venezuela, who visited the Soviet Union in 1966, in *Der Tog,* April 13, 1966: "Stalinistishe Gaboim Varfn on a Shrek oif di Shul Idn" (Stalinist Beadles Hold the Synagogue Jews in Fear).

29. *JEE,* Dec. 1965, p. 60.

30. See Nikita Struve, *Le Chrétiennes en USSR* (Christians in the USSR) in Chapter 13, who says: "The gross cruelty of Stalin's day has passed but the slyness of his methods remains. No one is directly punished just for being a Christian, but underhand methods are found for hurting those who take a leading part in church life."

31. Details in *The New York Times,* October 13, 1959; *Maariv,* Tel Aviv, October 16, 1959; *JEE,* November 1959.

32. *JEE,* November 1959, p. 13.

33. According to paragraphs 7, 8, and 9 of the *Instructions of the People's Commissariat for the Interior,* of October 1, 1929. These prohibitions are not specified in the *Law on Religious Associations* of April 8, 1929.

34. See, for instance: Shlomo Ben-Israel, "Eindrukn fun a Raise in Rusland" (Impressions From a Trip to Russia) (in the *Daily Forward,* September 10, 1966); also, B. Z. Goldberg "Arum Riger Shul" (Around the Riga Shul) (in *Der Tog,* August 18, 1966): "I have never heard complaints that congregations need money," wrote Goldberg.

35. Shneiderman, *op. cit.*

36. Ben-Ami, *op. cit.,* p. 66.

37. Ben-Israel, *op. cit.*

38. *Ibid.*

39. Even Shushan, *Sipuro Shel Maso, Esrim Yom be-Brit ha-Moatzot* (The Story of a Trip, Twenty Days in the Soviet Union) (Tel Aviv, 1964, p. 67).

40. *Moskovsky Komsomolets,* April 4, 1960, reprinted in *JJP,* Vol. 1, No. 2, p. 9.

41. A. A. Gershuni, *Yahadut be-Rusiah ha-Sovetit* (Judaism in Soviet Russia) (Jerusalem, 1961, pp. 63–4).

42. Goldberg, *op. cit.,* p. 90.

43. *AJYB,* 1953, p. 332.

44. *AJYB,* 1963, p. 350.

45. *JEE,* Mid-September, 1959.

46. "The Deceived Victims of Zionist Propaganda" (in *Znamia Kommunizma,* January 6, 1960).

47. *Yalkut Mogen,* Tel Aviv, May 1964.

48. *JEE,* Nov. 1964, pp. 22–3.

49. *Znamia Kommunizma,* August 19, 1964; and *YYN,* No. 17, 1964, p. 2.

50. These incidents are described in greater detail in *JEE,* December 1965, pp. 66, 67, 71.

51. *JEE,* December 1965, p. 65.

CHAPTER 3

Holidays and Observances

Holidays played an essential role in the preservation of Jewish religion and of the Jewish people; for hundreds of years the rhythm of life in a Jewish community evolved around the Jewish calendar with its once-a-week day of nearly absolute physical and spiritual rest, and with its holidays of various moods and meanings. The well-known dictum of Ahad Ha'am, the modern Hebrew writer and philosopher, that "the Sabbath has kept alive the Jewish people more than the Jewish people has kept [alive] Sabbath, adequately exemplifies the importance of the Sabbath in Jewish history.

Characteristic of the Sabbath and of most Jewish holidays is the fact that a large number of the observances are fulfilled in the home, outside the synagogue. While for some holidays, like Rosh Hashonah and Yom Kippur, the home-observed rites are not very significant, for other festivals the observances performed at home are the central part of the holiday. For instance, on Passover, the Seder, the festive meal with the prescribed ten points of the ritual and the reading of the Hagadah (the story of Passover) at the table is the focal point of the Passover observances. Also on Hanukah and Purim, the prayer services and celebrations at the synagogue take second place to the rites and festivities concentrated in the home—the lighting of the candles on Hanukah; plays, masquerades, and the exchange of gifts on Purim.

The attendance on the Sabbath and holidays in the synagogues and houses of prayers has been, in the Jewish communities, almost universal until the coming of the era of modernization in the nineteenth century.

The Sabbath

Before the October Revolution Russian Jews lived in a largely self-contained economy, particularly in the smaller towns. This was especially true in regard to the patterns of Jewish employment. The majority of Russian Jews were self-employed as merchants and craftsmen. Most of the remaining were in the employ of other Jews.

Jews were neither employed by the government and its agencies, nor could they find work, except in rare cases, in large industrial establishments.

Whether Jews were self-employed or in the employ of fellow Jews, their day of rest was Saturday. Saturday was the established and recognized day of rest in all Jewish hamlets (shtetlekh) and in the Jewish neighborhoods of larger towns. So widely accepted was the fact that Saturday is the universal day of rest for the Jews in East Europe, that never was the weekly market-day held on Saturdays in towns inhabited by Jews, because the non-Jewish peasants would not be able to sell their products to or buy from the Jews.

The secularization of Jewish life in the early twentieth century made visible inroads in the previously almost total observation of the Sabbath, but it was not until the October Revolution that Saturday ceased to be the generally observed day of rest of the Jewish population in Russia. The whole economic structure of the country had radically changed in the wake of the revolution. The government became the almost sole employer; Jews were not discriminated against any more in employment, and they had access to all available positions.

Nonetheless, the eradication of the Jewish Sabbath was a slow process, and a large proportion of the Jewish population resisted the change as much and as long as they could.

At first Jews even dared to protest the forcible imposition of Saturday as a workday and of Sunday as a day of general rest for all. Characteristic in that respect is the written protest of the Poltava Jewish community council (the kehilah), before it was disbanded by the government against the provision incorporated in the Law of 1922 regulating workers' rights and working conditions which in paragraph 109 established Sunday as the only day of rest. The protest of the Poltava kehilah was based on the contention that the imposition of a universal day of rest on Sunday suppresses the right of personal national autonomy and is in violation of the principle of freedom of conscience; the protest hinted that Sunday is essentially a religious day of rest observed by only one religious faith and imposing it on members of other religious cults is unfair and incompatible with the freedom of conscience.[1]

In an article titled "Not Saturday but Sunday" in *Emes,* the central organ of the "Jewish sections" (Yevsektsiia) evaluates the Jewish resistance to the imposing of Sunday as a general day of rest in the following manner: "The experiences from the anti-Saturday campaign disclosed that we were, almost everywhere, confronted with motives originating not from religious but nationalistic superstitutions: why does not the Russian worker give up Sunday?" [2]

In some factories the weekly day of rest, changed—for a short time—from Saturday, not to Sunday, but to another day of the week. For instance, a report in *Emes* informs that "the workers in the tobacco factory in Kremenchug decided by a great majority to change the day of rest from Saturday to Monday." [3]

Because so many Jewish workers had resisted the shifting of the day of rest from Saturday to Sunday (and in some plants to another day of the week), a prominent Jewish communist leader saw fit to point out that "the campaign against the Saturday rest day is and should be conducted exclusively from the economic point of view. It is not anticlerical arguments that ought to be the point of departure but arguments of economic necessity—this question was formulated in the directives of the Central Bureau as well as in the press and at meetings." [4]

The Soviet Yiddish press reported both "failures" and "great successes" in the anti-Saturday campaign. In 1923, *Emes* reported from Minsk,

> If a year ago some workers hesitated whether to work or not, now they do not hesitate any more. Bearded elderly Jewish workers are standing on Saturdays on the scaffolds, paint houses in the market place, are not afraid of God and are not ashamed of people. [5]

Nahum Chanim, leader of the Socialist-oriented Jewish fraternal organization "Workmen's Circle" in the United States, visited the Soviet Union in 1928, five years after this article appeared, and reported that although the Sabbath was being observed in the small towns in the homes "like in the good old days," on the streets the day of rest is hardly observable. [6]

Many small Jewish *artels* (producers' cooperatives of artisans) were still closed on Saturdays until 1929. [7] The resistance to making

Saturday a workday was much more stubborn, and had a better chance to succeed, if only temporarily, in places where all or most workers were Jews—in certain *artels,* for instance, and in the Jewish kolkhozes where many of the members remained religious and observant.

The majority of the Jewish peasants in the old "colonies" (villages) and in the newly established villages did not want to go out to work on the Sabbath, even after the establishment of the kolkhozes. This situation had changed in the 1930s. Pressure on the *artels* which still held onto Saturday as their day of rest had increased. More and more *artels* changed their day of rest to Sunday by "the voluntary decision of the collective," which in fact were thinly disguised orders from the Soviet authorities.

Many observant Jews succeeded in keeping the Sabbath by taking up lines of employment which would make it possible to avoid working on that day.[8] For instance, the positions of night watchmen were greatly cherished by religious Jews and former members of the clergy, because doing physical work on the Sabbath was not required in these positions. In addition, this kind of work offered a chance for intermittent study of the Torah in the quiet of the night. So large was the proportion of religious Jews in this very badly paid occupation that a *bon mot* then current in the Soviet Union was that to get a night watchman's job you had to be a former rabbi, and when the day comes that rabbis will be asked to take over their honored positions again each rabbi would be asked to prove that he had been a night watchman.

The number of Jews who wished to and also were able to, observe Sabbath as a day of rest has constantly decreased, and their number is apparently very small now. Some orthodox Jews still manage not to work on Saturday by taking up the same old occupations. In addition to the occupation of watchmen and night watchmen (an occupation in which a proportionately larger number of people were employed in the Soviet Union than in most other countries), observant Jews try to get positions where the time of work cannot be controlled: for example, as agents selling books, and as buyers and providers *(zagotoviteli)* for offices and institutions.

In rare cases, when a person is ready to face all consequences and the management is afraid to lose the services of a skilled and competent worker, a compromise is sometimes worked out. *Sovetskaia Torgovlia,* the organ of the Soviet merchandising establishment, disclosed an interesting case which involved a persistent and determined young man who refused to work on Saturday. His name was Vladimir Riabushin, an artist for Ukrotorgreklama (apparently a branch of the Ukranian trade advertising agency). "You can see him," reported the newspaper, "each Saturday in one of the Dnepropetrovsk squares in dark clothes with a Talmud in his hand." The writer called Riabushin *sektant* and not *Yudeist,* and it is difficult to surmise whether this man allegedly studying the Talmud was a Jew or a member of some "Judaic" sect.

The newspaper scorned the acquiescence of the agency to the artists obstinate refusal to work on Saturday and the decision which permitted him to rest on Saturdays and to work instead on Saturday nights, "as the firm was unwilling to lose the services of a good worker." "This practice is absolutely inadmissible," said *Sovetskaia Torgovlia,* "because it disrupts work discipline and presents a bad example." [9]

In the Soviet Union, synagogue attendance has decreased considerably, in part as a result of the continuing process of urbanization and secularization and in part due to the administrative antireligious restrictions imposed by the authorities. The present attendance at prayer services in the Soviet synagogues varies considerably, from one holiday to another, with some notable exceptions following the pattern of attendance prevailing in countries outside the Soviet Union.

Attendance at three weekday daily services, *shaharit, minha,* and *maariv* (morning, afternoon and evening prayers), is generally slight. Usually, not more than a few dozen elderly people are seen at these services, even in the great synagogues of Moscow or Leningrad. This is not unlike the situation in the United States and other western countries where the assembling of a "minyan" (a quorum of ten males for communal prayer) on a weekday is often a hard task.

Attendance is larger at the Friday night and Saturday morning services. The number of worshipers grows even higher during the three festivals of Sukkos, Passover, and Shevuos. [10] Particularly large becomes the number of worshipers on the days when Yizkor, the prayer for the dead, is said. Here, too, the pattern is not unlike the one familiar in Jewish communities in other countries, with the difference that the number of persons mourning the departure of members of their families is proportionately much larger in the Soviet Union; there is hardly a Jewish family there which has not lost close relatives at the hands of the German invaders in the last war.

The largest number of worshipers assemble on the two days of Rosh Hashonah, on Yom Kippur, and on Simchas Torah. The high attendance on Simchas Torah is the only exception to the pattern prevailing in other Jewish communities the world over.

Rabbi Levin of the great Moscow synagogue told a visitor that on the holidays the synagogue is full, on the Sabbath several hundred people come to the prayer services, and on weekdays 100–150 persons come to pray.[11]

The High Holidays

The High Holidays, Rosh Hashonah and Yom Kippur, particularly Yom Kippur, have exerted a dominating, almost mystical power in the long and torturous Jewish history. Jewish lore and literature include many stories of heretics and of Jews converted to other religions who, on the day of Yom Kippur, could not resist the mysterious impulse to visit a synagogue, and of marranos who paid with their lives for arranging Yom Kippur prayers in Catholic Spain.

Rosh Hashonah and Yom Kippur, the two holidays of solemn prayers in the synagogue, along with Passover which was the most important home holiday, were therefore the prime targets of anti-religious propaganda and harassment of religion in the Soviet Union. Many, if not most, Soviet Jews have long resisted or evaded working on the two days of Rosh Hashonah, and even more have done so on Yom Kippur. The resistance was strongest among the Jewish artisans in the "producer's cooperatives" and in the Jewish kolkhozes—the places of work where Jewish workers were a majority and the organizational framework allowed for a certain measure of self-rule.

Perhaps the most characteristic example of resistance is the fact that in 1921 the typesetters of *Emes,* the central organ of the "Jewish sections" of the Communist party, refused to work on the High Holidays, and the newspaper did not appear on that day. A year later, just before the High Holidays, an "explanation by a group of typesetters" was printed in *Emes* in which the suspension of the newspaper in the previous year was explained in this manner: "Last year part of the typesetters did not come on the *Yomim Noroim* [Days of Awe, High Holidays], and the others who did come were so exhausted from starvation after the hunger years that they could not take upon themselves the responsibility for the appearance of the *Emes* on these days." [12]

The tenacity of Jewish kolkhoz members in observing the High Holidays is illustrated by the following event. The "Collectivization Day" established by the government to be fêted on October 14 fell, in 1929, on Yom Kippur. Knowing that the Jewish kolkhozniks would not voluntarily participate in the festivities, the Executive Committee of the Supreme Soviet saw fit to change the date of the Collectivization Day for the Jewish kolkhozes, so that the "Jewish members could participate in celebrating their holiday of their own free will and not because they were forced to." [13] It is noteworthy that the decision of the Supreme Soviet was taken against the voiced opinion of the "holier than the Pope" Jewish Yevsektsiia, who had insisted on not postponing the day of celebration.

The Yiddish organ of the "godless," *Der Apikoires* (No. 12 of 1932), in its summary of the "anti-High Holidays campaign," complained that the Jewish members of the kolkhoz "Forward to Socialism" in Khislavitz did not go out to work on both days of Rosh Hashonah, and that after a search of several weeks they happily found a cantor for the services for that holiday. "In a tailors' *artel* only 6 out of 29 workers reported for work," wrote the periodical and "a similar situation prevailed at the shoemakers' *artel.*" The situation is a little better, says *Der Apikoires,* in Berdichev, because "a staff to prevent absenteeism on the High Holidays has been organized and has worked well." [14]

The Yevsektsiia's program of activities for Yom Kippur included the organization of meetings and concerts on Yom Kippur night, and of so-called "Yom Kippurniks"—voluntary work on high-priority projects. Sometimes communist officials forced their way into the synagogues and made inflammatory and derisive antireligious speeches. [15] In the first decade of Soviet rule, when there was still hope of resisting the antireligious onslaught, abusive anti-Yom Kippur marchers often met staunch resistance; fist-fights erupted, followed by arrests and court sentences. [16]

In the course of time, however, the harsh administrative measures against religion, the fear of consequences in case of resistance, the deprivation of educational opportunities for the families of resisters, and the constant antireligious propaganda (which had an appreciable effect only in regard to the young Jewish generation) have taken their toll. Attendance at High Holiday worship services in the synagogues declined considerably during the following decades. The dwindling attendance was aided by the progressively growing scarcity of Jewish prayer houses, and by the ever-growing sanctions for workers' absenteeism, which culminated in the 1940 law imposing fines or jail sentences for more than twenty minutes of tardiness to work (*progul*).

Nonetheless, the awareness of the High Holidays, and especially Yom Kippur, is still deeply imbued among great numbers of the older and the middle-aged Jewish generation who respond, almost instinctively, when the High Holidays come. Some Jews attend the full service; some show up for the *Yizkor;* and some just stand a few minutes among the crowd of worshipers. Characteristic of this attitude is the following item which appeared in *Birobidzhaner Shtern* (the only Yiddish-language newspaper which appears in small format several times a week in the Jewish Autonomous Region Birobidzhan). The Yiddish writer H. Rabinkov, who is active in the "atheist movement," describes his discussion with several Jews in this manner: "You may conduct with us as many antireligious meetings as you can stand, but you are wasting your words. We are, you should know, like those cavalry horses: when they hear the trumpet, on they go. The same with us: as soon as Rosh Hashonah and Yom Kippur come, on to the synagogue we go *i nikakikh* [and nothing will hold us back]." [17]

In the still-existing synagogues the attendance at High Holidays services was invariably high even in recent years. Synagogues could not accommodate all who came to worship. The *New York Times* reported that on Yom Kippur in 1963 during the Kol Nidrei services "several thousand worshipers spilled over into the streets near the synagogue." [18] The largest Moscow synagogue had a capacity crowd of two thousand worshipers on both days of Rosh Hashonah of 1966, according to press reports. [19] At the Yom Kippur services an overflow crowd of two thousand people had to be content to stand outside the synagogue building and listen in on the prayers. Also, at the two smaller Moscow synagogues, people were standing outside the building, although not in such great numbers as at the central synagogue.

The majority of the worshipers were old and middle-aged persons, although a good number of young people were among those present.[20]

During the 1966 High Holidays, foreign correspondents and visitors saw "thousands of young Russian Jews" assembled in the immediate vicinity of the central synagogue of Moscow during the services. One of the correspondents had a conversation with a young man in the crowd who told him that he had come there "in search of himself." [21]

On the High Holidays many religious Jews, otherwise meek and law-abiding citizens, boldly take their chances in defying Soviet law, and assemble "illegally" for community prayer wherever legal permission for holding religious services is not given to them, although Soviet law provides that prayer meetings organized for special occasions, even when not held in "places especially adapted for religious purposes and organized by believers who have not formed a religious society or a group of believers," are still legal if "notification is given to the authorities regarding each meeting separately." [22] But very rare are the cases when groups organized for High Holiday worship will dare to submit such notification to the authorities, and seldom do the authorities take cognizance of such notification.

The number of private prayer meetings organized for the Rosh Hashonah and Yom Kippur services in private homes and in rented quarters is apparently high, although, obviously, the exact number is impossible to determine. In some localities the authorities will tolerate *ad hoc* services, provided they are small, inconspicuous, and certain to dissolve after the Holidays. In other places, or in the same localities at other times, they will clamp down and interrupt the services, sometimes punishing the organizers and leaders of the prayer meeting, and sometimes limiting themselves to a stern warning. Accounts of "illegally" held Yom Kippur services are found in reports of a number of visitors to the Soviet Union; we have a detailed description by a Soviet Jew of such services which was smuggled out of the country and published in the form of a book.[23] In the episode described the police interrupted the services, wrote down the names of those present, and impounded all prayer books.

Another case in which Jews applied for permission (although according to the law only "notification" is required) and services were held in spite of an explicit denial of permission was reported by an Israeli visitor who participated in the illegal prayer meeting.[24]

The Russian-born Australian Jewish writer Judah Waten, a recipient of several Australian literary prizes, described a conversation
with his cousin in the Soviet Union, in the left-wing *New World
Review*. The cousin told him that she attended the synagogue more
often than her husband, because she enjoyed the services and enjoyed
meeting Jews: "On the New Year and Yom Kippur the synagogue is
packed and people stand out in the street. You would be surprised at
the people you would meet there. Professors, writers, doctors, army
officers." [25]

The number of Soviet Jews who attend Yom Kippur services or
are present for a while near or in the synagogues and the "illegal"
minyanim is, of course, impossible to determine. However, it can
be stated with certainty that they number in the hundreds of thousands.

Simchas Torah

Simchas Torah, "the rejoicing in the Torah," is a one-day holiday
celebrated upon the conclusion of and the immediate beginning of the
re-reading of the Five Books of Moses in the synagogue.

Simchas Torah was celebrated in the Jewish communities of East
Europe more exuberantly than were the three Festivals (Passover,
Shevuos and Sukkos) when the Torah injunction is also to rejoice
(vesomahto behagekho).

Each member of the community was awarded, on Simchas Torah,
the honor of being called to the Torah reading and of carrying the
Torah scroll in a procession. While children in the procession held
paper flags, young and old sang and danced. On that day it was
permissible, even recommended, to "wet the throat with something
stronger than tea," and the prohibition against men and women
mingling in the synagogue was overlooked.

In the Soviet Union the character of Simchas Torah and its mode
of celebration have evolved in a somewhat different manner from that
in which it was celebrated before the October Revolution and from
the way it is celebrated today in other countries. In the Soviet Union,
it has become the gay festival for Jewish youth. Although Simchas
Torah was always a joyful holiday in which old and young participated, there was another holiday which was celebrated even more
merrily in Jewish communities of Eastern Europe, and was only
slightly connected with the Torah and religious observances. This was

Purim, which was celebrated mainly by carnivallike dramatics *(Purimshpiln),* exchange of gifts, and feasting.

Why then has a holiday which is celebrated in honor of the Torah become the holiday of the secularized nonreligious Soviet Jewish youth, and not Purim, the only Jewish holiday which the rigid Jewish communist leadership seldom attacked and had even a faintly sympathetic attitude to (in view of its irreverent folk character and because the Yiddish theater evolved from the *Purimshpil)?*

The destruction of secular Yiddish culture, a rather long process finally terminated in 1948, has made this situation possible. When all Jewish secular leaders and the Yiddish literary figures were either killed or arrested, all links between Jewish secular culture and Jewish youth ceased to exist. There was no way of renewing these links eleven years later, when a feeble restoration of Yiddish culture was allowed, because in the interim the organizational and linguistic forms of communication were destroyed. Yiddish was no longer the language of the younger Jewish generation. By contrast, the synagogue has retained both its existence and the old forms of its functioning; this was the only institution in which the amorphous desire for Jewish identification was able to fulfill itself. Jewish religious believers, however old and frightened they were, still sang and danced clumsily on Simchas Torah, and the youngsters could join them, while Purim, precisely because it was more secular and because it needed for its existence a Jewish milieu, was disregarded.

While a very large attendance in the synagogues on the High Holidays is typical for all Jewish communities the world over, an equally large turnout on the holiday of Simchas Torah is a purely Soviet phenomenon which developed in recent years due to these special circumstances. This became the occasion for associating as Jews, and for participating in folk singing and folk-dancing, for which all other Soviet nationalities have so many secular occasions. The songs young people sang on Simchas Torah near the synagogues were for the most part not religious songs, their dances were not religious dances, and their use of musical instruments on a holiday is forbidden by Jewish law and custom.[26]

Reportedly, as many as thirty thousand Moscow Jews of all ages, men, women and children (the presence of children at religious celebrations is a rarity in the Soviet Union) assembled on the day of

Simchas Torah, October 18, 1965, in the Moscow synagogue and in neighboring streets. The daytime services were attended mostly by elderly people, but starting at six o'clock in the evening, throngs of middle-aged and young people in their holiday best filled the synagogue and the streets around it. They sang and played Yiddish and Hebrew songs on harmonicas and guitars, and many danced with the scrolls of the Torah in their arms until midnight. Those present at the Simchas Torah celebration a year before said that the number of young people this time was much higher than in the preceeding year.[27]

A report from 1964 has put the number of persons who assembled near the Moscow synagogue at 50,000.[28] Reports from 1963 estimated that "during the Simchat Torah services 15,000 Jews, mostly young people, sang and danced in front of the synagogue."[29] The correspondent of the Paris *Le Monde* reported at the time that "the Jewish crowd in Moscow was more enthusiastic than ever."[30]

The writer Eli Wiesel who visited the Soviet Union in 1965 and witnessed the Simchas Torah celebration in Moscow reported: "I saw young and old, students and teachers, soldiers and officers singing 'Lomir ale yneinem dos yidishe folk mekabel ponim zain' [Let us all together welcome the Jewish people]."[31]

Here is another description of a Simchas Torah celebration as witnessed by one foreign visitor:

> After the first marching round ended, the cantor and some from the crowd started singing on a gay note. The microphone was grasped from the hands of the cantor and some people ventured to sing into it Yiddish folk songs and Hasidic songs. The next marching rounds were conducted in a much faster and gayer tempo. Those who now carry the scrolls are not necessarily old people, and are not regular worshipers. Someone begins dancing and immediately a circle is formed, elderly people, men, women, youngsters of both sexes come into the dancing circle, the circle becomes larger and a second and third circle emerge inside the large cirle. Tens and tens of people join hands and move to the melody of *"Vetaher Libenu"* [Cleanse Our Hearts] and "David the King of Israel Lives" [these are the first words from prayers, which were adopted by the Israel youth for folksinging]. The dance gradually evolves into something which resembles an Israeli hora. The old gradually disappear from the circle and before long only young people remain. The dancing groups look now like a typical student crowd, and a question comes to my mind: Who are these

youngsters who dance with such enthusiasm? Is this evening just one single event in their lives, an occurrence without significance? We were later told that on the Simchas Torah night a similar performance, even on a larger scale, has taken place in Leningrad, perhaps because the Leningrad synagogue is larger, or perhaps because in Leningrad western winds blow stronger. And when you hear about similar phenomena in other cities too, you begin thinking that the presence of the young people on this evening is not at all an accident and that the roots of it go very deep. Yet, it is difficult to get to talk to the youngsters. After all is finished they disappear into the night and you don't see them, or the like of them, again till next year. The "big holidays" have passed and the synagogue sinks again in the grayness of the Russian winter. Again old people assemble on weekdays and Sabbath, and deep down in their hearts they know that in spite of their lowliness, the passing years, and the affronts they have to face, it is they who are the keepers of the thousands-of-years-old glowing coals of Jewish tradition which turn into a fire a few times a year.[32]

The Hebrew writer and the wife of a former Israeli diplomat in the Soviet Union, Yemima Chernovitz-Avidar, was at the Moscow synagogue at the very time when the Simchas Torah celebration—Soviet-style—originated, and related the occasion in the following words:

Like waves in a stormy sea the people burst out dancing into the street. And the outside crowd, which could not make a way for itself into the synagogue, greeted those coming out with the traditional song "Lomir ale yneinem di Yidn mekabel ponim zain," as if a festive welcome would have been arranged here for representatives of the Jewish people, who went out openly on the street as Jews, as members of a people who desire to live. The dancers formed circles inside circles and the blowing of the horns of the cars trying to get through were of no avail. The street was closed and the crowd was in command.[33]

In 1966 the majority of the crowd were again young people, and the Jewish songs and dances continued well into the night to the tunes of guitars. Many said that they had never been to a synagogue before and they decided to come here on Simchas Torah night "for the only reason—that it is a Jewish holiday and they are Jews."[34]

Why do not Soviet authorities interfere with this exuberant way of celebrating a Jewish holiday on the streets of large cities, when heavy obstacles are put in the observance of many "quieter" religious rites, and when celebrations outside the house of prayer could easily be impugned as interfering with public order, and as such are forbidden according to Soviet law?

(Article fifty-nine of the Law on Religious Associations of April 8, 1929, requires a special permission "for the performance of religious processions as well as the performance of rites in the open air." Article sixty of the law states that "permission is not required for religious processions which are an inevitable part of the divine service and are made only around the prayer building, provided they do not disturb normal street traffic." [35])

Does the Soviet government not interfere with the Simchas Torah celebrations outside the synagogue because it considers them an "inevitable part of the divine service," or perhaps for the opposite reason—that dancing and singing is not regarded as a procession and religious rite, which, indeed, it is not? Or do the authorities allow the mass gathering because a sudden reversal would have an adverse effect on public opinion abroad, and a question would be raised as to why the celebration was suddenly prohibited after it was allowed for several years? Or is the Soviet tolerance due to the recognition that an annual safety valve is needed for the suppressed feelings and emotions of the Jewish youth, frustrated by the awareness that they do belong to one of the many Soviet nationalities and are not given the means to express themselves? We can only guess.

From the Soviet point of view, the mass outpouring of Jewish youth in front of synagogues should be regarded as a defeat of the Soviet antireligious propaganda. We surmise, however, that the Soviet authorities prefer to suffer a setback on the "Jewish religious front" than a setback in the area of "Jewish nationalism." Jewish religious avenues of expression are still preferable, according to present Soviet attitudes, to the fanning of "Jewish separateness" and of Jewish "nationalistic sentiments." Jewish "nationalism" is presently a greater evil than Jewish religion in the eyes of Soviet policymakers.

Significantly, at the time of relative religious liberalism in the 1920s, Soviet authorities were not so tolerant of similar street celebrations on Simchas Torah. A case in point is reported by A. Gershuni.[36] In a small Soviet town, after the conclusion of Simchas Torah services in the synagogue, the worshipers started dancing on the street, whereupon young people, among them some members of the Komsomol, joined the dancing circle. This so enraged the local

Party officials that an investigation was initiated which "discovered" that "Party work in town was in a state of disorganization, and this in turn was the fault of the local rabbi." The rabbi was charged with "counterrevolutionary propaganda" and was reportedly saved from severe punishment by one of the judges who "covered for him."

Passover

The Jewish Communists, who in the first 20–25 years of Soviet rule were in charge of antireligious propaganda in the "Jewish sector," have concentrated their most stringent efforts to combat the observance of both the High Holidays and Passover.

Not only was the outpour of printed antireligious propaganda for the two holiday seasons much higher, but different forms of propaganda were developed for each holiday. For instance, on Passover the towns and hamlets with heavy Jewish populations were the scenes of parades with placards, caricatures, flags, and marching in the streets of the Jewish neighborhoods and near the synagogues.[37]

Jewish Communists have also tried to combat the deeply entrenched tradition of Passover festivities by substituting the traditional seder with a "seder" of their own, a "Red seder." At a "Red seder" white challah was served (instead of the everyday bread), antireligious speeches were presented, and a "Red Hagadah" was read. The "Red Hagadah" began with the following paraphrase of the traditional text. *"Ho lahmo anio"* [this bread of affliction]—for a crust of bread has every capitalist bought our sweat and blood. Forced by starvation, we became 'voluntary' slaves of the capital."[38]

It is apparent from the anti-Passover pamphlets and articles that the Jewish militant atheists were repeatedly confronted with questioning by believers and some nonbelievers as to why Passover should be considered a "reactionary celebration" when it commemorates the flight from slavery into freedom. It has been repeated over and over in publications and lectures that "Passover is not a freedom holiday but a holiday of spiritual slavery"[39] and that "Science contradicts both the clerical and the nationalist Hagadah."[40]

The Jewish Communists introduced not only "trials against Passover" but also "political trials" against those celebrating Passover. For instance, *Emes* reported about one such trial "held in the Tailors' Club against workers who baked matzohs and arranged seder celebrations."[41] A group of workers, noted the newspaper, reported their neighbors who celebrated the holiday. "Some of the celebrants," charged the indictment, "did it because of their religious beliefs, others because of nationalistic convictions, and still others because of petit-bourgeois sentiments [in consideration of the father-in-law and wife]." The verdict against those who celebrated Passover because of religious convictions was the severest: to evict them from the house cooperative and to expel them from the trade unions until the time when they "will free themselves from the rabbinical influence." The "petit-bourgeois" had the lightest sentence: to study in an evening school.[42]

Why has Passover remained the "high season" for Jewish anti-religious propaganda and the object of repeated restrictions on the observance of its rites?

There are a number of valid reasons to justify the special attention given by Soviet authorities to Passover:

1. On Passover the center of observances is located in the home and not in the synagogue. Whereas synagogues can be closed down or easily controlled, the same cannot be done, or cannot be done so easily, with homes. Consequently, a home-centered holiday is more difficult to combat and more effort is needed to eradicate it.

2. Passover, which recalls the march of Jews from slavery to the Promised Land, has strong *"nationalistic overtones"*; it symbolizes the struggle of the Jewish people for national and religious liberty. The idea of the return to Zion is epitomized in the final sentence in the Hagadah: *Le-shono ha-booh be-Yerusholaim* (Next year in Jerusalem). To this day, this phrase is one of the most often repeated lines in the Jewish antireligious propaganda. It serves to illustrate that Jewish religious believers are disloyal to the "Socialist homeland."

3. The seder and the eating of matzohs are still, in spite of the growing secularization of Jewish life, almost universally observed by Jews the world over, if sometimes only in a rudimentary form. These observances, as much as the day of Yom Kippur, are occasions when the bonds uniting all Jews come vividly to the fore, perhaps as a result of the collective Jewish memory of persecution and sufferings inflicted in the course of centuries on these very days. The Soviet regime is obviously opposed to any worldwide ties

among Jews, and the more universally an observance is adhered to the more grounds for the attack on it.

4. The attractiveness of Passover and of the seder ceremony in the form of a family gathering is an additional reason for combating it. Since eating matzohs is an integral part of the seder and of the holiday, the baking of matzohs, or receiving them from abroad, were under constant attack by the Soviet authorities, and were intermittently forbidden or restricted.

These actions and the vehement campaigns against Passover have for the greater part of the fifty years of Soviet rule focused the attention of Jewish communities abroad on the "matzoh problem" in the Soviet Union. Consequently, this aspect of Jewish religious life in the Soviet Union has been in recent years explored, discussed, and written about in greater detail than other aspects of Jewish religious life in the Soviet Union. Our discussion here of the matzoh problem will, therefore, be more concise than its importance would otherwise require.

The struggle of Soviet Jews to secure matzohs for Passover started almost as early as the beginning of Soviet rule.

At times the difficulties in obtaining matzohs were a result not only of particular governmental prohibitions but were due to the specifics of the Soviet economic system, where manufacturing and distribution of goods is monopolized by the government. That this monopolist had an unfavorable, to say the least, attitude to religion and religious practices provided an additional contortion of fate. At the end of the 1920s, with the collectivization of agriculture and severe food shortages, austere rationing of bread was introduced. Flour was not sold by the government and the Jews were unable to obtain either matzohs or flour with which to make matzohs. The authorities were unwilling to make an exception for Jews and to sell them flour instead of bread during the eight days of Passover. As a result of a worldwide Jewish protest and many interventions, and partly to alleviate the bitter shortages of food at home, the Soviet government finally permitted Jewish organizations abroad to donate and ship large quantities of matzohs to the Soviet Union for the Passover of 1929. The Soviet Government demanded and received additional benefits: that the cost of transportation be paid in hard currency, and that an import duty of up to two rubles for each kilogram of matzohs received be imposed.

Securing matzohs became easier in later years with the improvement of the economic situation and the possibility of obtaining flour in the black or "gray" market. Generally, the synagogues were allowed by the authorities to make necessary arrangements for the baking of matzohs, although government-sponsored propaganda against Passover and matzohs was always simultaneously conducted, and various chicaneries were used and pressures exercised against those who baked, distributed, and bought matzohs.

Restrictions and prohibitions on the baking and obtaining of matzohs have begun to be felt with greater force since Stalin's death in 1953. Ironically, official Soviet policy in regard to the "matzoh problem" was much more liberal under Stalin's ruthless reign than in the post-Stalin "thaw." For instance, in the years of Stalin's rule matzohs were often obtainable in the stores (all stores in the Soviet Union are publicly owned). The restrictions on the baking and distribution of matzohs in the post-Stalin period, although undoubtedly centrally inspired, were at first not of a general character; they were spottily applied in certain areas and in various forms, the methods of harassment largely left to the discretion of the local authorities.

Since 1957 total restriction of matzoh baking in the Jewish communities and in certain chosen areas have become more and more common; in 1959 the authorities banned the baking of matzohs in the large Jewish community of Kharkov, the second largest city in the Ukraine. Since then the restrictions on matzoh-baking have covered increasingly wider areas.

In 1961, the ban on matzoh-baking spread to all areas of the Soviet Union, with the exception of Moscow, Leningrad, Central Asia, and the Caucasus. Finally, in 1962, the baking of matzohs was, for the first time in Soviet history, totally prohibited in the whole country, with the last-minute exception made for a few Jewish communities of the "Oriental" Jews. Not only was the baking of matzohs prohibited in the synagogue-owned matzoh bakeries, but baking them at home has become a dangerous undertaking, if even a minute quantity of the matzohs are sold or given to others. In 1963, eight Jews were arrested for selling very small quantities of matzohs, and four of them were sentenced to prison terms by the Moscow court.

Concurrently, a campaign was conducted against receiving matzoh parcels from abroad. Jewish organizations anxious to alleviate the plight of those who would rather go hungry than eat bread on Passover undertook to send parcels of matzohs (which included in addition to matzohs a few other Passover food items) to individual Soviet Jews. The receivers of the parcels were induced to refuse accepting the gifts from abroad; "irritated" recipients of parcels wrote letters to the press. "Take your rags back," wrote *Pravda Vostoka* of March 17, 1964 (reprinted in *Izvestiia* and *Birobidzhaner Shtern*). Characteristically, in the Yiddish-language *Birobidzhaner Shtern* the following paragraph printed in the Russian newspaper was omitted: "Who needs matzoh from England, don't we have our own? Or does anyone forbid us to bake them? Eat your matzohs yourselves, gentlemen, and leave us alone." Apparently, the facts were too well-known to the readers of the Jewish newspaper. Some other headings of articles in newspapers .were: "Spare us your care—an answer to uninvited benefactors"; "Take back your gifts, gentlemen." [43]

At almost the same time as the Soviet government has initiated its actions which later culminated in the total deprivation of matzohs for Soviet Jews, information was provided by the Soviet government for a special study initiated by the United Nations Commission on Human Rights. According to the information received:

> The government states, that by order of the USSR government, on days preceding particularly important holidays such as Easter in the case of the Old Believers and Roman Catholics and Passover in the case of the Jews, the shops of the State trading organizations sell special types of bakery products, such as "kulichi" (Easter cake) for Christians, *matzohs (unleavened bread) for Orthodox Jews, etc.* to enable worshipers to perform the appropriate ritual. [our italics][44]

According to this information the government not only allows the baking and selling of matzohs but is taking upon itself the task of distributing matzohs (along with ritualistic food items of other religions) through its network of stores. This information was blatantly untrue.

The ban on matzohs and the arrest of people accused of baking matzohs has aroused public opinion abroad; even Western Communist parties voiced their displeasure.

In 1965 some restrictions were lifted in deference to foreign public opinion; in 1966 the baking of matzohs was allowed in some capitals of the Soviet Republics, in a few large towns and in the "Oriental" Jewish communities. The prohibition has remained in force, however, in all other parts of the country, including many towns with large Jewish communities.

Rabbi Levin of the Moscow central synagogue reported on March 2, 1966, in an unprecedented telephone interview with the Jewish Chronicle of London, that "all Moscow Jews who will bring their own flour will be able to bake matzohs in the special bakeries at the synagogues." [45]

According to this report those who wished to have matzohs for Passover had to bring their own flour and to register their names at the bakery. The registration of the names might have been necessary because the baking was done for individuals on order. Nonetheless, the registering of persons who availed themselves of religious articles was, no doubt, a disquieting procedure for Soviet citizens.

Matzohs were also allowed to be baked in that year in Moscow, in Vilna (capital of the Lithuanian SSR), Riga (capital of the Latvian SSR), Kishinev (capital of the Moldavian SSR), Kiev (capital of the Ukrainian SSR), Minsk (capital of the Belorussian SSR), in Leningrad, and in Odessa. In addition, matzohs were also baked in Tbilisi (capital of the Georgian SSR) and in several other Jewish communities in the Caucasus and in Central Asia. Reportedly, 80–90 tons of matzohs were baked in Moscow; 15 tons in Odessa; and in Leningrad "enough for more than 10,000 people." [46]

The Soviet press agency Novosti assured in its press release that the supply of matzohs was sufficient for "everyone who wished to have them." This assertion is highly questionable. Even if the official figures of matzohs baked in the particular towns are not exaggerated, it is doubtful whether, for instance, a supply of 15 tons would satisfy the needs of the Odessa Jews. [47] It is quite certain that the amount of matzohs which were reportedly baked in the few large towns could not satisfy the needs of the hundreds of thousands of Soviet Jews who live in other cities and towns of the Soviet Union which did not have matzoh bakeries at all.

The observance of a seder privately at home is, of course, allowed by Soviet law; Soviet authorities have not contested the legality of celebrating a seder or of reading the Hagadah in one's home. Nevertheless, these Passover home observances, when they become known to the officials dispensing power, authority, or favors, often hurt the person who arranged or participated in them.

At times the punishment or the disfavor comes swiftly after the "deed" becomes known; more often it shows up later, and the cause and effect are not always visible and possible to prove. Outright dismissals from work for holding a seder were sometimes reported,[48] but such cases are not typical, "delayed action" being the rule. Frequently, no reaction is forthcoming and there is only fear and an aura of incertitude hovering over the head of the person known to have arranged or participated in a "religious rite."

To avoid repressive measures, or their possibility, many Soviet Jews hold their seder in secret, in disguise, or in a very rudimentary form. As it happens in other countries outside the Soviet Union, many nonreligious Jews in Russia also wish to hold or participate in a traditional seder. A noted Yiddish poet from Poland who spent several years in the Soviet Union as a World War II refugee—in the period when Soviet attitudes toward religion were most liberal—describes in a poem a marrano-type seder being held in the guise of a "family gathering."

> And for the neighbor who pretends not to know; even for him beware; for the Jew in the same house; the non-Jewish guests went home; and as through magic all changed in an unexpected way; the doors are closed, the windows covered; in the candlesticks holiday lights are lit; a holiday shine suddenly fills the room; the table cleaned, the bread gone; a tablecloth, a matzoh on it too; the table now looks so pious.[49]

If this was the manner of celebrating a seder during the period when the war against religion was suspended, one can surmise how much stronger were the fears to celebrate a seder in times of open antireligious warfare.

In 1966 the attendance at synagogue services on the first night of Passover was reportedly much higher than it was in the preceding years.[50] There are no memorial services on the first two days of Passover, and Passover is no more a solemn holiday than the other two festivals, Shevuos and Sukkos. The reason for the increased attendance on Passover may, perhaps, be found in the unconscious desire to "adapt" one more important holiday in addition to the two already existing important holidays—Yom Kippur and Simchas Torah. While Yom Kippur expresses to the Jews in the Soviet Union the purely religious component of Jewishness, and Simchas Torah became the expression of the Jewish ethnic and folk character, Passover signifies the "national" component of Judaism.

Passover responds more tellingly to the "national Jewish" longings felt by a significant part of the Jews in the Soviet Union, not only because of its implicit strong motif of national freedom, but also because the constant striving of the Soviet Jews for their right to eat matzohs on Passover becomes symbolic of the overall struggle of Soviet Jewry for the preservation of their national continuity.

This hypothesis is reinforced by the fact that, for the first time in many years, a large number of *young people* came to the Moscow synagogue on the Passover night of 1966. As reported by the press, the crowd was so large that many people had to stay outside the synagogue. The assembled young people, for the first time in the Soviet Union, initiated the dancing and singing of Jewish folk songs on a Passover night.[51] If Simchas Torah has been traditionally celebrated in the Jewish milieu with dancing and singing, Passover was never celebrated in East Europe by dancing and singing in the streets.

There is reliable information from tourists that the rabbis were very apprehensive of this new display of support by Jewish youth. They feared it might provoke displeasure and possible restrictions of what had been tacitly tolerated by the authorities on Simchas Torah. The young people were, therefore, asked by the oldsters to disperse; they apparently understood the validity of the apprehension and complied.

The Passover tradition is one of the more durable expressions of Jewish religious life in the Soviet Union.

Sukkos

Sukkos, the Feast of Booths or Tabernacles, is one of the three Festivals and is celebrated for seven days in the Holy Land and eight days in the Diaspora. Partaking of meals in provisionally erected booths and the blessing of the *esrog* (citron) and *lulav* (a palm-branch flanked with sprigs of willow and myrtle) are the principal rites of the Sukkos holiday.

Even before the advent of the October Revolution in Russia the practice of erecting booths *(sukkos)* in house yards or on balconies had decreased in the larger towns. After the revolution, the practice all but disappeared in the large cities and became rare in the smaller ones; booths of a religious character were too conspicuous a sight in a country which opposed religion.

In the 1920s some religious Jews were still allowed to receive *esrogim* and *lulavim* from friends and relatives in Palestine or in other countries, and they managed to observe the commandment of saying the benediction over the "four species" *(esrog, lulav,* myrtle, willow). This became progressively more difficult. A description of a peculiar arrangement made by two neighboring towns to share in the use of one *esrog* by dispatching, every day of the eight-day holiday, a non-Jewish messenger who carried the *esrog* from one town to the other was published in the *Emes* (October 8, 1922).

At certain times the packages with the Sukkos objects of the cult sent from abroad were not delivered to the addressees; at all times the names of the recipients of foreign mail were taken down for future reference and possible use. In later years an *esrog* (which grows only in tropical lands) has become a rarity in the Soviet Union. Since most *esrogim* and *lulavim* are imported from Israel, Soviet authorities are particularly apprehensive about their use by Soviet Jews.

A report from Jerusalem in the *Jewish Chronicle* of August 4, 1950 mentioned that rabbis of "several" Soviet Jewish communities had written to the Israeli Ministry of Religious Affairs requesting *esrogim* for the holiday of Sukkos.[52]

The Moscow and Leningrad rabbis were permitted to receive an *esrog* and a *lulav* from the Rabbinate in Israel; most smaller Jewish religious communities had great difficulties in acquiring these items.

In the fall of 1959 the Israeli Chief Rabbinate shipped to several Jewish communities in Soviet Russia 185 parcels containing the "three species" *(esrog, lulav,* and myrtle—the fourth plant, the willow, was not sent because it withers quickly). The Soviet postal services, which in the past admitted these parcels, returned them this time to Israel and the Soviet custom authorities labeled the packages: "Forbidden for import." Several similar parcels mailed to private addresses were reportedly delivered.[53]

An Israeli visitor reported seeing many people outside the Central Moscow Synagogue on Sukkos because the synagogue was too crowded to accommodate all who came to worship. The several thousand worshipers present in the synagogue "had no more than three or four *lulavim* and not one of these had the specifications required by religious rules. Where are the *esrogim* and *lulavim*—why have you not sent them to us this year?—people asked us. We knew that hundreds of *esrogim* were sent to the Soviet Union but had not reached their destination." [54] The visitor entered "the only *sukkah* in Moscow," which was located in the backyard of the synagogue. "No one would dare to erect a *sukkah* in or near his home. The one little hut was too small for the hundreds who wanted to enter it and say the traditional blessing *Leishev be-sukkah* (to sit in the *sukkah*)." [55]

"If accidentally an *esrog* or *lulav* reaches the old rabbi of one of the congregations," says another visitor, "this is so great a find *(metziah)* that the rabbi watches over it with trembling care lest it be destroyed by the hundreds of hands waiting to touch and caress it on the holiday." [56] It was, however, reported by Rabbi Zvi Bronstein of Brooklyn that on his visit to the Soviet Union in 1966 he was allowed to distribute a number of Israeli *esrogim* among rabbis and lay religious leaders of Jewish communities in the Soviet Union.[57]

The situation is different in the communities of Oriental Jews in Central Asia and in the Caucasus. The *esrog* and *lulav* are rarities there, too, but the observance of the holiday in booths is still extensive. A group of American rabbis who represented the Rabbinical Council of America reported after their visit to the Soviet Union that in the town of Kulashi, Georgian SSR, "of 2000 Jewish families, 1200 still celebrated the traditional Holiday of Tabernacles by spending eight days in rude temporary huts." [58]

Shevuos

Shevuos, the only Festival lasting two days and not eight, commemorates the giving of the Law on Mount Sinai.

While Shevuos is from the religious point of view as important and meaningful a holiday as the other two Festivals of Sukkos and Passover, it is not associated with symbols and symbolic rites such as the matzohs, *esrog,* and Sukkos booths. The decorating of houses and synagogues and eating of dairy dishes on Shevuos is an observed custom but has not the power of religious injunction. For that reason Shevuos has not attracted as much attention from Soviet authorities or Soviet antireligious propagandists as have other Jewish holidays.

Attendance of worshipers at the Shevuos prayers is, as a rule, not very large, except on the second day of the holiday when Yizkor, the prayer for the departed, is recited (any occasion when Yizkor is said attracts many worshipers). Whereas 400–500 persons was the average number of worshipers on the first day of Shevuos in the large synagogues of Moscow and Leningrad, the number of worshipers in the Moscow synagogue on the second day of Shevuos was 2500 (in 1964), as reported in the Israeli press.[59]

Hanukah

Hanukah is celebrated for eight days in commemoration of the Maccabean victory over the Greeks, and the miracle when a cruse which contained only enough oil to light the menorah for one day burned in the restored Temple for eight days. Hanukah has been considered in the Jewish communities of East Europe as a *minor holiday*.

Because it was a minor holiday, a holiday little distinguished from week days (working is permissible on Hanukah), and perhaps also because Hanukah did not lend itself very well to antireligious propaganda, as its theme is the struggle against foreign invaders and oppressors, it has rarely been discussed or attacked in the Soviet press and literature.

The mode of celebrating Hanukah has changed in the last several decades in the countries outside the Soviet Union. Due to the influence of Zionism and also to the fact that the holiday falls on or near Christmas, much luster and importance have been added to this holiday as observed today in Israel and in the United States. Among Soviet Jews Hanukah is hardly noticeable. The lighting of the candles is observed by only a small number of Orthodox Jews. In addition to the fact that lighting candles in one's home is a conspicuous act of religious adherence, it is difficult to secure the small Hanukah candles. Although the Soviet government allows non-Jewish cults to manufacture candles for the needs of their rites, and to sell them at a profit to the adherents of their faith, no such rights are granted to Jewish religious associations. Hanukah candles are not produced legally in the Soviet Union, either by religious associations or by private persons.

Old Jews, some of them part-time clergymen, occasionally engage in producing and selling the holiday candles. The Soviet press will "expose" from time to time the "manufacturers of candles" and accuse them of "profiteering." Thus, for example, *Znamia Kommunizma* of Odessa charged "the former employee of the Odessa synagogue Auerbach with manufacturing candles at home" and "selling them on Hanukah to believers at speculative prices." The newspaper accused him also of selling Jewish calendars at "exorbitant prices" and attacked the Odessa religious association for being "tightly linked to the "private persons" engaged in the undertakings.[60]

Purim

Purim, a one-day holiday commemorating the downfall of a plot to destroy the Jews in ancient Persia, although it is considered a minor holiday, was celebrated in Jewish communities the world over with great merriment and joy.

Purim was principally the holiday of the "simple people" and of the children. On that day, rabbis and "learned men" would take second place and forgivingly acquiesce to "mischievous" behavior, such as drinking, wearing masks, staging plays, and reciting irreverent satirical parodies—otherwise looked askance at in the Jewish communities of Eastern Europe.

Although Purim was the most secular of all Jewish holidays (not only is the celebration secular in its mode, but the Megilah, the Book of Esther which is read on Purim in synagogues or in private homes, does not even mention the name of God), Jewish Communists in the Soviet Union, even at the height of secular Jewish cultural activity, did not "adopt" Purim as a Jewish "folk holiday."

Purim is now all but forgotten and is rarely celebrated in the Soviet Union. The reading of the Megilah takes place in a number of synagogues, and, as custom requires, noisemakers are twirled at every mention of the name of Haman. It was reported that in 1964 a group of children from the American Embassy visited the Moscow synagogue on Purim and participated in the twirling of the noisemakers.[61] It should be added that in most other Jewish communities, except

Israel, where it is celebrated with masquerade parades, Purim has become an almost forgotten holiday, too. The prerequisite for the holiday to be perpetuated seems to be a self-contained Jewish community, or at least the existence of densely populated Jewish neighborhoods which are able to perpetuate the Jewish lore; in most countries these do not exist any more.

The Prayer of Kadish

Kadish, the prayer for the dead, is said daily by mourners during the period of one year, and on the anniversary *(yarzeit)* of the decease of a member of the immediate family. The custom is still observed by many Soviet Jews, in synagogues and in privately held prayer meetings, organized *ad hoc* by sympathetic Jews who wish to enable the mourner to recite the Kadish. Many Jews observe the reciting of Kadish for their departed parents, although they do not come to synagogues on other occasions, including even Yom Kippur. Presumably many nonreligious Jews observe the occasion not as a religious ceremony but as a fulfillment of the explicit or understood wishes of their departed parents.

Characteristic of this attitude is the report by Judah Waten, the left-wing Australian writer, who was told by his cousin that although she often attends services in the synagogue, her husband "attends services only once a year, on the anniversary of the death of his parents at the hands of the Nazis." [62]

Prayer Meetings Commemorating the Victims of the Holocaust

Prayer meetings, or assemblies in synagogues, with a varied liturgical-literary program to commemorate the death of the six million Jews killed in the Holocaust, have become widespread in Jewish communities the world over. Although a prescribed day of mourning is not yet sanctioned by religious authorities, a need to find adequate forms and appropriate religious rituals for the occasion has made itself strongly felt. Some elements of a nonprescribed ritual have already developed: the lighting of six candles (for the six million dead); the saying of the prayers for the dead (Yizkor and Kadish); and the chanting of Psalms are the accepted nucleus of the emerging ritual.

Surprisingly, in spite of the almost complete lack of contact between the Jewish communities in the Soviet Union and in other countries, a similarity in the observances of the Day of Remembrance is apparent at the not too frequent occasions when these commemorations took place. Six candles were lit in the synagogue, the same prayers were said, and, for this occasion only, secular Yiddish literary readings related to the Holocaust (such as "The Song of the Perished Nation" by Itzhak Katzenelson and poems by Haim Nahman Bialik) and speeches by lay members of the Jewish community were allowed in the synagogue.

The attitudes of the Soviet authorities toward the observance of the Day of Remembrance is ambiguous. On one hand, the official Soviet position encourages recalling Nazi atrocities (and the danger of neo-Nazism); on the other hand, Soviet policy is apprehensive of evoking "Jewish-national" sentiments, which are certain to emerge when the raw nerve of Jewish suffering is touched. Remembrance of those who died because of their Jewishness is bound to provoke deep-seated Jewish emotions and elicit boldness of expression not likely to come out on other occasions. This is true even when the commemoration of the Nazi victims is tied to a current political campaign. For example, at a meeting held in the Moscow Synagogue in 1964, protesting the impending end of the statute of limitations for the German war criminals, after six black candles were lit suitable speeches were presented. One of the speakers was a decorated war invalid and a graduate of the Moscow Yeshivah. The theme of his speech touched a very bold and startling chord. His theme was: "Resistance through Jewish history." The meeting was concluded by reading an excerpt of Bialik's "Megilat ha-Esh." [63]

The holding of this meeting was presumably suggested or agreed to by the Soviet government because it lent support to its campaign against West Germany; but once the meeting began, the assembly took a different turn. Facts from Jewish history, usually slanted or distortingly presented in the Soviet Union, were recalled, and a poem by the national Hebrew poet, was read. No more meetings of that kind were reported.

There is not yet a generally accepted date for the commemoration of the victims of the Holocaust. Generally, it is the day when the Warsaw ghetto uprising started, but the date is variously interpreted.[64]

In the first postwar years the commemoration was observed in the Soviet Union on Victory Day (May 9). A foreign correspondent who witnessed the commemorative services held in the Moscow synagogue after the war ended in 1945 wrote the following: "Some of the present were old people . . . most were middle-aged, and almost all of these in military uniforms. Medals and decorations earned on the battlefields sparkled on dozens of chests. I saw on one of them the highest military decoration, 'Hero of the Soviet Union' . . . . When Rabbi Schlieffer recalled the Jewish victims he broke down in tears." [65]

Special prayer meetings in remembrance of the victims of the Holocaust are presently held in the Soviet Union occasionally and irregularly.

A Peculiar Soviet-Jewish Performance of a Religious Ritual in the Reading of the Torah

In several Soviet synagogues a peculiar manner of the reading of the Torah has developed. While the general practice in the East European synagogues, as well as in other countries, is for one reader to read the weekly portion of the Torah in the central section of the synagogue, in some Soviet synagogues the reading is done simultaneously by several readers in different parts of the same hall. The apparent purpose of this practice is to make it possible for a much larger number of people to be honored by being called to the Torah. An American tourist who was present in the Leningrad synagogue on a Sabbath reported that the reading of the Torah was done in four places simultaneously. An additional explanation for the strange practice given to him was that it enabled worshipers, former residents of various lands and provinces (Polish, Ukrainian, and Galician Jews), to assemble for at least part of the services in separate and more intimate groups. [66]

Notes

1. A. A. Gershuni, *Yahadut be-Rusia Ha-Sovetit* (Judaism in Soviet Russia) (Jerusalem, 1961, p. 80).

2. *Emes,* Moscow, April 6, 1923.

3. *Emes,* April 27, 1923.

4. A. Merezhyn, "A Correct Tactic" (in *Emes,* December 25, 1921).

5. *Emes,* September 25, 1923.

6. Nahum Chanin, *Sovet Rusland, Vi Yikh Hob Yir Gezen* (Soviet Russia, As I Saw It) (New York, 1929, p. 42).

7. E. Gershuni, *op. cit.,* p. 123.

8. The organ of the Jewish "godless," *Der Apikoires,* of January 1, 1933, complained in a correspondence from the town of Nevel, Vitebsk district, that in the local factories "some workers establish their own days of rest on Saturday and Jewish religious holidays, besides the regular days of rest" (Jacob Leshchinsky, *Dos Sovetische Yidntum, Zain Vergangenheit un Kegnvart* [Soviet Jewry, Its Past and Present], New York, 1941, p. 314).

9. Iu. Grachev, "Na Povodu u Sektanta" (On the Leech of a Sectarian) (in *Sovetskaia Torgovlia,* November 30, 1963, as photostated in *Yevrei i Yevreiskii Narod* (hereafter *YYN*), No. 14, 1963, p. 1).

10. Sukkos, the Holiday of Tabernacles, is celebrated in the autumn, Pesach (Passover) falls in the spring, and Shevuos, commemorating the giving of the Torah on Mount Sinai, comes seven weeks after Passover. (The spelling of the holidays here follows the Ashkenazic pronunciation used in Eastern Europe).

11. S. L. Shneiderman, "In der Moskver Groiser Shul" (In the Great Synagogue of Moscow). (Yidisher Kemfer, December 29, 1965)

12. *Emes,* October 8, 1922.

13. Gershuni, *op. cit.,* p. 103.

14. Leshchinsky, *op. cit.,* p. 315.

15. Gershuni, *op. cit.,* p. 83.

16. The October 11, 1923, issue of the Yiddish—language *Veker* of Minsk reported: "The clericals of Borisov [Belorussia] received a good lesson last year, and have spent some time in a 'secluded place' but this has not prevented them from acting again as 'God's cossacks' this year. A large group of children, of old men and young and old women, burst out of the synagogue throwing whatever objects their hands could get hold of at the marchers." (Leshchinsky, *op. cit.,* p. 311.)

17. H. Rabinkov, "Notitsn fun an Ateist" (Notes by an Atheist) (in *Birobidzhaner Shtern,* September 23, 1962).

18. *New York Times,* September 29, 1963.

19. *The Day-Morning Journal,* September 18, 1966.

20. *The Day-Morning Journal,* September 26, 1966.

21. *Jewish Chronicle,* January 14, 1966.

22. Paragraph twenty-two of the Instructions of the People's Commissariat of the Interior, of August 1929 (published in *Sobranie Uzakonenii i Razporazhenii Rabochevo i Krestianskovo Pravitelstva* (A Collection of Statutes and Decrees of the Workers' and Peasants' Government), No. 35, 1929; texts also in N. Orleanskii, *Zakon o Religioznikh Obiedinieniakh* (The Law on Religious Associations), (Moscow, 1930; English translation of text in *Church and State Under Communism,* Special Study Prepared by the Law Library of the Congress for the U.S. Senate, Washington, 1964).

23. Yehudi Sovieti Almoni, *El Ahai be-Medinat Israel* (Anonymous Soviet Jew, To My Brothers in the State of Israel) (Jerusalem, 1957, pp. 122–6).

24. Michael Shashar, *Israeli Be-Moskva* (An Israeli in Moscow) (Jerusalem, 1961, pp. 117–24).

25. *New World Review,* December 1965.

26. Joseph Schechtman tells in *Star in Eclipse* (New York, 1961) about the utter embarrassment of Jewish youngsters when they were asked to perform their "national songs and dances" at a Song and Dance Festival in a summer camp and were unable to do so, because they never heard of them.

27. *Der Tog,* New York, October 20, 1965; *Davar,* Tel Aviv, October 20, 1965.

28. *American Jewish Year Book* (hereafter *AJYB*), New York, 1965.

29. *New York Times,* September 29, 1963; *AJYB* (New York, 1964).

30. *JTA Bulletin,* October 18, 1963.

31. Told at the memorial for the Babi Yar victims organized by the Congress for Jewish culture, September 26, 1966, in New York, and reported in *Der Tog,* September 28, 1966.

32. Ben-Ami, *Bein ha-Patish ve--ha-Maagal* (Between the Hammer and the Sickle) (Tel Aviv, 1965, pp. 69–71).

33. Yemima Chernovitz-Avidar, "Simchas Torah be-Moskva" (in *Davar,* October 10, 1965).

34. *The Day-Morning Journal,* New York, October 8, 1966.

35. "O Religioznych Ob'edineniiakh" (in *Sobranie Uzakonenii i Rasporiazhenii Rabochekrestianskovo Pravitelstva RSFSR* (On Religious Associations in the Collection of Statutes and Decrees of the Workers' and Peasants' Government of the RSFSR), No. 35, 1929, text No. 353).

36. Gershuni, *op. cit.,* pp. 69–70.

37. See, for instance, the descriptions of street parades and "trials" in *Emes,* April 11, 1923.

38. M. Altshuler, *Hagode far Gloiber un Apikorsim* (Hagadah for Believers and Atheists) (2nd imp. ed., Moscow, 1927).

39. M. Altshuler, *Kegn Peisech, Materialn far Propagandistn un Fortreger tsu der Anti-Peisech Kampanie,* (Against Passover, Materials for Propagandists and Lecturers in the Anti-Passover Campaign) (Moscow, Tsentraler Farlag, 1929, p. 17).

40. *Ibid.,* p. 18.

41. *Emes,* April 19, 1923.

42. *Ibid.*

43. *Sovetskaia Moldavia* (Soviet Moldavia), March 3, 1964; *Vechernii Kiiv* (The Evening Kiev) March 3, 1964.

44. *Study of discrimination in the matter of religious rights and practices.* Commission on Human Rights, U.N. Sub-Commission on Prevention of Discrimination and Protection of Minorities, *op. cit.,* p. 11.

45. As reprinted in *Der Tog* of March 7, 1966.

46. According to a report distributed by the Soviet Press Agency *Novosti* and items in the *Jewish Advocate,* Boston, March 31, 1966; *Davar,* Tel Aviv, April 6, 1966; *Der Tog,* New York, March 15, 1966; *Morning Freiheit,* New York, February 2, 1966.

47. The Jewish population of Odessa and its district numbered 121,377, according to the census of 1959. Fifteen tons, or 33,000 pounds, of matzohs would provide an average of less than one third of one pound of matzohs for every person for an eight-day supply. If we even consider that a large part of the Jewish population of Odessa did not want matzohs, the supply was obviously much too limited.

48. For instance, it was reported that after the Passover of 1959 some people who held the traditional services in their homes lost their employment (*Jews in Eastern Europe* [hereafter *JEE*], November 1959, p. 24).

49. Yosef Rubinstein, *Hurban Poiln* (Poland Holocaust), (Cyco, New York, 1964, p. 24).

50. *Der Tog,* April 6, 1966.

51. *Ibid.,* April 12, 1966.

52. *AJYB,* 1951, p. 331.

53. Schechtman, *op. cit.,* p. 127.

54. Shashar, *op. cit.,* p. 103.

55. *Op. cit.,* p. 102.

56. Ben-Ami, *op. cit.,* p. 63.

57. *Der Tog,* August 19, 1966.

58. *New York Times,* August 8, 1956.

59. *Yalkut Mogen,* August 1964.

60. *Znamia Kommunizma,* January 24, 1964; also reported in *JEE,* November 1964.

61. The *New York Herald Tribune* February 27, 1964.

62. *New World Review, op. cit.*

63. *Yalkut Mogen,* Tel Aviv, June 1965, p. 22. The lighting of six candles symbolizing the six million Jewish victims has been initiated in the D.P. camps in Germany. From there the practice has spread to other countries, including the Soviet Union.

64. April 19, according to the general calendar; the 27th day of the month of Nisan, according to the Jewish calendar.

65. Léon Leneman, *La Tragedie des Juifs en URSS* (The Tragedy of Jews in the USSR) (Paris, 1959, pp. 13–4).

66. Itzhok Fein, "Beim Davenen in Leningrad" (At the Prayers in Leningrad) (in *Yidisher Kemfer,* September 2, 1966).

CHAPTER 4

Religious Rites and Ceremonies

Kosher Slaughtering (Shehita)

According to Jewish religious law, animals which are permitted for consumption must be slaughtered in a specified manner by a man licensed to do it, a *shohet*. The *shohet* is required to follow a special course of studies dealing with kosher slaughtering and to pass the respective examinations; he is permitted to practice his profession only upon receiving a certificate from a recognized religious authority.

The *Shohet* uses a special knife, the *halaf,* which he must examine for flaws before slaughtering, and he must apply this knife to a specific spot on the animal's neck. After the slaughter, he must closely examine the animal's inner organs for signs of disease. A *shohet* is therefore also called *shohet u-bodek* (or *shub*)—a slaughterer and examiner. Upon discovering diseased organs in the slaughtered animal, the *shohet,* in accordance with the corresponding articles of the laws, pronounces the animal unfit for consumption *(treif).* The *shehita* laws were intended to both assure a less painful manner of killing animals and to safeguard the health of the consumers.

Thus, a *shohet* performs the menial task of killing animals and fowl; in addition, he examines them for their fitness for consumption (according to Jewish religious law). His function was considered of such importance from the Jewish religious point of view that *shohtim* were considered important members of the Jewish clergy.

The Soviet authorities shared this opinion. They included *shohtim* in the same category as rabbis—as *lishentsy* (deprived of civil rights), in spite of the official legal instructions that those religious functionaries who also perform menial tasks are not to be deprived of their civil rights.

Ritual slaughterers in the Soviet Union were harassed, jailed, and deported, along with rabbis, during the periodical waves of anti-religious persecutions. Many were deported to the remote regions of Siberia and to central Asia.

101

A Jewish actor who lived as a refugee in Frunze, the capital of Kirgizian SSR in Central Asia, during World War II recounts his conversation with a deported *shohet:* " 'At home in Bobruisk [Belorussian SSR] I was a *shohet,'* he said, 'so they have deported me here as an antisocial element. I am now slaughtering fowl for several dozen Jewish families living here, rarely do I slaughter cattle. A number of deported Jews live in the surrounding towns, and they, too, eat kosher. Each Thursday I take my *halafim* and visit them. It was probably God's will that I should be deported here so that Jews in Kirgizia could have kosher meat. The local authorities are not concerned about my ritual slaughtering.' " [1]

There was never an official general prohibition of *shehita* in the Soviet Union, but many obstacles and prohibitions have been effected since the inception of Soviet rule. In some areas total prohibitions of *shehita* have been issued and later revoked. For instance, on April 20, 1920, the Poltava office of the Commissariat for food supplies issued a prohibition of *shehita* which was later reversed. The restrictions abated at the time of the NEP (New Economic Policy) in the 1920s. [2]

The two commonly asked questions which arise concerning *shehita* in the Soviet Union are: Is kosher slaughtering legal, according to Soviet law? Is it still performed?

Two visitors to the Soviet Union, both natives of Russia and well informed, reported the following:

"My wife asked whether it is possible to get kosher meat in Russia. The answer was that this is impossible, but there is a *shohet* who secretly [*shtilerheit*] slaughters chicken." [3]

The other visitor reported: "There are two *shohtim* at the Odessa synagogue. In Kiev, I was introduced to the *shohet,* who doubles as a *mohel* and is practically never in demand in either capacity." [4]

According to the first account, kosher slaughtering is not allowed, but there is a certain demand for kosher meat which is met by the clandestine *shohtim.* According to the second account, kosher slaughtering is allowed, but there is hardly any demand for it.

What is the actual situation? The state of kosher slaughtering in the Soviet Union seems to be, to a large degree, similar to the situation with regard to circumcision. There is no legal prohibition against *shehita,* but the practice is looked down upon by the authorities, and harassment and restrictions are often applied. The *scope* of the restrictions and the *degree* of harassment is largely left to the discretion of the local authorities.

Apparently, Soviet authorities grant permission to a restricted number of *shohtim* in selected localities: in the capitals of Soviet republics, in a few large towns frequented by foreign tourists, like Leningrad and Odessa, and in the communities of Oriental Jews. Permission to perform kosher slaughtering is often revoked from those few functioning as *shohtim*.

Nonregistered *shohtim* who perform kosher slaughtering can be punished by the authorities on several grounds. First, a kosher slaughterer deals in services, killing the animals for an established fee. Therefore his trade or business, if at all permitted, should be registered with the local Soviet officials and he should pay taxes on his income (taxes on allowed trades or businesses are extremely high). If he is not registered as a person conducting a business or service, he is open to criminal charges. Second, his establishment must be subject to sanitary control. The local authorities may find, if they wish, sufficient reasons to prohibit his services, or to impose fines just on sanitary grounds—for endangering the health of the consumers. And finally, the *shohet*, if he is not registered as a clergyman, can be disciplined for his part in the performance of a religious rite. Only clergymen registered by the authorities may perform religious rites—and kosher slaughtering is considered a religious rite.

Thus, a situation was created where the practice of kosher slaughtering is legal but the legality is enjoyed only by a small number of people in a selected number of places. In places where kosher slaughtering is clearly legal, as in Moscow and Leningrad, petty harassment and chicaneries are either an existing reality or a potential threat; not every Soviet citizen will dare to come openly, carrying his hen in his arms, to the slaughterer's house (which is usually located in the synagogue yard).

A visitor to the Soviet Union reported that "in Moscow ritual slaughter was taking place, but in another city that was mentioned to me, permission for a *shohet* to move to that locality was refused, and thereby the re-introduction of *shehita* was frustrated." [5]

The picture which emerged from the reports was: in the large cities *shehita* is usually permitted, although severely restricted due to the small number of *shohtim* allowed to function; in the smaller localities *shehita* is usually nonexistent.

A Soviet Jew whose letters were smuggled out of the Soviet Union and published in book form in Israel gave a detailed description of "illegal" slaughtering in the Soviet Union.

> Most of the still existing slaughterhouses, like most of the synagogues, were closed down in the course of the antireligious strictures steadily applied by the Soviet authorities—because the slaughterhouses were like thorns in the eyes of the local rulers, and not without reason: before the Jewish holidays, and especially before Yom Kippur, thousands of people, mainly women, lined up near the slaughterhouses.
>
> An end had come to the slaughterhouses in our town, yet people still line up with their fowl when the holidays come, but now they are in fear; not so much of being disclosed, but in fear for the fate of the *shohet,* in case his doings should be discovered. Punitive action will be sure to follow.[6]

Nonregistered *shohtim,* who still operate in the Soviet Union, will resort to their trade either because of religious zeal, in order to make it possible for religious Jews to eat kosher meat, or because of economic necessity when no other occupations are accessible to them. In the particular case described above, the *shohet* was forced to take up his forbidden profession after an interval of four years, because of severe financial difficulties. His son's role in the operation was to form a line of the waiting women, to keep them still, and to lead, inconspicuously, two persons at a time to the place where the slaughtering was performed. Waiting women had to refrain from talking "because noise could provoke undesired attention and endanger the old *shohet,*" who was the provider of the whole family.

According to the Soviet press, the prevailing fee for slaughtering a hen was in the postwar years 2–4 rubles (in old rubles, before the revaluation of the currency), 4 rubles for a goose, and 15–45 rubles for slaughtering a calf. Before the holidays, the fee was reportedly higher.[7] In most of the country the available kosher meat would be restricted to fowl, as kosher cattle-slaughtering is extremely rare.

How many Jews are able to adhere fully to *kashrut* in their meat consumption is impossible to ascertain. Their number is probably small. From many sources we do know, however, that the number of Soviet Jews who desire kosher meat for the Jewish holidays, particularly for the High Holidays, is substantial. From some items in the Soviet press we gather that there are even Jews of the younger generation who observe *kashrut*.

Nauka i Religiia, the mouthpiece of antireligious propaganda in the country, tells of a letter sent by a woman reader to the periodical. She complains that when she married her husband, who was a teacher in an evening school, he did not reveal to her his religious convictions. Now, he forces her to observe Jewish religious rituals and "when she brought home nonkosher food he chased her out from the house." [8]

There was positive information about the existence of slaughterhouses and functioning *shohtim* in a number of Soviet cities. There was a *bet shehita* (slaughterhouse) in the Moscow synagogue, and two *shohtim* functioned there in 1965.[9] A slaughterhouse for poultry existed at the Leningrad synagogue, and was sometimes shown "proudly" to prominent visitors.[10] The Kuibishev newspaper *Volzhskaia Komuna* named two *shohtim* who "almost monopolized the supply of meat to believers" and there was another person, the *shames* (sexton) of the synagogue who also performed kosher slaughtering and competed with the *shohtim*.[11]

A slaughterhouse reportedly existed in Kiev, the capital of the Ukranian SSR. It was located, as in most other localities, in the ward of the synagogue. The late Jewish journalist, Chaim Shoshkes, saw a young man bringing a hen to the Kiev slaughterhouse, and when he tried to take a picture of the "rather unusual sight," the young man stopped him by saying: "I came here to kill a chicken, and now you are going to kill me?" [12]

There was one *shohet* in Minsk, but observant Jews considered bringing to town another *shohet* from Vilna. A feuilleton in a Soviet newspaper reconstructed an imaginary conversation which had supposedly taken place between the leaders of the Minsk synagogue concerning this new *shohet*. "If he comes he will take away Naftali Kagan's means of livelihood. Naftali earns 3–4 rubles per cockerel," objected one of the leaders of the congregation.[13]

A feuilleton was published in a Gomel (Belorussia) newspaper concerning a certain Shmuil Gershon Shmaievich Sorkin whose "heart has long been beating sweetly at the sound of hens clucking, cocks crowing, and ducks quacking." He practiced ritual slaughtering, said the newspaper, "along with performing circumcision and organizing illegal Jewish prayer houses. On Jewish religious holidays, Sorkin earns more than one thousand rubles." [14]

If this information is true, it would indicate that at the rate of three rubles per fowl, which was the prevailing fee, 300 pieces of fowl were slaughtered for the Jewish holidays by one *shohet* in Gomel. The Jewish population in Gomel was reported to number 18,500 (or around 5700 families).[15] The proportion of Jews observing *kashrut,* at least during the holidays, seems from this information to be not negligible (it might even be much higher than indicated here, if we allow for the well-substantiated assumption that an amount of kosher slaughtering always escapes the attention of the local Soviet authorities.)

Travel Notes, published in the Yiddish literary magazine *Sovetish Heimland* reveal that there was a *shohet* in the industrial town of Sverdlovsk (in the Ural). An elderly woman told the writer: "My daughter-in-law [non-Jewish] searched the whole town till she found a *shohet,* and she cooked up for me a kosher chicken soup." [16]

A journalist visiting the city of Lvov (Western Ukraine) was told by the rabbi (prior to the closing of the Lvov synagogue in 1962) that about 300 of the approximately 3000 families living in town observe *kashrut,* and on the High Holidays about 1000 families, or one third of the total, bring their fowl for *shehita.*[17]

Prior to the closing of the synagogue in 1960 there was a small slaughterhouse in Orgiev, Moldavia.[18] Alma-Ata, the capital of the Kazakh SSR, had a *shohet,* according to a report by a visitor in 1965.[19]

Kosher meat is not being sold in stores. Private trading is prohibited, and state shops do not want to handle kosher meat. The only kosher shop which existed for a time in Moscow was closed down on a flimsy pretext, according to a well-informed source.[20]

The Soviet press conducted, in 1961, a strong campaign against the "widespread religious practices" among Central Asian *(Bukharan)* Jews, particularly in the Jewish quarters of the cities of Samarkand and Bukhara (Uzbek SSR) which, it was charged, remained immune to the influences of modern Soviet life. An item in the Moscow *Nauka i Religiia* suggested that kosher slaughtering was widespread among Central Asian Jews: "Rabbi Alaiev specializes in slaughtering chicken. People stand in his yard in a regular line, they think a chicken can be fried only when I. H. Alaiev takes her life." [21]

Central Asia seems to be one of the few places in the Soviet Union where kosher slaughtering of cattle, and not only of fowl, occurs. If we are to believe the accounts of the Soviet press, the slaughtering of cattle there is done on a grand scale. "Just during the first half year of 1962 they [i.e., the *shohtim* whose names were given in a previous paragraph] killed more than 800 heads of large horned cattle [in the town's slaughterhouse allegedly given to their disposal] at a fee of 2½ rubles a head. Four meat stands in the 'Zelenii Bazar' and in the center of the town sell kosher meat." [22]

This information pertains to only one town in the Uzbek SSR, Bukhara, where the Jewish population, including European Jews, numbers not more than 10,000 souls. Large-scale kosher slaughtering of cattle was also allegedly taking place in the town of Samarkand, Uzbek SSR. [23]

Kosher slaughtering of both fowl and cattle also takes place in the communities of the *Mountain Jews* in the Caucasus. In a Russian translation of a short story written in the Tat language by one of the most noted Jewish Tat writers, Mishi Bakshiev, we find this passage: "The people complain about Rabbi Insat, who slaughters fowl, takes money, slaughters cattle, takes money." [24] In the same passage a unique custom of the Mountain Jews relating to *shehita* is described: "In the yard of one rabbi a bag hangs on a nail. When the believers bring a chicken for slaughtering they pluck a few feathers from the chicken and throw them in the bag. This is, so to speak, an addition to the kopecks which the rabbi takes for each hen; afterwards he makes pillows from the feathers and sells them at the bazaar." [25]

There are no indications in the Soviet press or from visitors that operations in kosher slaughtering of cattle are also carried out in the European segments of the Soviet Union. If and when such an operation is conducted, it is probably a quick and secret affair, and the meat from the slaughtered cattle is sold to trusted persons only. Whereas an individual who brings to the *shohet* a fowl which he bought in the open market does not violate Soviet law if he is the sole consumer of the slaughtered fowl, the private kosher killing of cattle is another matter. In this latter case the person usually also sells the meat to other people, and this constitutes a violation of the rules concerning private trading. The Samarkand newspaper rebuked the local militia "which does not lead a struggle against those who engage in the unwarranted slaughter of cattle and trade in kosher meat." [26]

However, the crusade by the Soviet authorities to eradicate kosher slaughtering is not as fierce or as passionate as the war against circumcision. Apparently *kashrut* is considered to be a rite less crucial for the survival of Jewish religion and "Jewish separateness" than the rite of circumcision.

Recapitulating what has been said: The observance of kashrut in meat consumption is limited to a relatively small group of Soviet Jews, except for the High Holidays season when their number increases considerably. The communities of the Oriental Jews in Central Asia and the Caucasus are an exception to the rule: most Oriental Jews consume kosher meat. In these parts of the Soviet Union *shohtim* are permitted to function almost freely; although kosher slaughtering of cattle is not permitted officially, it is frequently done "on the side."

However, in most towns of the Soviet Union *shohtim* are not found or are not permitted to function. The number of qualified *shohtim* is shrinking constantly. The Moscow Yeshivah where several students have been trained as *shohtim* is now defunct.

Ritual Bathhouses (Mikvahs)

Ritual bathhouses existed in almost every Jewish community in East Europe. Often they were the only bathhouses accessible to the Jewish population, and sometimes they were the only communal bathhouses in town.

It was customary for the whole Jewish male population of the community to use the *mikvah* once a week before the advent of the Sabbath. Very pious Jews submerged themselves in the cold waters on the mikvah (or river) in the early morning on weekdays as well, as an act of purification. Women were required by Jewish religious law to bathe in the mikvah after their monthly periods.

After their ascent to power, the Soviet authorities tried to close the mikvahs; the method they adopted to eradicate this religious practice was different than in other antireligious campaigns. Rather than objecting on religious grounds, they chose to close the bathhouses on sanitary and hygienic grounds. Many mikvahs were destroyed or have remained in a state of utter neglect in the aftermath of the civil war and of the 1918–1922, pogroms, and the general pauperization of the Jewish population. Sizable funds were required to rebuild and keep the bathhouses in a condition that would satisfy the sanitary authorities. These funds the Jewish population was unable at that time to raise. Yet, in some instances when the local Jewish population managed to collect the required means and proposed to repair the damaged or neglected bathhouses and to keep them in a sanitary condition, the local authorities were still unwilling to approve the improvements.

However, Jewish religious leaders tried to keep as many mikvahs functioning as possible. In the mid-1920s these endeavors were considerably increased, as the economic situation of the Jews improved after the introduction of the New Economic Policy (NEP). Particularly energetic action was displayed by Rabbi Zorvitzer, a confidant of the Lubavicher Rebe, who devoted himself to this task. He organized the rebuilding and restoring of many ritual bathhouses, among them one in Moscow.[27]

The problem of ritual bathhouses came up on the agenda of the only conference which Soviet rabbis were allowed to convene, and which took place in the town of Korostyn (Volyn province of the Ukraine) in 1926. Rabbi Grossman spoke to the assembled rabbis and religious lay leaders on the difficulties and obstructions made by the authorities to prevent the normal functioning of the mikvahs. However, he expressed hope that the authorities would no longer interfere, and would allow the mikvahs to function.[28]

In 1933, a correspondent from the town of Nevel, Vitebsk district (Belorussia) ruefully informed *Der Apikoires,* the organ of the Jewish *"militant godless,"* that "the local clericals have sent a lobbyist [khodatai] to the district authorities and have received permission to build a mikvah."[29] In the period preceding the Soviet-German War in 1941, an unspecified number of mikvahs were still in existence in the Soviet Union.

After the end of the war in 1945, few ritual bathhouses remained intact in the previously German-occupied territory. In Moscow, Leningrad, and in a few other large towns, and in the Oriental Jewish communities of Central Asia and the Caucasus, mikvahs, although reduced in number, were still functioning.

The attacks on ritual bathhouses continued after the war. They were conducted on the same grounds as before the war—as being unsanitary and constituting a health menace to those using them. Surprisingly, the argument that Jewish bathhouses propagate national separateness, an argument so persistently used in the case of circumcision, has rarely been raised in the Soviet press.

Voiovnichi Ateist (The Militant Atheist), the organ of Soviet atheists in the Ukraine, attacked in 1963 the mikvahs as being, along with circumcision, "another ritual dangerous to health, since the water remains unchanged for weeks, and tens and hundreds of religious Jewish women, among them, naturally, women affected by various illnesses, submerge themselves in these waters." [30]

If what *Voiovnichi Ateist* asserts is true, then "tens and hundreds" of Soviet Jewish women still used mikvahs, forty-five years after the Revolution.

In an article entitled "In the clutches of antiquated customs," the Samarkand (Uzbek SSR) newspaper *Leninskii Put* reported on May 27, 1961, that the local doctor in charge of sanitation "has ordered the liquidation of this nest of infection [mikvah]." [31] The Jews of Samarkand, however, protested the closing of the mikvah, and when no positive answer was received, some "religious fanatics" threatened the doctor. [32]

The existence of a mikvah in Moscow was confirmed by several foreign tourists. The bath was reportedly open for women three times a week. One tourist reported: "They proudly showed me ... the costly mikvah (ritual bath for women)." [33]

Vechernii Leningrad, the afternoon Leningrad paper, attacked Rabbi Lubanov of the local synagogue, and charged him with arranging a position in the synagogue for his wife "as a supervisor of the mikvah." This is plain "featherbedding," maintains the newspaper, because visitors to the synagogue seldom see his wife fulfilling her duties, but she receives 80 rubles regularly each month. [34] Mikvahs have been reported to function in Kiev [35] and in Riga, capital of Latvian SSR. [36] A Jewish journalist described "a newly built mikvah, with tubs, showers, and an electric heater" in Lvov, before the synagogue was closed down by the authorities. He was told that the mikvah is used "by men and by only few women." [37]

In *Nauka i Religiia* an item appeared about a Jewish woman who had complained to a newspaper that her husband, whom she had only recently married, forced her to use the mikvah, but she refused when she saw in the mikvah "a woman with an eczema on her body." [38]

On the basis of reports by foreign visitors and of items published in the Soviet press, we may conclude that several mikvahs function in the Oriental Jewish communities and in several large towns of European Soviet Union, and that these bathhouses are attended by a relatively small number of men and women. The wonder is that mikvahs, by now quite rare in Western countries, still exist in the Soviet Union.

Religious Weddings

The Decree of January 23, 1918, "On the separation of the Church from the State and the School from the Church," which is the basic legislative act regulating the position of religious cults in the Soviet Union, radically changed the legal status of religious weddings which had thereto prevailed. Article eight of the decree abrogated all legal validity of weddings registered by clergies of various faiths, stating that "All civil acts are performed exclusively by the civil authorities of the department for the registration of marriages and births." [39]

Local Soviet authorities interpreted the law in the sense that they were now empowered to remove forcibly all acts of registry from churches and offices of religious associations. In many localities clergymen were forbidden to make any entries of marriages, even in the form of private notes. Often religious wedding ceremonies were prohibited altogether.

As a result of these restrictive measures which violated existing Soviet law, a series of protests were sent in the early years of Soviet rule to higher Soviet authorities, and as a consequence of the protests and appeals, a number of decisions and legal interpretations were issued.

For instance, in 1918 Rabbi I. A. Melamed of Vitebsk protested the acts of the local "Jewish section," the *Yevsektsiia*. He subsequently received "clarification" from the Eighth Department of the Commissariat of Justice, dated August 12, 1918, which stated:

> In reply to your telegraphic and then written appeal [*obrashchenie*], in the name of supposedly [*iakoby*] many thousands of religious Jews protesting the activities of the Vitebsk National Jewish Section [*Natsionalnaia Yevreiskaia Sektsia*] we clarify the following . . .

(The first two points of the reply concerned the applicant's status of Public Rabbi [*Obshchestvennyi Ravvin*], and the third point dealt with registrations of wedding:)

> In view of the fact that you have surrendered five official books of civil registry, the People's Commissariat of Justice does not find any fault in your making registrations of religious ceremonies conducted by you, insofar as this is done in private manner and with the consent of the parties concerned and no fee is exacted for the furnished document.[40]

The "Circular on the Problem of Separation of Church from State" issued on December 1918 by the People's Commissariat of Justice[41] stated, "the so-called church wedding represents a religious ceremony of a private character," which is to say that entries of wedding ceremonies made in church registries, which do not have an official character, are permissible, and that the religious act and the entry of the wedding in a nonofficial registry book is permitted but does not have judicial power.

A later circular of the Commissariat of Interior Affairs (NKVD) (April 7, 1924, No. 149) informed the Bureau of Civil Registry (ZAGS) that "servants of the cult who perform rites of baptizing, weddings, etc., before the registration of births, weddings, etc., by organs of ZAGS are not transgressing law, if they do not assume functions of judicial persons." In addition, the Commissariat of Justice resolved that the local authorities have no right to forbid the performance of church rites "under the condition that the church rites and ceremonies be performed in church or at the home of the believers"; special permission is required for performing the rites in public.[42] Nevertheless, in spite of the clear wording of the numerous interpretations, clergymen were often persecuted both for entering the ceremony in a private book of registry and for performing the ceremony.

In 1956, the Soviet government submitted information to the Commission on Human Rights of the United Nations concerning the status of religious marriages in the Soviet Union. The Soviet report quoted the previously cited Article Eight of the Decree of January 23, 1918 and stated: "When a citizen chooses . . . to be married in the church according to the rites of his religion, the State regards these acts as private matters and does not interfere with them. These acts have no legal force." As to divorces, only those granted and registered by the competent civil authorities are recognized as valid, says the report.[43]

For some years after the October Revolution Jewish weddings were, in most cases, still performed according to Jewish law and custom, particularly in the smaller towns. N. Chanin, the Russian-born American Jewish labor leader, visited the Soviet Union in 1928 and noted in his published report:

> The Jewish *hasunah* [wedding] has changed very little. In the old times there were, perhaps, more musicians; the *hupah* [canopy] was placed in the synagogue yard and the young couple were accompanied on their way by the musicians. Today, the ceremony is done more quietly, more unostentatiously, but the ceremony itself has the same religious content as it had in previous years. An exception is the Komsomol members of whom Jews say with bitter irony "they have registered" [instead of married].[44]

The rate of Jewish intermarriages was at first relatively low, and in not a few cases Gentile partners converted to Judaism.[45] The situation later changed and the intermarriage rate increased from year to year; a Jewish source has given the figure of 8½ percent of all marriages performed in the year 1926.[46] By contrast, an available official Soviet source cited the rate of intermarriage for the Jewish population in 1927 as 27.2 percent for males and 19.8 percent for females.[47]

Intermarriages undoubtedly increased in frequency in the 1930s, and at the same time religious wedding ceremonies decreased. This was a result of the harsher administrative measures taken against religion in general, and due to the incessant antireligious indoctrination young people were receiving in the schools, youth clubs, and places of work, as well as to the increased contacts of Jews with non-Jews.

The traditional ceremony prescribed for a Jewish wedding is that it be performed outdoors, under a canopy *(hupah)*, with a rabbi or other member of the clergy officiating. A wedding in the Jewish *shtetl* (hamlet) was a great event, a gay and joyful occasion in which all, or most of the community, participated. The *hasunah* has been for centuries a fountainhead of Jewish folk music and folklore, perpetuated by the Jewish *klezmorim* (musicians) and *badhonim* (singers and satirists), without whom a Jewish wedding would be deprived of its unique character.[48]

At present, the traditionally colorful, communal affair of the *hasunah* has all but disappeared in the Soviet Union. It has been substituted by the lifeless and colorless "registration act" at the office of civil registry (ZAGS). However, the Soviet authorities have recently realized the necessity of adding more color to the matrimonial ceremony, and as a result "wedding palaces" have been built, with rooms for the bride and halls for the guests, banquets, and dancing.[49] Needless to say, no prescribed ceremony could revive the genuine folk creativity which was perpetuated at the wedding ceremonies in the communities of Eastern Europe.

Yet Jewish weddings with the proper religious ceremony under a *hupah* are not yet extinct in the Soviet Union. They are still performed, although infrequently and in most cases surreptitiously. The fact that a Jewish religious wedding ceremony must not necessarily be effected in a synagogue and must not necessarily be performed by a rabbi, makes the performance of the rite easier. By the same token, obtaining information on weddings becomes more difficult. It may be assumed many perform the ceremony in private and are careful to keep the fact secret.[50]

Several larger Soviet synagogues have a special *hupah zal* (wedding hall). One visitor to the Leningrad Choral Synagogue reported that the synagogue has an "elegant hall where they said religious weddings are frequent." [51] Another visitor saw in the Leningrad synagogue "a separate room for weddings; a huge Star of David hangs on the wall; inside stands a magnificent canopy *(hupah)*, also the arc for the Holy Scrolls, shelves with religious books, and a piano." [52] From another source we have a report that on the one-day holiday of Lag baOmer two wedding ceremonies were performed at the Leningrad synagogue, and eight couples registered to wed.[53] Considering the fact that in Leningrad 168,641 persons in the 1959 census declared themselves to be of Jewish nationality, and that Lag baOmer is the first day after an interval of thirty-three days when Jewish weddings are not to be performed according to Jewish law, the rate of religious weddings in Leningrad is very low.

In Odessa, an American visitor was told: "Very few dare to marry in the synagogue; during the preceeding five months, only one wedding has taken place there."[54] An Israeli was present at a wedding ceremony in a small synagogue of a Moscow suburb. He described it in the following words:

> In the evening some two dozen old Jews assembled. The groom and the bride came separately, in their everyday attire so as not, God forbid, to attract attention when entering and leaving the synagogue. The groom was confused, it was apparent from the expression on his face that he had consented to the ceremony only on the wishes of his bride and her parents. . . . After the *hupah* ceremony was over someone opened a bottle of wine, another one took out from under his coat a few herrings. A quick "Lechaim" and the assembled hurriedly dispersed, as if saying one to another, "Nu, nu, let's quickly finish the affair and beware of an unfriendly eye."[55]

In Kiev, a visiting journalist reported "weddings are not performed in the synagogue; those who still insist upon a religious ceremony observe it quickly, almost stealthily, in the privacy of their homes."[56] It is also evident from these reports that young people, when they do consent to a religious ceremony, are apprehensive of possible consequences for their careers, and prefer, therefore, to have the ceremony done as inconspicuously as possible. Apparently religious marriages, like other religious observances, are more frequent in the towns of the Ukraine and Belorussia than in Russia proper, since the Jewish population in these parts of the Soviet Union remain more attached to the Jewish traditional way of life than do the highly urbanized and culturally assimilated Jews of Moscow and Leningrad. The percent of Jews who have declared Yiddish as their native tongue is 2 to 3 times higher in the Ukraine and Belorussia than in Moscow, Leningrad, or in the western districts of the RSFSR.

Most of the larger towns and none of the smaller towns in the European parts of the Soviet Union (where 90 percent of the Soviet Jews live) have neither synagogues nor rabbis. Consequently, the religious wedding ceremonies which take place in these localities are probably performed by nonclergymen. Such persons, if they are not registered as clergymen, would be punished by the Soviet authorities for performing religious functions. Nevertheless such "illegal" practices persist, as evidenced from dispatches in the Soviet press. For example, the periodical *Kommunist Moldavii* alleged that "The former Rabbi I. S. Eppelbaum continues to perform religious rites, weddings, divorces, etc." [57]

While in Leningrad a magnificent wedding hall is located in the synagogue, in the more remote regions of the country, religious marriage ceremonies are exposed in the press and their legality is questioned. In a letter published in the Bukovina newspaper *Radianska Bukovina* (September 9, 1960) a certain B. Langer calls for the closing of the synagogue in the capital of Bukovina, Chernovtsi. One of the reasons why the synagogue should, in his opinion, be closed down is that in the synagogue "Illegal marriage ceremonies are performed, issuing the necessary certificates which are more 'legal' than those of Zags."

It is common knowledge that letters of this kind are inspired, if not directly written, by Soviet agencies or the newspapers themselves. In this case too, the letter reflects the opinion of the local Soviet authorities, which, in contradiction to existing Soviet law, states that marriage ceremonies in houses of prayer are "illegal." The certificates of marriage, if issued by the clergymen, have, of course, no official validity; they cannot, therefore, be "more legal than the certificates issued by Zags [the Registry of Civil Acts]," as the angry letter in *Radianska Bukovina* asserted. Apparently, the ire of the newspaper was provoked by the fact that these religious ceremonies still hold greater significance for the parties involved than do the registration at the marriage license bureau. This may be true not only for the Jews of Bukovina.

It is, of course, impossible to ascertain the rate of marriages performed with a Jewish religious ceremony. There are, however, some indications that the attraction of a traditional Jewish marriage ceremony is still great even among Jewish parents who are themselves nonbelievers. The late Zalmen Yefroikin, himself a nonreligious Jew (a former leading member of the Jewish Socialist Bund and the "Workmen's Circle" in the U.S.), in describing his visit to the Soviet Union, recounted a conversation with a Soviet Jewish Communist who insisted that the wedding of his daughter should take place in the synagogue, although this was for him, a member of the Communist Party, "a very risky thing to do." [58]

If one can believe the Soviet press, even vestiges of the old, almost extinct way of marrying through matchmakers *(shadkhanim)* still survive even in the large cities of the Soviet Union. The newspaper *Volzhskaia Kommuna* of Kuibishev (a wartime capital of the Soviet Union after the Soviet government's evacuation from Moscow), in describing the lively activities of the local synagogue, tells of the wife of the sexton *(shames),* who "engages in matchmaking and arranges the meeting of the brides-to-be in the synagogue." [59]

Among the Oriental Jews (Bukharan, Georgian, and Mountain Jews, where religious observances are more entrenched and the attitude of the authorities toward religion more lenient, religious marriages are almost commonplace. *Leninskii Put,* a newspaper published in Samarkand, Uzbek SSR, stated matter of factly that young couples marry in the synagogue." [60] *Nauka i Religiia,* the organ of the Soviet atheist organization *Znanie* chides the ritual slaughterer Mani Adminov of Samarkand, who deals "with equal zeal in performing wedding ceremonies—if only money is paid." [61]

Ben-Ami, who visited the Jewish communities of the Caucasus and Central Asia, emphasizes the striking differences in wedding ceremonies between the Western and Oriental Jewish communities. In the latter "there is no doubt that along with registering their civil marriage young couples go to the *hakham* [rabbi] and are married in a religious ceremony. The ceremony under the *hupah* is performed in a festive manner, in the presence of all members of the family; even when the groom or bride do not wish, on personal grounds, to make the affair very public, they will not renounce the religious ceremony. The large, still partially patriarchal family will simply not recognize them as man and wife without the religious rite of marriage." [62]

The Mountain Jews of Caucasia are in this respect as in other phases of their religious life, in an in-between position—i.e., somewhat worse than the situation of other Oriental Jews, and somewhat better than that of the European Jews. The tenacious press campaign against the Jewish religion in 1960, which climaxed with the short-lived "blood libel" affair in Buinaksk,[63] had as its first aim the closing of the synagogue in Buinaksk (Dagestan ASSR, RSFSR), which was charged with inspiring "the survival of harmful rites, such as circumcision, old-custom marriage ceremonies, etc."[64]

Administrative and social pressures are much stronger when applied to the Western Jews who live in the Asian and Caucasian parts of the Soviet Union, than to the Oriental Jews who live in the same provinces. Yet, the Western Jewish population of the Oriental areas do benefit to a certain extent from the greater religious liberty existing in these provinces.

The Western European (Ashkenazic) Jewish community of Tashkent, capital of the Uzbekistan SSR, has substantially increased in size due to the influx of wartime evacuees who remained there after the war. The Soviet press has frequently complained that the synagogue of the Ashkenazic Jewish community and its clergymen (there exists in Tashkent another synagogue of the Oriental Jewish community) have too free a hand in performing various religious rites, and this "very lively business allows the clergymen to amass large profits." *Pravda Vostoka* complained in an article that Cantor Anatol Linkovsky of the Tashkent synagogue "sings at weddings and funerals and with every nuptial and funeral prayer a few hundred rubles find their way into his pocket."[65]

The Soviet press seems not to be aware of one obvious contradiction in its own propaganda. If religious observances, at least among European Jews, were as near extinction as the Soviet spokesmen assure, how could religious functionaries amass large profits from the performance of these observances?

Some flashes of insight in the religious life of Soviet Jewry and in problems connected with particular religious observances such as religious weddings, can be gained from the *responsa* of Soviet rabbis to questions posed to them by Jews in the Soviet Union.

In a book of religious essays and *responsa* published in 1966 in Jerusalem[66] Rabbi Chaim Shraga Kalish, former rabbi of Kharkov, has attempted to settle the problem of whether a wedding without a *minyan* (ten male Jews) is valid, insofar as Jewish boys and girls belonging to the Komsomol may frequently feel embarrassed to participate in a religious ceremony.

Another contributor, Rabbi Mordechai Dov Eidelberg, former rabbi of Nikolaiev, submits his opinion regarding an inquiry of a young man, reportedly a Communist, whether he may perform the wedding ceremony on Hol hamoed Pesach (when weddings are not allowed), because he is about to move to another town where it will not be possible to arrange a Jewish wedding.

Summary

The performance of religious weddings according to Jewish religious rites and Jewish custom, as well as divorces conforming to Jewish canonical law, are perfectly legal by Soviet law.

Soviet law states, and subsequent legal interpretations have made it evident, that entries of marriage made in synagogue registries, and the issuing of religious certificates of marriage *(ksubos)* have no official validity, but are fully legal practices not punishable by Soviet law. In fact, however, most marriage ceremonies, except in the Oriental Jewish communities, are arranged and performed secretly or in half-secrecy. Apprehension and fear of jeopardizing the future of the young couple in case of the discovery of their religious marriage is preeminent.

The decline in the number of religiously performed Jewish marriages is dramatic. A practice which previously has been universally observed has shrunk considerably. It is difficult to appraise how high the present rate of religious marriages is among the Jewish population in the Soviet Union. Religious marriages are more frequent in the later-acquired Soviet territories, and are widely practiced in the Oriental Jewish communities. Most young people are probably indifferent to the religious rite of marriage, especially when performed surreptitiously, without decorum, and in fear. The reaction would certainly be different if the wedding were performed openly, with the colorful traditional wedding songs and dances and ceremonies which for centuries were part of the Jewish way of life.

Although according to Jewish law the rite of marriage is validly performed even without the participation of a clergyman if certain basic requirements are met (two witnesses, putting a ring on the finger of the bride, and pronouncing the *harei at* (avowal), the full and unequivocal completion of the rite requires also the drafting of a marriage license *(ksuba)*, and the fulfilling of several other requisites which can be performed only by a qualified person. The acute shortage of religious personnel in the Soviet Union, particularly in the smaller communities, has become an important factor limiting the incidence of religious marriages. Jewish practice and custom has demanded and expected a person qualified to conduct a marriage ceremony *(mesader kdushin)* to participate in the rite. A ceremony otherwise performed, although valid according to Jewish religious law, has not gained general acceptance.

Because of the shortage of religious personnel; because the fear to perform and to take part in the religious wedding ceremony; and because the rite involves mostly young people who are especially vulnerable to pressure generated and exercised by the regime, prospects for the perpetuation of Jewish religious weddings in the Soviet Union are very slight.

Bar-Mitzvah Rites

The Hebrew term *bar-mitzvah* refers to the accepting of adult religious responsibilities by Jewish males who reach the age of thirteen. On the first Sabbath after his thirteenth birthday the bar-mitzvah boy is supposed to chant in the synagogue the portion from the prophets *(Haftorah)* and the respective blessings, whereupon his father pronounces his thanksgiving for being henceforth relieved from the responsibility for the transgressions of his son.[67] Beginning with this day, the boy is considered an adult in matters of religious commandments, and is eligible for the required quorum of ten in the community prayers *(minyan)*.

Traditionally, as the occasion was practiced in the East European countries, the bar-mitzvah boy was supposed to deliver, in addition to his *Haftorah* reading, a learned speech based on the scriptures, and after the end of the Sabbath service all worshipers would partake in a modest reception at the synagogue. The custom of arranging elaborate festivities, the bestowing of expensive gifts on the celebrant, as well as bas-mitzvah celebrations for girls, as we know them presently in the U.S. and other countries, are relatively new developments, not known to the Jews of Eastern Europe.

In the Soviet Union, the rite of bar mitzvah has presently all but disappeared, except in the Oriental Jewish communities.

The reason this observance has vanished faster than any other Jewish religious rite in the Soviet Union perhaps may be explained by the fact that the bar-mitzvah rite involves the young Soviet citizen while he is in his formative years. Whereas the methods of combating religious beliefs of the old and the middle-aged have varied from very severe to, occasionally, mild, there was no wavering in the regime's determination to protect the young generation from "religious indoctrination," and to prevent them from being "subjected" to religious rites, particularly those performed in public.

The rationalization of the regime's right to interfere with the decisions of the parents in the religious upbringing of their children is construed in the following manner: persons not of age are not able to exercise their free will and choice; therefore, their participation in religious rites is an undue enforcement and a violation of their "natural" right to be brought up free of "superstitious beliefs." Consequently, it is the "sacred duty" of a solicitous socialist government to defend the young and the powerless from the encroachments upon their inherent rights as individuals.

There is seldom found a Jewish father or mother who will dare to submit their son to the dangers and consequences of standing up in the synagogue and publicly pronouncing what amounts to a declaration of allegiance to the religious community.

A retired Soviet professor told his visiting American friend: "Bar-mitzvah is out of the question, neither do the parents want to take the risk, nor do they want to cause inconveniences to their son." [68]

A Leningrad Jewish clergyman said to a visitor from Israel: "Bar-mitzvah?—an unheard of thing. Woe to the father who will take his son to the synagogue." [69]

A visitor in Leningrad was told that the number of bar-mitzvah celebrations in the synagogue during the year was "no more than five." [70]

When the son of Rabbi Liberman of Rockville Center, N. Y., visited the USSR with the American delegation of rabbis in 1966, he was called to the Torah and recited the blessings in the Moscow Central Synagogue, and aroused extraordinary excitement and wonder. The assembled worshipers exclaimed "It is a long, long time since a boy has come to worship to our synagogue." [71]

According to Rabbi Arthur Schneir, who in 1968 visited the Soviet Union as a member of the three-man group representing the Interfaith Appeal of Conscience Foundation of New York, "circumcision in the Soviet Union has become a thing of the past," and "there has been only one bar-mitzvah in Moscow in the past 15 years. That occurred last summer. People are afraid to hold them, a member of the congregation told me at the central synagogue. The only ones not afraid to be seen here are the old men who say 'we have nothing to lose.'" [72]

There are reliable indications that circumcision has not yet become entirely "a thing of the past" as Rabbi Schneir asserted, but his pessimistic views concerning bar-mitzvah are indeed there. Because this religious function takes place in public, not only must the father bear the consequences, but it is also very difficult for the youngster to wash off the stigma of having actively participated in the perpetration of "Judaic prejudices." He will have to prove time and again that the act was forced upon him by his "brutal and fanatic parents."

Some visitors to the Soviet Union have observed that the religious Jews inhabiting the later-incorporated Western territories, particularly the Jews living in the provinces of Bessarabia, Bukovina, and the Baltic States of Lithuania and Latvia, have tried to assert their right to conduct religious ceremonies involving the young in their synagogues. For instance, the journalist B. Z. Goldberg reported:

> Ceremonies involving the religious indoctrination of the young, like bar-mitzvahs, practically extinguished in Russia proper, were still the practice in . . . the Soviet Baltic republics, Moldavia, and other parts of Eastern Ukraine, and a certain defiance was in the air, a determination to hold onto the ancient faith. [73]

Such attempts were indeed made, as indicated by the indignant Soviet press. The defiance of the perpetrators was, however, handled "properly" by the local authorities.

Sovetskaia Moldavia of Kishinev disclosed that boys have been called in the synagogue of Falesti to chant the parts of the Torah for their bar-mitzvah. [74] The occurrence is described in detail:

Sioma Kizhner is reading a prayer. Elderly men nod their heads approvingly. One should think so. The boy reads in clear Hebrew language. Who among the young knows Hebrew at present? Nobody. But Sioma has mastered it. And so has Aronchik Rokhlar. On reaching the age of thirteen Sioma Kizhner and Aron Rokhlar underwent a "bar-mitzvah" ritual. These boys are good pupils, they wear red ties [i.e., they belong to the "Pioneers"]. They were nevertheless forced to learn prayers in the synagogue and to observe religious rituals.

The newspaper makes the information more poignant by divulging the name of the teacher who taught the boys the "prayer," and the names of all parents whose children have taken instruction for the bar-mitzvah observance. "The elders tell them," notes the newspaper, "to use cunning and to pretend; otherwise those who taught them the prayers will be incriminated for teaching religious dogma to juveniles. The boy puts on *tefilin* every morning and then removes the *tefilin* and puts on a red Pioneer tie. The struggle between school and synagogue has been going on for more than one year." [75]

The "struggle" was solved not in the boys' hearts but by a huge, widely publicized public trial at which all "offenses" of the Falesti Jewish clergymen were exposed. The accused clergymen, some of whom were arrested, were forced to publicly denounce and to further desist from religious practices, such as circumcision and private religious instruction. The last remaining Felesti synagogue was closed down, and religious believers were henceforth sufficiently intimidated not to protest any future acts of encroachments upon their loudly pronounced religious freedom.

The situation is again much different in the Oriental Jewish communities of Georgia and Central Asia

Ben-Ami, an Israeli citizen, visited many Oriental Jewish communities. After stating that the bar-mitzvah ritual is in the process of extinction in the European parts of the Soviet Union, he describes the conditions existing in this respect among the Oriental Jews:

You see another picture in the synagogues of the "Oriental Jews." I have visited the synagogues in Tashkent, Buchara, Samarkand, Tbilisi, Kutaisi, Baku, and in the other communities of the Caucasus and Central Asia, and there was hardly a Sabbath without a bar-mitzvah celebration. A Jewish boy dressed in his best will excitedly step up on the *bimah* [platform]; accompanied by his father he will recite the blessings in a good enough Hebrew in the Sephardic pronunciation, as the congregation and, of course, all the members of the ramified family will respond with a loud *amen*.[76]

The author muses about where the boy could have learned to read Hebrew and to chant the *Haftorah*. His impression was that the instruction was conducted inside the large patriarchal family which "transmits the fundamentals of tradition from generation to generation." There are indications from the Soviet press and from visitors that instruction is conducted not only in the homes.

But, as the case may be, even if this instruction is sometimes also given by rabbis and other clergymen, it can not impart more than the fundamentals, if it is conducted clandestinely and in fear of being disclosed.

In summing up it can be said that, except for the Oriental communities, the rite of bar-mitzvah is almost extinct in the Soviet Union. The near-extinction is due largely to government pressure and harassment. Yet, it may be assumed that in addition to extremely rare public celebrations in the open synagogues, a limited number of bar-mitzvahs are conducted in rudimentary form in makeshift houses of prayer and assemblies *(minyanim)*.

Notes

1. Sheftl Zak, "Yidn un Yidishe Hertser in Kirgizia" (Jews and Jewish Hearts in the Kirghiz Republic) (in *Folk un Velt*, October 1965).
2. A. A. Gershuni, *Yahadut be-Rusiah ha-Sovetit* (Judaism in Soviet Russia) (Jerusalem, 1961, p. 75).
3. Zalmen Yefroikin, *A Bazukh in Sovet Rusland* (A Visit to Soviet Russia) (New York, 1962, p. 86).
4. Joseph Schechtman, *Star in Eclipse,* (New York, 1961, p. 125).
5. Hans Lamm, "Jews and Judaism in the Soviet Union" (in *Studies on the Soviet Union,* Munich, Vol. 5, No. 4, 1966, p. 104).
6. Yehudi Sovieti Almoni, *El Ahai be-Medinat Israel* (Anonymous Soviet Jew, To My Brothers in the State of Israel) (Jerusalem, 1957, pp. 118–22).
7. *Sovetskaia Belorussia,* February 4, 1960, and March 3, 1960; *Gomelskaia Pravda,* July 24, 1960.
8. *Nauka i Religiia,* No. 11, 1961.
9. Schechtman, *op. cit.,* p. 20.
10. Schechtman, *op. cit.,* p. 119; Michael Shashar, *Israeli be-Moskva* (An Israeli in Moscow) (Jerusalem, 1961) p. 48). Shashar reported seeing in the yard of the Leningrad synagogue, several old women who brought chicken to be slaughtered by the *shohet* for Yom Kippur.
11. "Pod Svodami Sinagogi" (Under the Vaults of the Synagogue) (in *Volzhskai Komuna,* September 9, 1961).
12. Chaim Shoshkes, *Fun Moskva biz Ever Hayarden* (From Moscow to Transjordania) (Tel Aviv, 1961, p. 136).
13. *Sovetskaia Belorussia,* "Under the Synagogue Vaults," February 4, 1960.
14. "Hens Bring Money—Religion Opium for the People" (in *Gomelskaia Pravda,* July 24, 1960).
15. The number of Jews in Gomel, as given by the *American Jewish Year Book,* 1965, p. 423. The average number of a Jewish family, according to the Soviet census of 1959, has 3.2 (*Vestnik Statistiki,* Moscow, No. 11, 1961, p. 95).
16. Chaim Malamud in *Sovetish Heimland,* August, 1965.
17. Shoshkes, *op. cit.,* 1961, p. 153.
18. As stated in a letter by former Cantor I. Godysh of Orgiev, renouncing Jewish religion in *Sovetskaia Moldaviia,* August 6, 1960.
19. I. Timoner, in *The Day-Morning Journal* of New York, November 15, 1966.
20. *Jews in Eastern Europe,* November, 1963, p. 26.
21. *Nauka i Religiia,* No. 10, 1961, p. 47.
22. *Ibid.,* p. 28.
23. *Nauka i Religiia* (No. 10, 1961, p. 47) reported: "In Samarkand Jewish clergymen manage to arrange the slaughtering of cattle through dependable slaughterers."
24. *Dagestanskaia Pravda,* August 8 and 28, 1963.
25. *Ibid.*
26. *Leninskii Put,* May 27, 1961, *JEE,* December, 1962.
27. Gershuni, *op. cit.,* p. 92.
28. *Ibid.*
29. *Der Apikoires,* January 1, 1933, quoted by Jacob Leshchinsky in *Dos Sovetishe Yidntum* (New York, 1941), p. 92).
30. *Voiovnichi Ateist,* No. 8, 1963; *Yevrei i Yevreiski Narod* (hereafter *YYN*) No. 13, p. 9.

31. *JEE*, December 1962, p. 31.
32. *Ibid.*
33. Schechtman, *ibid.*
34. M. Berman and M. Yoffe, "Pod Seniu Talesa" (Under the Cover of a Tales) (in *Vechĕrnii Leningrad,* October 27. 1962, as quoted in *YYN* No. 10, p. 4).
35. Schechtman, *op. cit.,* p. 126.
36. Shashar, *op. cit.,* p. 59.
37. Shoshkes, *op. cit.,* p. 152.
38. *Nauka i Religiia,* No. 11, 1961.
39. "Ob otdelenii tserkvi ot gosudarstva i shkoly of tserkvi," Dekret Soveta Narodnykh Kommissarov, January 23, 1918 (in F. Garkavenko, *O Religii i Tserkvi* (On Religion and the Church) (Moscow, 1965, pp. 95–6); English translation in J. G. Curtiss, *The Russian Church and the Soviet State,* Boston, 1953, p. 333).
40. *Voprosy Istorii Religii i Ateizma,* No. 5, 1958, p. 41.
41. "Tsirkular po voprosu ob otdelenii tserkvi ot gosudarstva," VIII Otdel Narodnovo Komissariata Iustitsii Articles fifteen and sixteen of the Circular; O Religii i Tserkvi, *op. cit.,* pp. 100–5.
42. Interpretation of V Dept. of NKYU of January 20, 1922, No. 32. See P. V. Gidulianov, ed.; *Otdelenie Tserkvi ot Gosudarstva* (The Separation of Church from State) (Moscow, 1924, p. 268).
43. *Study of discrimination in the matter of religious rights and practices* (summary of information relating to the USSR. U.N. Commission on Human Rights, Sub-Commission on Prevention of Discrimination and Protection of Minorities, p. 10).
44. N. Chanin, *Sovet Rusland, Vi Yikh Hob Yir Gezen* (Soviet Russia, As I Saw It) (New York, 1929, p. 43).
45. Reportedly, Rabbi Maze of Moscow had in the first years after the Revolution converted to Judaism 367 Russian girls (Gershuni, *op. cit.,* p. 114).
46. *Ibid.,* on the basis of information in "Naftulei Hador," p. 336.
47. M. S. Dzhunusov, "K Kharekteristike Protsessa Sblizhenia Sovetskikh Natsii v Khode Sotsialisma i Kommunizma" (On the Characteristics of the Process of Drawing Together the Soviet Nationalities in the Course of Building Socialism and Communism) (in *Istoria SSR,* No. 3, 1962, pp. 37, 39–42, 46). The corresponding figures for the Armenians are 39.5 percent for males and 17.4 percent for females.
48. The noted Soviet Yiddish writer David Bergelson, one of the innocent victims killed in 1952 by the Soviet government, wrote movingly and with insight on the meaning and the originality of the Jewish wedding and wedding ceremony in his review of the play "Freilechs" which was the last performance of the Moscow Yiddish Art Theater before it was closed down by the Soviet authorities in 1948. The play was based on the music and folklore of a *hasunah.*
49. The wedding ceremony is now called "The beginning of new life" as the confirmation has been given the name "Coming of Age" ceremony. See "Struggle Against Religion in Latvia" (in *East Europe,* January 1965).
50. For an illustration of weddings thus performed see: Shashar, *op. cit.,* p. 45.
51. Schechtman, *op. cit.,* p. 119.
52. Even Shushan, *Sipuro Shel Maso, Esrim Yom be-Brit ha-Moatzot* (The Story of a Trip, Twenty Days in the Soviet Union) (Tel Aviv, 1964, p. 119).
53. Shashar, *ibid.*
54. Schechtman, *ibid.*
55. Ben-Ami, *Bein ha-Patish ve-ha-Magal* (Between the Hammer and the Sickle) (Tel Aviv, 1965, p. 154).
56. Schechtman, *op. cit.,* p. 126.
57. *Kommunist Moldavii,* No. 7, 1960, pp. 73–5. *Jews and the Jewish People* (hereafter *JJP*), No. 2, p. 6.

58. Yefroikin, *op. cit.*, p. 59.

59. *Volzhskaia Komuna*, "Pod Svodami Sinagogi" (Under the Synagogue Vaults), September 9, 1961, *YYN*, No. 5, p. 6.

60. *Leninskii* Put, May 27, 1961, in *JEE*, December 1962, p. 31.

61. *Nauka i Religiia*, No. 10, 1961, p. 47.

62. Ben-Ami, *op. cit.*, p. 154.

63. An article in the local paper had accused Jews of using Moslem blood in the preparation of matzohs. The article was repudiated two days later.

64. *Kommunist*, Buinaksik, July 30, 1960. *JJP* V. I, No. 2, p. 1.

65. *Pravda Vostoka, Tashkent*, December 2, 1960. *JJP* V. 6, No. 2, p. 6.

66. Zvi Harkavy and Avraham Shevli, eds., *Shomrei ha-Gahelet* (Guardians of the Glowing Coals), *op. cit.*, (Jerusalem and New York, 1966).

67. "Barukh Shepotrani Meonsho Shel Ze" (Blessed be Thou that I am now exempt from the punishment for him").

68. Itzhak Fein, "Mit Sovetishe Yidn" (in *Yidisher Kemfer*, November 25, 1966).

69. Shashar, *op. cit.*, p. 45.

70. Elie Wiesel, *The Jews of Silence.*

71. *Der Tog*, New York, July 18, 1966.

72. Rabbi Arthur Schneir, "Time Runs Out for Russia's Jews" (in *Look, New York*, Nov. 29, 1966, p. 103).

73. B. Z. Goldberg, *The Jewish Problem in the Soviet Union* (New York, 1961, p. 133).

74. "Under the Synagogue Canopy" (in *Sovetskaia Moldavia*, April 28, 1960).

75. *Ibid.*

76. Ben-Ami, *op. cit.*, p. 152.

CHAPTER 5

Objects of the Ritual, Prayer Books, and Religious Publications

The production of Jewish religious articles necessary for the observance of Jewish rituals—prayer shawls, phylacteries, Torah scrolls, mezuzahs, and also prayer books and Jewish calendars—has not been permitted, nor has their importation from abroad been allowed. Objects for Jewish rituals now found in the Soviet Union either date from the Tsarist period or were left there by foreign tourists as gifts.

The supply of religious articles was adequate in the initial period of Soviet rule. The number of observant Jews and the possibility of observing the faith diminished and some of the ritual objects and religious books from requisitioned synagogues found their way into the remaining houses of prayer or into the hands of worshipers.

Soviet law requested that objects of the cult and religious books be transferred to members of the confiscated house of prayer, if the members were willing to "take responsibility for the objects while the government remained the legal owner of the entrusted objects." [1] In many cases there were no persons willing to take upon themselves this responsibility and be subjected to continuous control by government agencies. This would have made the possessor of religious articles vulnerable to persecution if the religious objects were used in other than "legal" prayer groups; also, as government property, the objects had to be properly preserved.

However, there have been numerous cases in which the local authorities refused to hand over religious objects and books from confiscated synagogues to former members of the dissolved religious association. The objects were either destroyed or diverted to other uses.

On some occasions Soviet authorities confiscated religious books even when the synagogues in which these books were used had not been closed. Religious books which were not prayer books were often confiscated on the grounds that a synagogue is a house of prayer and not a house of study. The books were sent to paper factories as raw material, and, occasionally, burned in stacks in public, much to the discomfort of some Communists for whom it brought to mind the medieval burnings of books.[2]

The notion that the publication of Jewish religious books in the Soviet Union was suspended as soon as the Bolsheviks took over is not correct. Religious books, excluding Bibles and Talmuds, were published until 1928, that is, for eleven years after the Revolution. However, the books were published in increasingly smaller numbers and with increasingly greater difficulties.

The last published Jewish religious publication in the Soviet Union (until 1956 when a prayer book was printed) was *Yagdil Torah*, a collection of articles and essays on religious problems by Yehezkel Abramski, the head of the rabbinical court in Slutsk. It was printed in the government-owned printing plant of *Komunotrast* in Bobruisk, Belorussian SSR.[3]

The first issue of this collection, which numbered eighteen pages, appeared in the Hebrew month of Tishri, 5687 (1927), the second and last collection in the month of Adar, 5688 (1928); they were edited by Rabbi Shlomo Yosif Levin of Novozivkov.

The last Hagadahs for the Passover were published in 1927 and in 1928, both in Bobruisk.[4]

The last prayer books *(sidurim)* were published in 1927 and 1928, in Berdichev (Ukrainian SSR) and in Leningrad.[5]

An annual Jewish calendar was published in Bobruisk in 1928 for the Jewish year 5688. A crude calendar which had been printed privately from movable type appeared also for the year 5690. (Several pocket calendars were issued by the Moscow and Leningrad synagogues after 1956.) The last *mahzor* (prayer book for the High Holidays) was published in Berdichev in 1926.[6]

The last published religious discourse in book form was a commentary on Maimonides' works by Yitzhak Krasileshchikov; it was printed in Poltava in 1926.[7]

Humashim (The Five Books of Moses) and editions of the Bible and Talmud were never allowed to be published in the Soviet Union.

The accelerated campaign against Jews and Jewish religious institutions in the late 1920s brought a definite end to the publication of Jewish religious literature, prayer books, and calendars. At the same time the importation of Bibles from abroad, in any language, was officially prohibited by the Soviet government.[8]

When an American Jew contacted Moscow Radio and asked when the last Torah was published in the Soviet Union, he received, after a year's delay, the strange reply: "The Torah is written by hand, we do not publish it. We publish annually a calendar for the Jewish Religious Association of Moscow." [9] Of course, the Torah scrolls kept in the arks of synagogues are written by hand on parchment but the *texts* of these Torah scrolls, which are part of the Bible, have been published in innumerable editions since the discovery of the printing press. The substitution of a "yearly calendar we publish" for the Bible is so primitive that it is almost incredible. As a matter of fact, the statement that calendars are published is also untrue. The Moscow and Leningrad synagogues published tiny pocket calendars for a few years only.

Equally baseless were the two reasons for not publishing the Bible given by P. A. Dogorozhny, the Vice Chairman of the Soviet Council of Religious Cults, to Rabbi E. Rosenberg of Toronto: 1) The Hebrew alphabet is too strange and esoteric for the printers in the State publishing houses (as if other publishing houses existed in the Soviet Union); and 2) if the Russian Jews want a Bible, they should ask for it. "Since they haven't asked for it, we must assume that they don't need one." [10] This reply is reminiscent of one given by the woman in Sholem Aleichem's story who, when asked by her neighbor to return a borrowed pot, answered that, first of all, she never borrowed a pot, and, second, the pot was badly broken anyway.

Yet, in spite of the impossibility of seeing their works printed, Jewish scholars have not ceased to study and to write essays and discourses on religious subjects. A number of these manuscripts have had the good fortune to become available outside the Soviet Union and have been published in other countries: a book entitled *Yehave Deo* (expressed opinion) by Rabbi Zvi Makovsky of Militpol, which includes a number of responses characteristic of conditions of Jewish life in the Soviet Union, was published in Israel, as was a volume dealing with topics of religious philosophy, *Mikhtvei Mehkar u-Bikoret* (Letters of Research and Critique), by Shmuel Alexandrov, published in 1932 in Jerusalem.[11]

In 1930, the Soviet government requested that "voluntary" donations of valuable objects of religious cults be made to the impoverished state treasury. Golden and silver bells were taken down from church towers and precious vessels removed from the Russian Orthodox Church. Jewish synagogues, especially those in the smaller towns, did not have any valuable religious objects; even the richer synagogues in larger towns were endowed with a relatively small quantity of silver or golden objects of cult, in sharp contrast to most Russian Orthodox and Catholic churches. Jewish Communists felt, however, that political considerations demanded that the same campaign be conducted in the "Jewish street" irrespective of the insignificant returns expected. The Soviet authorities were careful to persecute with equality. Thus, if a church had to "donate" its golden ritual objects, then the synagogue in the hamlet was forced "to make a gift" of its copper candlesticks. The Yiddish communist press led by the Moscow *Emes* demanded that synagogues "sell" to the government their religious objects, the menorahs (candlesticks), lamps, books, prayer shawls (*talesim*), and phylacteries (*tefilin*). Jewish children were "mobilized" to help in the "sales campaign." The true character of the campaign was best revealed by the name adopted for it by the Communists: "Battle against God." The battle was replete with bulletins from the "frontline." As expected by everyone, including the Communists, the proceeds from the "sold" goods were utterly negligible.

The shortage of religious books and objects considerably increased after the German-Soviet war, with the complete annihilation of hundreds of Jewish communities, and dispersion of the hundreds of thousands of Jews who were saved from German slaughter. After innumerable petitions and many years of delay, Rabbi Schlieffer of the Central Moscow Synagogue succeeded, during a short respite in the Soviet antireligious campaign, in obtaining permission in 1956 to publish 3000 copies of a prayer book in a photo-offset reproduction.[12]

The new *sidurim* were very quickly sold out, so quickly that a Jewish journalist who visited the Soviet Union three years later, in 1959, reported of Jews approaching him stealthily and asking for a *sidur*, being ready 'to pay any price he would have asked."[13] The shortage of prayer books soon became as acute as it had been before Rabbi Schlieffer's book was published.

The document which the Soviet government submitted in 1956 to the Commission on Human Rights of the United Nations, providing information on the state and status of religion in the Soviet Union, related to *inter alia,* the publications and devotional literature issued in the Soviet Union by those religious cults not centrally organized, of which the Jewish religion is one: "The various religious centers and religious communities in the Soviet Union which do not form part of a religious center have the right to publish such devotional literature as they require; to enable them to do so, the State supplies them with the necessary paper and affords them the use of printing plants." It is further stated in the submitted information that a "sidur (prayer book) for worshippers of the Jewish faith is now being published." [14]

It will not take much effort to show that in the case of the Jewish faith the right to publish "such devotional literature as they require" has· remained a right only on paper.

The Soviet authorities have never admitted that a shortage of devotional material exists, and the Soviet press has not stopped attacking Jewish tourists for "disseminating religious articles among Soviet Jews," invariably asserting that there is no shortage of these articles, while simultaneous attacks are directed against synagogues and Jewish religious leaders for "black market dealings" in religious objects and prayer books, which are allegedly in large supply. [15]

Attacks on tourists and on Israeli diplomats for distributing religious books and articles became most widespread during the years 1959–1965, a period of massive assault on Jewish religion. [16] On October 18, 1966, two secretaries of the Israeli Embassy in Moscow, Yehudah Katz and Meir Biran, were accused by the newspaper *Komunist Tadzhikstana* of having enticed the worshipers of the Dushanbe (Tadzhik SSR) synagogue to take from them "propaganda material." The propaganda material consisted of prayer books and religious articles. [17]

Observations made by almost all foreign visitors sufficiently illustrate the unquestionable shortage of prayer books and religious articles.

The Israeli journalist Ben-Ami saw Jews who were using "all kinds of discolored rags, tattered pieces of old prayer shawls in various phases of disintegration." [18] Another Israeli visitor, Michael Shashar, described in his book how old Jews "wearing ancient phylacteries and faded *taleisim* kissed his *talis* and implored for a mezuzah." The shortages are so great, noted the author, that an observant Jew joyfully pays 200 rubles (a worker's wages for one week) for a prayer book and 1500 rubles for a prayer shawl.[19] A young man approached Shashar outside the Moscow synagogue after the Sukkos services and said: "I am 25 years old, in a month I will be married and I don't have a *talis;* perhaps you can get one for me." [20] Two hundred rubles, notes Shashar, was the black market price for a *sidur* even in Leningrad, a town frequently visited by Jewish tourists from abroad.[21]

The American Jewish journalist, Joseph Schechtman, corroborated this information:

> A middle-aged Jew told me: what we miss most are prayer books and prayer shawls. A complete prayer book costs between a hundred and a hundred and fifty rubles (from ten to fifteen dollars at the tourist rate of exchange). And for a *talis* one has to pay a thousand rubles and more. Even a *mezuzah* has become an expensive item.[22]

The situation in the Jewish communities outside the large cities of Moscow and Leningrad was even worse. Schechtman was told by a Jew in Kiev: "What we miss most are *sidurim* and *taleisim.* I have heard that three thousand prayer books have been printed by the State Publishing House for the Moscow religious community, but not a single copy has reached us. Nobody cares for a provincial Jewish community which very few foreign tourists visit. You can see the wornout condition of the few *sidurim* and *mahzorim* we still have. And to buy new ones is nearly impossible as prices are prohibitive, 100–150 rubles on the black market." [23] The lack of prayer books, which are the most often used religious books, was felt more keenly than the lack of those religious books used only for study or special occasions.

In 1960 several synagogues joined the Moscow synagogue in a request to allow the printing of a new edition of the *sidur,* but no answer to their request was received.[24] When, in Moscow in 1961,

Rabbi E. Rosenberg of Toronto asked Pavel Anotolovich Daghorozny, Vice Chairman of the Soviet Council of Religious Cults, what was holding up a new edition of a prayer book, he replied "most probably a paper shortage." [25]

Promises to print a new edition of the *sidur* were repeated by Soviet spokesmen in later years. The promises were at times vague and at times explicit. Rabbi David Hollander of New York reportedly received a promise from two officials in the Ministry of Culture on March 1965 that a sidur would be printed, and restrictions in the furnishing of religious articles would be eased. In August 1965, half a year later, Rabbi Levin of Moscow declared that he himself had received assurances that a new edition of the 1956 sidur would be printed. [26]

In August 1965 Aron Vergelis, the editor of the Yiddish-language monthly *Sovetish Heimland,* reportedly said that a *sidur* was being printed at his journal's printing plant. [27] Another visitor to the Soviet Union related: "When we asked the present Chief Rabbi of Moscow about prayer books, he pointed to a pile lying at his side, and replied: 'with God's aid we are going now to press; here you see the plates.' " [28]

Two Christian clergymen, a Catholic, the Reverend Thurston M. Davis, editor of the Jesuit weekly *America,* and Dr. Harold A. Bosley, minister of Christ Church, a Methodist, and Rabbi Arthur Schneier, all members of the Appeal to Conscience Foundation, an organization founded in 1965 to aid restoration of religious freedom for Jews in the USSR, reported upon their return from the Soviet Union in January 1966 that they had been promised by Peter Makaratsev, of the Soviet Council of Religious Cults, that 10,000 Hebrew prayer-books, to replace all old, tattered copies, would be printed "as soon as technical arrangements could be completed." [29] In 1967 the *sidur* was not yet ready. Its printing seemed to be technically more complicated than sending a sputnik into orbit.

The printing of a prayer book was visibly obstructed; the production of objects for use in Jewish rituals was nonexistent; and the importation of these articles from abroad was forbidden as well. In the spring of 1960, parcels from Israel containing *taleisim* and *tefilin* were returned to their senders marked "undeliverable." When a number of Canadian Jews attempted to send prayer books and other ritual necessities to their relatives in the Soviet Union, Soviet consular officials in Canada informed them that the import of such articles was not allowed.[30]

Jewish calendars are another item in very short supply in the Soviet Union. Calendars are essential to observant Jews, especially in smaller communities where there are no rabbis and no synagogues. Without calendars, religious Jews do not know on which days to observe Jewish holidays, and are deprived of other information relevant to religious observances.

Jewish calendars are a very popular item in all Jewish communities the world over; they are often given out free by various organizations and businesses, or are sold in pocket size for a few pennies each. In the Soviet Union, Jews were forbidden, except on a few occasions, to issue calendars. Therefore, some older and retired persons with a knowledge of Jewish religious law had from time to time engaged in writing calendars by hand and selling them for a small price. These activities were not overlooked, neither by the Soviet press nor by the Soviet authorities. The "writers" of the calendars were attacked in the newspapers, and not infrequently subjected to penalties for engaging in "private enterprise."

For instance, the newspaper *Sovetskaia Daugava* of March 3, 1959, criticized "Rabbi Baruch Eliashberg who had purchased several dozen notebooks at 15 kopeks apiece, split them into two, and fabricated religious calendars which he sold at 5–10 rubles each." [31]

Only two Jewish religious communities were allowed, in some years, to publish mimeographed calendars. The Moscow Jewish community issued, after an interval of many years, a calendar for the year 5717 (1956–1957), and for the year 5718 (1957–1958). A handwritten Jewish calendar for the year 5722 (1961–1962) was mimeographed and distributed by the Leningrad Jewish religious community. A calendar was printed again by the Moscow Jewish Religious Association in 1963 and in 1964. The small four-by-three-inch booklet of thirty-five pages in Yiddish and Russian included, in addition to the months and days, information on the time for lighting Sabbath candles, as well as the dates of important Soviet anniversaries. Two prayers are included in the calendar. The prayer for peace, in Hebrew and Russian, and the prayer for the dead, the Kadish, in Hebrew and in a Russian transliteration.[32]

Apparently, some of the calendars published in Moscow are sent to

Jewish religious associations in other towns. *Znamia Kommunizma* (October 27, 1963) of Odessa tells of 200 calendars that arrived at the local synagogue and deplored that "their sale was immediately organized, exactly on a holiday and at a higher price, breaking two laws at the same time, the religious and the state law."

Because of their small size and minimal cost, calendars are given out by tourists more freely and with greater ease than prayer books. Nonetheless, a shortage of calendars has always existed.

Israeli diplomats were often accused of "spreading Israeli and anti-Soviet propaganda" because they had distributed calendars to Soviet Jews. As one Israeli diplomat who had served in the Soviet Union for a longer period of time told an interviewing journalist, "It happens sometimes that an old Jew meets an official from the Israel Embassy and implores him: 'Have pity, spare a calendar, so I will know when to observe Yom Kippur.' The official is unable to resist the Jew's request and gives him a calendar. The old man is consequently detained by a militiaman, and later an announcement will be issued that 'the Israel diplomat has maintained contact with the Soviet populace and has spread anti-Soviet propaganda.' " [33]

On September 1, 1966, an article in *Sovetskaia Moldavia,* written by F. Maiatsky, known for his virulent writings against the Jewish religion, attacked the Jewish calendar which was published in the Russian language in Israel. The calendar was, in his opinion, a product of "dirty swindles of bourgeois ideologists who are forging history." The forgery, he said, is demonstrated by the fact that the calendar recalls the confining of Jews in Tsarist Russia to a certain area of the country, but fails to mention that the October Revolution has abolished this restriction. Apparently Maiatsky was irked by the fact that the Russian calendar allowed Soviet Jews to receive information on various facts of Jewish history. [34]

Soviet spokesman consider the Israeli calendars as "literature hostile to the Soviet people" for the following reasons: "It contains no mention of such dates as the great October Socialist Revolution, or the Holiday of the workers of the whole world, May 1, or of the decree signed by Lenin, directed at uprooting anti-Semitism." Also, the calendar does not include news about Israel's ties with West Germany and "does not mention the Nuremberg race laws, the German death camps, etc." [35]

The policy of the Soviet regime which provides religious articles for non-Jewish religious cults differs from the policy which the government adopted for the treatment of Jews. Several examples will illustrate the differences.

The Moscow Patriarchate of the Russian Orthodox Church was allowed to publish a complete edition of the Russian translation of the Bible in 1956 in 50,000 copies.[36] In 1957 a Baptist edition of the Bible was printed in 10,000 copies.[37] As mentioned before, no Hebrew Bible has been printed in the Soviet Union since the October Revolution. The Russian Orthodox Church was granted the right to publish a monthly periodical of about eighty pages, the *Journal of the Moscow Patriarchate,* with material pertinent to religious matters, in editions of 15,000–25,000 copies. Another periodical, the *Pravoslavnii Visnik* (Russian Orthodox Herald) is published in the Ukrainian language in Lvov, in an edition of 3000 copies.[38] The Armenian Church established a new printing press in 1956. The Armenian community in the U.S. raised the funds and the Soviet government gave permission to the Armenian Church to receive and use the money for the press.[39]

The ban on the importation of Jewish religious articles contrasts significantly with the handling of similar packages sent to German Lutherans in Siberia, observes one writer. In January 1959, the Evangelical Church in Western Germany announced that it was receiving up to one hundred letters a day from German deportees in Siberia, acknowledging shipments of Bibles and religious literature.[40]

A review of Soviet Jewish religious literature would not be complete without mentioning the interesting collection of rabbinical *Responsa* and studies on homiletics and Torah problems which was published in 1965 in Jerusalem under the name of *Shomrei ha-Gahelet* (The Guardians of the Glowing Goals).[41] Contributors were former Soviet rabbis who emigrated from the Soviet Union and settled later in other countries (mainly Israel), and several rabbis still living in the Soviet Union and in several other countries of the communist bloc.

For the first and only time Soviet rabbis were allowed to publish their works, although still not in the Soviet Union itself. Among the Soviet contributors were the late rabbi of the Central Moscow Synagogue, Solomon Schlieffer, the present rabbi of the synagogue, I. L.

Levin, and Rabbi A. H. Lubanov of Leningrad. Among the contributors from countries of the Eastern bloc were Eliyahu Katz, the rabbi of Bratislava (Czechoslovakia), and the rabbis Shik and Weiss of Budapest (Hungary).

There are indications that many more rabbinical works were written in the Soviet Union and that they were not allowed to be published either within the country or abroad. B. Z. Goldberg remarked in his book: "It cannot be ascertained how many manuscripts on religious topics were written in the Soviet Union, as it cannot be known how many secular Jewish works were written since 1948. Yet it cannot be doubted that manuscripts of religious books do exist. I myself know about several. Others know about more." [42]

The right of the Soviet Jews to secure ritual objects and religious books, at least to the same degree as other religious cults in the country are able to do, is a most important issue—demanded by Soviet Jews in low voices, and more loudly by other Jews. The facts of discrimination against the Jewish religion in this particular field are so unequivocal that they cannot be denied by phrases extolling the freedom and absolute equality of all religions in the Soviet Union, and by assertions that religious discrimination cannot exist in the Soviet Union because the Soviet Constitution forbids it. Denying obvious facts will convince neither friend nor foe, no matter how obdurately the denial is made.

Notes

1. Tsirkular Po Voprosu Otdelenii Tserkvi Ot Gosudarstva, January 3, 1919; F. Garkavenko, *O Religii i Tserkvi* (On Religion and the Church) (Moscow, 1965, pp. 100ff); see also article forty of the Law on Religious associations of April 3, 1929, *Sobranie Uzakonenii i Pasporiazhenii Rabochekrestianskovo Pravitelstva RSFSR*, No. 35, 1929.

2. A. A. Gershuni, *Yahadut be-Rusiah ha-Sovetit* (Judaism in the Soviet Union) (Jerusalem, 1961), p. 93.

3. *Yagdil Torah, Maasaf Torani Mukdash Le-Hidushei Torah, Pilpulim Behalakha Lemaase. Aruch u-Mesudar al ydei Yehazkel Abramski,* Vols. 1, 2 Bobruisk, 1968 (Yosef Cohen, *Pirsumim Yehudiyim be-Verit ha-Moatzot 1917–1960* [Jerusalem,1961, p. 38, No. 32]).

4. *Seder Hagada shel Pesah ym Pirsumim Nifloyim,* Bobruisk, *Beis mishar shel Yaakov ha-Kohen Ginzburg,* 1927; *Hagada shel Pesakh mit Yivri Teitsh Oif Reinem Zhargon,* etc., Bobruisk, Izdanie Magazina Ginzburga, 1928. (Cohen, *op. cit.,* p. 18, No. 121, 122.)

5. *Sidur Tefilat Yaakov Hasholem,* Bobruisk, Yaakov Ginzburg. Printing plant "Radianskii Shliakh," 1927; *Sidur Tehilat Adonai,* 5th ed. Leningrad, Z. Kalmanson, 1928. (Cohen, *op. cit.,* p. 25, No. 184, 185.)

6. Cohen, *op. cit.,* p. 19, No. 145, 146 and p. 22, No. 149.

7. Yitzhak Aizik Krasileshchikov, *Sefer Tvunah be-Mishne Torah leha-Rambam,* Vol. 1 Poltava, 1926. (Cohen, *op. cit.,* p. 22, No. 153.)

8. By order of the Commissariat for Foreign Trade, later confirmed by the Council of Peoples' Commissars (Gershuni, *op. cit.,* p. 131.)

9. *Yalkut Mogen,* August 1964, p. 14.

10. *Jews in Eastern Europe* (hereafter *JEE*) No. 8, 1961.

11. Gershuni, *op. cit.,* p. 126.

12. Salo Baron, *The Russian Jews under Tsars and Soviets* (New York, 1964, p. 340); *American Jewish Year Book,* 1957 and 1958, chapters on the Soviet Union; B. Z. Goldberg, *Yidn in Ratn-Farband* (Jews in the Soviet Union) (Tel Aviv, 1965, p. 142).

13. Goldberg, *ibid.*

14. "Study of Discrimination in the Matter of Religious Rights and Practices" (United Nation's Commission on Human Rights, *op. cit.,* p. 14).

15. Such allegations were directed against, for instance, the Central Synagogue in Moscow (*JTA Bulletin,* October 18, 1962), against the Minsk synagogue (*Minskaia Pravda,* April 3, 1961, in an article "Under the Dark Vaults of the Synagogue").

16. A characteristic example is the article "Erusalimske Iarmulki" in *Radianska Bukovina,* August 8, 1960, and the several articles and letters to the editor that followed the article.

17. "Soviets Accuse Israelis of Distributing Sidurim" (in *Der Tog,* October 19, 1966).

18. Ben-Ami, *Bein ha-Patish ve-ha-Magal* (Between the Hammer and the Sickle) (Tel Aviv, 1965), p. 65.

19. Michael Shashar, *Israeli be-Moskva* (An Israeli in Moscow) (Jerusalem, 1961, p. 35). Other instances are related on p. 47. (A mezuzah is a parchment scroll placed in a container and nailed at the doorposts in homes inhabited by Jews.)

20. *Ibid.,* p. 102.

21. *Ibid.,* p. 130. Other references on the shortage of prayer books may be found in Shashar, *op. cit.,* pp. 47, 59, 60.

22. Joseph Schechtman, *Star in Eclipse* (New York, 1961, pp. 126–7).

23. *Ibid.,* p. 126.

24. Goldberg, *ibid.*

25. *Jews in Eastern Europe* (hereafter *JEE*), No. 8, 1961.

26. *Der Tog,* New York, August 12, 1965.

27. *Jewish Chronicle,* January 28, 1966.

28. Hans Lamm, "Jews and Judaism in the Soviet Union" (in *Studies on the Soviet Union,* Munich, Vol. 5, No. 4, 1966, p. 194).

29. *Jewish Advocate,* Boston, June 23, 1960.

30. Schechtman, *op. cit.,* p. 128.

31. *JEE,* No. 4, 1960, p. 16.

32. Cohen, *op. cit.,* pp. 19–22; the author saw a copy of the 1964 calendar in the New York Yivo Institute.

33. *Yidisher Kemfer,* New York, September 2, 1966.

34. *Der Tog,* September 2, 1966.

35. *Trud,* March 11, 1964, as quoted in *JEE,* December 1964, p. 46.

36. Walter Kolarz, *Religion in the Soviet Union* (New York, 1961, p. 94).

37. *Ibid.,* p. 321, *Bratskii Vestnik,* 1958, No. 1, p. 33.

38. Kolarz, *op. cit.,* p. 94.

39. *Ibid.,* p. 173.

40. Schechtman, *ibid.*

41. *Shomrei ha-Gahelet* (Guardians of the Glowing Coals) (Jerusalem and New York, 1966). One of the two editors, Avraham Sheuli, is reportedly the pseudonym of Abraham Byk, former rabbi and former staff member of the pro-communist New York daily *Morgen-Freiheit.*

42. Goldberg, *op. cit.,* p. 197.

CHAPTER 6

Circumcision

Circumcision in Jewish Religious Law

Circumcision, in Hebrew *milah* ("the cutting away of the foreskin"), is a religious rite performed on Jewish male children on the eighth day after birth. According to religious tradition circumcision was enjoined upon Abraham and his descendants as "a token of the covenant" concluded with him by God for all generations *(brit milah).* In ancient times the operation was performed by a surgeon, *rofe,* who was later called by a specific name, *mohel.* The *mohel* became an indispensable institution in every Jewish religious community.[2]

Few Jews went uncircumcised in the course of Jewish history and until recent years the notion of an uncircumcised Jew was a contradiction in terms. So tenacious and deep was the Jewish attachment to the idea of circumcision that when a Greek ruler, in his attempt to eradicate the Jewish religion, probhibited the rite, many Jews risked death rather than obey the prohibition. An ancient chronicler describes vividly this martyrdom: "They put to death certain women that had caused their children to be circumcised. And they hanged the infants about their necks, and rifled their homes and slew them that had circumcised them" (*Maccabees* L 1, 60–63). Few Jewish rituals were observed so faithfully or were until recent years so universally a distinguishing mark of Jewish males.

Circumcision, although important and deeply rooted in Jewish tradition, is not a sacrament which gives the Jewish male his religious character as a Jew. According to Jewish law *(Halakhah)* any child born to a Jewish mother is a Jew by birth. For instance, Jews in the Soviet Union who are not circumcised are still considered Jews by Jewish law.

Circumcision is not exclusively a Jewish rite for it is also practiced by Moslems, who perform the operation on males of various ages. In recent decades the practice has spread to non-Jews and non-Moslems as a result of an increased belief in its value as a prophylactic measure.

The Legal Aspect

Contrary to general impression, circumcision, as practiced by Jews and Moslems, is not prohibited by law in the Soviet Union. There is no explicit legal provision against it in the enactments dealing with religious matters or in the criminal codes of the Soviet republics. Article 227 of the new criminal code of RSFSR comes closest to a prohibition and could be construed by the authorities to apply to circumcision. One of its provisions makes punishable "the performance of religious rites connected with inflicting harm to the health of the citizens." "Inflicting harm to the health" can be variously interpreted, of course. However, to our knowledge article 227 has not been invoked to prosecute the performance of circumcision as practiced in the Soviet Union by Moslems and Jews, except in cases where a medical complication followed the operation. The very authoritative Journal *Sovetskoie Gosudarstvo i Pravo* (Soviet State and Law) contains the following examples of what constitutes "inflicting harm" under article 227: "The harm would be done in the process of zealous prayer or long fasts, or by refusal to receive medical help, and also as a result of bringing sacrifices to expiate for sins." [3] Circumcision is, significantly, not included here.

It is reasonable to assume that circumcision has not been included in the category of activities "inflicting harm" because it would entail a prolonged fight, too troublesome to conduct and too arduous to win, against a well-entrenched religious rite practiced by 25–30 million Soviet Moslems. [4] It would also be difficult to make circumcision legal for one religious group and not for the Jews as well.

However, other pressures are brought to bear upon the Jewish people. Members of the Communist Party who, it is discovered, have a circumcised child—whether the operation had been performed with or without the parents' knowledge—are expelled. Expulsions from the Communist Party for such transgressions are not applied to Moslem Communists.

Every case of medical complication, real or alleged, resulting from circumcision is used, under the Criminal Code, to prosecute the person who performed the operation. The *mohel* is charged with inflicting harm to the life or health of the child.

Pressure is applied against *mohelim*. Warnings to desist are given;

expulsion from their living quarters or their town may occur; or, in extreme cases, there may be detention and arrest. Practices of this kind are responsible for the impression which prevails among many Soviet Jews—that is, that circumcision is against the law. Therefore, when performed by Jews in non-Moslem areas, the rite is usually done in secret.

Discriminatory action may be taken against parents or close members of a family which allows the performance of circumcision. Some of these actions consist in demotions from positions, denial of job advancements, loss of priorities for acquisition of a new apartment, or denial of permits for vacations in resort areas.

An Israeli who had the opportunity to visit parts of the country that are not accessible to the average tourist, describes the plight of the *mohel* in the Soviet Union in the following manner: "The war on circumcision is waged in an indirect way. The fight is conducted not only against the rite itself but also against those who perform the rite. After apprehending the *mohel,* who is usually an old man, they would ask him: 'Say, is it true, or not true, that on that day and in that place you performed a surgical operation on a Soviet citizen, eight days old, by the name of so-and-so?' When the *mohel* admits the fact, they would then ask him: 'Now, where is your surgeon's diploma, and who gave you the permission to perform surgery on human bodies?' And if the bewildered *mohel* replies that he has been doing this kind of 'surgery' for decades, they will tell him in an unequivocal way that he has been violating Soviet law, and if they catch him again doing this sort of thing he will be arrested and severely punished." [5] The fact that a *mohel* is usually not immediately prosecuted but first threatened with arrest and prosecution is an added indication of the illegality of this procedure by the local authorities. If circumcision were a breach of Soviet law, prosecution would immediately follow its discovery, as in the case of criminal offenses such as theft or forgery.

The Medical Position

The official Soviet medical position concerning circumcision is that the practice is a barbaric, savage ritual, detrimental to the health of the infant. No mention is made anywhere that the practice of circumcision in Western countries has gained wide acceptance among non-Jews and non-Moslems due to the growing evidence of its hygienic and prophylactic qualities; and that circumcision has become a routine practice in many hospitals, where up to 80 percent of all newborn males in some urban areas of the U.S. and 95 percent of the males born in Australia are routinely circumcised.[6]

The attitude of Soviet medical science to the medical aspects of circumcision is interesting. Several medical studies pointed toward the fact that circumcision is highly effective in preventing cancer of the urogenital organs. Very prominent among the researchers in this field is Dr. Abraham Ravich, an American urologist, who has devoted many years to the study of the correlation between cancer of the urogenital organs and circumcision. Dr. Ravich has read several papers on the subject at medical conferences and has published the results of his findings and the findings of other scholars on this subject in several medical journals.[7] As a practicing urologist for thirty-five years in the Jewish section of Brooklyn, he accumulated 16,000 case studies of patients of which 90 percent were Jewish, and found not a single case of cancer of the penis, vulva, or vagina among the Jewish patients. Dr. Ravich also cited the report by Professor M. Caine and Dr. J. Singer in which it was stated that they failed to find a single case of cancer of the prostate, bladder, or cervix in Yemenite Jews who had migrated to Israel in 1950. The incidence of cancer of the prostate gland among his Jewish patients was 1.7 percent, compared to 20 percent among non-Jews (of whom only 5 percent were circumcised). In his survey, cancer of the bladder occurred in 1.8 percent of the Jews and 4.7 percent of the non-Jews. Cancer of urogenital organs comprises 25 percent of all cancers in the U.S. and accounts for 60,000 deaths annually in the United States.

The health aspects of circumcision are now a frequent topic in the medical press of many countries and inquiries were made to discover if this problem is also being discussed in the medical press of the Soviet Union. The author of this study is indebted to several persons who provided their advice and made available information.[8] The Library of Medicine of the U.S. Department of Health, Education, and Welfare stated, in response to a letter of inquiry dated March 3, 1966, that they "cannot locate any translation project on circumcision." At the same time, a search of *Index Medicus* for the last three years gave no references for Russian research on circumcision. There was no specific reference to the subject of circumcision in the *Great Medical Encyclopedia* of the Soviet Union, and there was no mention of circumcision in the medical press of the Soviet Union. The only important study on the subject by a Soviet physician was located in a U.S. medical journal.[9] In this article the author, Dr. Shabad, admits that circumcision is of great prophylactic value to a certain kind of cancer. He states: "Another peculiarity of penile cancer is its dependence on circumcision. The literature contains reports of only 4 cases of penile cancer in Jews who have undergone ritual circumcision in the first days of life." Dr. Shabad also relates interesting results of a study made in the Kazakh SSR which showed that the incidence of penile cancer among circumcised Moslems was twenty times lower than among non-Moslems. The author concludes that the earlier in life circumcision is performed, the lower is the incidence of penile cancer. No mention is made about cancer in other urogenital organs. However, in conclusion Dr. Shabad does not recommend circumcision, but advocates another method which "has none of the disadvantages of circumcision."[10] One infers from close reading of his paper that the most important disadvantage of circumcision, and the greatest advantage of Dr. Shabad's method, is of a quite non-medical nature. His method, Dr. Shabad says, "is not considered a religious ritual custom and therefore is available to all ethnic groups of the world, independent of race and religion." The method of circumcision, Shabad admits, is also effective, as was shown by the aforementioned investigation in the Kazakh SSR. However, the author adds, its nonacceptance by all so-called "ethnic" groups would mean that "universal use of routine circumcision in newborns seems to be unrealistic."

On February 13, 1965, Dr. Ravich wrote to Dr. Shabad asking for detailed information about his recommended new method and suggested that a study be made "in the Soviet Union of the effect circumcision has on the incidence of cancer of the penis, prostate, cervix and bladder." Dr. Ravich invited "an exchange of opinions on this matter." Another letter on the subject was written to the Soviet Medical Academy. No reply was ever received to either letter.

Dr. Ravich gave us his opinion on the medical value of Dr. Shabad's method. He stated: "Dr. Shabad admits the effectiveness of circumcision against cancer of the penis but offers an alternative for those who are prejudiced against the procedure. . . . Under no circumstances can Dr. Shabad's method be as effective as early complete circumcision." It is clear that the Russians do not choose to be drawn into correspondence on the matter. This refusal to discuss and to reply to an inquiry of a medical authority in the field of circumcision; along with the indirect admission of a Soviet scientist that circumcision, though medically sound, cannot be used for other than medical reasons; and the fact that findings on the medical value of circumcision in the foreign medical press are never mentioned in the medical press of the Soviet Union, all point clearly to the conclusion that the Soviet medical profession consciously avoids discussing this medical problem for fear of clashing with an established policy of the regime. Not unlike the theories of the "geneticist" Lysenko which reigned supreme for many years before Soviet scientists were brave enough to attack them, the slogans of the "barbarity" and inherent "danger" of circumcision are still loudly voiced. In the case of circumcision, ideology still takes precedence over science. Soviet physicians shrink from recommending a proven prophylactic practice, because it is also a religious rite.

The Jewish population of the Soviet Union, has strongly resisted any efforts to eradicate the practice of circumcision since the beginning of the Soviet regime. The government and its Jewish arm, the *Yevsektsiia,* organized to "establish communism in the Jewish milieu," have stressed the alleged harmfulness of circumcision, the non-hygienic ways in which it is performed, and the lack of medical knowledge on the part of the *mohelim,* as well as the antireligious arguments.

The arguments against circumcision as hazardous to health evoked a responsive chord among many Jews until the 1920s and 1930s when the medical advantages of circumcision became known. Circumcision had always been performed by Jews as a religious rite, and not on medical grounds. It was generally considered that the national-religious considerations of the ritual outweighed the medical risks involved. Secularization of Jewish life provoked some protest against the "barbaric" practice, often by people whose ideologies were far removed from Marxism. The famous Jewish writer Sholem Asch, at the beginning of his literary career, campaigned against circumcision. Another *cause célèbre* was the fight of Victor Alter, the leader of the Jewish socialist Bund, against the Warsaw *kehilah,* the Jewish community organization. Alter did not have his son circumcised, believing the ritual to be a purely religious one and not of national Jewish significance. He insisted, however, that his son be included in the registry of the Warsaw *kehilah* on the grounds that the *kehilah* was an organization of all Jews, religious and nonreligious alike. It had been the practice of the *kehilah* to demand a certificate of circumcision before registering a newborn male.

The Fight Against Circumcision

In the first years after the October Revolution and to a lesser degree in the 1920s, many Jewish members of the Soviet Communist Party did not heed the demands of the Party and continued to consent to the circumcision of their sons. Discovery would have meant expulsion from the Party and lifelong suspicion, handicaps far greater than those levied against non-Party members. "Party trials" of members who had their children circumcised were staged in many places in the European part of the Soviet Union. Nevertheless, the Jewish masses and many Jewish Communists tenaciously followed the age-old custom. A secretary of a communist cell declared publicly that she preferred to be expelled from the Party than to have her son go uncircumcised.[11] It was not uncommon for Jewish Party members who wanted their sons to be circumcised to get a *komanidorovka* (a business assignment out of town) and arrange to have the circumcision take place during their absence. The parent claimed ignorance of all knowledge of the operation or assured the Party officials that the circumcision had been arranged against his wishes by the other parent or by the grandparents. Many a "dramatic performance" was staged by the "duped" father who returned home to discover his "barbarous act." Windows were opened wide for neighbors to witness the shoutings and protestations of "the outraged father," who was usually the Party member. Some of these fathers even called on the authorities "to put an end, once and for all, to this shameful practice."[12]

Yiddish communist periodicals in the 1920s and 1930s were filled with "discoveries" and vehement attacks against Jewish Party members, Komsomol members, and also nonmembers who occupied higher positions, for this "anti-party" transgression. Some of the transgressors were high up in the Party or government hierarchy.[13] Many Jewish Communists, however, were genuinely opposed to circumcision in general, and circumcision in their families in particular. In the families where circumcision was opposed by the Party member, it was often performed secretly at a later age either by one of the parents or by the grandparents. Especially prominent was the role of the grandmothers in keeping alive the time-honored Jewish rite. They were "more determined and less vulnerable to punishment and harassment than other members of the family." [14]

The pressures exerted by Communist organs and by local authorities in their fight against circumcision were generally in keeping with the current overall antireligious campaign which in the first decade of Soviet rule emphasized propaganda, and in the second decade emphasized administrative punitive measures. Propaganda "trials of circumcision" were prevalent in the 1920s, the last possibly that in Kharhov in 1928.[15]

An entirely different situation prevailed in the regions where Jews lived among Moslems. The Jews profited from the regime's permissiveness toward the Moslems in Central Asia and in the Caucasus who practiced the rite of circumcision. A similar attitude also prevailed in respect to the Jewish population of the non-Moslem Georgian SSR, which is inhabited mostly by Christians. The more stringent governmental policies were extended to "Western" Jews, compared to the more lenient attitude toward "Oriental" Jews. The regime was determined to eradicate Jewish "nationalism," which was significant among European Jews of the Soviet Union. The Soviet government concentrated its fight against the religious practices that had a Jewish national significance.

As a result of heavy pressure, the practice of circumcision in the European section of the Soviet Union steadily decreased in the 1930s. It is impossible to state what percentage of newborn Jewish males were circumcised in the Soviet Union on the eve of World War II, because estimates vary as widely as from 10 to 40 percent of the total number of newborn Jewish males.

The impression that circumcision was rarely practiced in that period could conceivably be false, judging by a small item published in

Emes of 1935. A correspondent from the then-existing "Jewish National Raion" of Novo-Zlotopol in the Ukraine complained that "there were in our Raion in the last several months, eleven cases of Communists and Komsomol members who circumcised their newborn sons." [16] A little arithmetic on the demographic data from the Raion allows us to draw some conclusion from this fact. The Jewish population of Novo-Zlotopol Raion numbered 8,349 in 1931 and 7,500 in 1939.[17] Approximately 8000 Jews lived in the Raion in 1935, and Communist and Komsomol members, with their families, made up approximately one fifth of the population, which was a greater percentage than the average for the country.[18] The annual birth rate in the Raion for that year we will assume to have been 3.5 percent, which is the estimated rate for the whole country in that period,[19] and assuming that half of this percentage will account for boys, the number of newborn boys in the Raion in that year would be 140 and in the Communist and Komsomol families, one fifth of that number, or approximately 28. If "several months" can be said to mean not more than half a year, the incidence of circumcision among the chilren of the Communist and Komsomol members of the Raion was as high as 78 percent (11 out of 14 boys).

Undoubtedly the incidence among non-Communists was higher, suggesting the possibility that, in 1935, 90 percent of the children of the Jewish population of that Raion were circumcised. If this calculation is correct, there was a greater incidence of circumcision than has been generally assumed. However, this sampling is from one district only; moreover, a "Jewish administrative unit" is not a sufficiently typical unit. Jewish cohesiveness, the observation of Jewish customs, and the number of students in Yiddish schools were more in evidence in the five Jewish administrative units of the Soviet Union than in most other parts of the country. Nevertheless, the above information allows us to assume that, although some details of the compilation could be challenged, it cannot be too far off course. There is a real possibility that a higher incidence of circumcision than has been assumed existed in the Soviet Union during the years preceeding World War II.

The campaign against circumcision was waged unceasingly. The atheist journal *Bezbozhnik* of July 1, 1938 reported, under the heading "Wild Customs Kill Children," that in Bobruisk (Belorussia) a child died and the *mohel,* Shulman, was sentenced to five years in prison. Where a child died in Uman, Ukrainian SSR, the *mohel* was sentenced to one and a half years of prison. In Kiev, *mohel* Magilevitch was accused of bringing about the death of several children.[20] The journal *Nauka i Religiia* notes in an article about circumcision that "several Judaic operators, accused of causing the death of several children, have stood trial in the Soviet era. Thus, when *mohel* Radunsky was tried in Leninsk in 1931, the court expert announced that he had established dozens of instances of infants dying of blood poisoning following circumcision. In 1937 in Uman, a Jewish minister Nogilevich (Magilevitch?) was sentenced for circumcising three children with a dirty instrument—and as a result they had suffered from blood poisoning."[21]

It is difficult to establish whether these facts and accusations were true. Information we have now on Soviet trials of that period, especially in cases where the regime had a political ax to grind, would cast great doubt on the evidence as it was presented, and on the guilt of the performers as it was established by the courts. The rite was usually performed in full or half-secrecy (except among Oriental Jews) and information on cases of circumcision usually came from people who wanted to ingratiate themselves with the regime, or by fanatical Communists who thought it to be their "sacred duty" to "bring to light" all activities discouraged by the regime. More reliable sources of information were the hospitals and clinics where children were brought for treatment.

The Detente and the New Onslaught

Very little is known about the practice of circumcision among the Jews during the years of 1941–1945. The birth rate among Jews in the war period was even lower than the much decreased birth rate of the Soviet population as a whole, for not only were most young and middle-aged Jewish men in the military, along with the non-Jewish men, but a proportionately larger part of the Jewish population of Belorussia, Ukraine and parts of the RSFSR were evacuated or had fled into territories unoccupied by the Germans. In the occupied territories hundreds of thousands of Jews were slaughtered by the invading German armies, among them many women whose husbands were in the military. In the course of evacuation, and in the new places where Jewish refugees settled, few possibilities existed for arranging religious rituals. *Mohelim* were hard to find and the primitive squalid conditions of the remote regions of the Ural, Siberia, and Asia were not conducive to the performance of this religious rite.

It is impossible to give a precise answer to the question: how widespread did the practice of circumcision become in the postwar years and how common is it now? Religious life in the Soviet Union is kept under cover, especially information concerning religious practices that have been singled out for extinction. The fact that the rite is not forbidden by the existing legislation does not prevent its being exposed to various kinds of harassment and persecution. Circumcision is presently widely practiced by Oriental Jews in the Republics of Caucasus and in the Central Asian Republics, where the lack of local persecution of Moslem circumcision makes it difficult for the Soviet authorities to adopt a harsh policy in respect to Jewish circumcision. In many places and in many instances the pressure against Jewish religious rites in the Moslem areas is nevertheless heavier than that against Moslem rites, including circumcision. Jews living in non-Moslem Georgia still enjoy a more lenient policy and circumcisions are performed quite openly with the participation of invited guests and family, sometimes even in the synagogue. A group of American rabbis headed by Rabbi David Hollander of the Bronx reportedly witnessed a religious circumcision rite in the synagogue of the Georgian town Kutaisi, attended by some 500 persons.[22] Many of those who have visited Georgia in recent years have gained the impression from their contact with Georgian Jews that nearly all newborn Jewish males are being circumcised in that republic.

Circumcision is also widely practiced by a large proportion of "Mountain Jews" in the Caucasus, despite the fact that the local authorities have conducted a campaign against the Jewish religion for some time. (The famous "blood libel" accusation was published in the Dagestan paper *Kommunist* along with the accusation that Jews hate Moslems and "thus provoke the hate of Moslems to Jews." *Kommunist* charged that the existence of the synagogue in Buinaksk inspired the survival of harmful rites "such as circumcision and old-custom marriage ceremonies."[23]

Judging from the area and the frequency of attacks in the Soviet press, the European provinces where circumcision is most widespread are the Moldavian SSR, and the former Bukovina and Transcarpathia provinces in the Ukrainian SSR, territories that formerly were part of Rumania and Czechoslovakia. At the time of the press campaign before the synagogue in Chernovtsi, Bukovina, was closed, several letters from readers were published in *Radianska Bukovina* on September 1960. One of the letters, signed by "M. Langer, building technician," stated that "it is known that a group of parasites make a living because of the synagogue, by performing the custom of *ob-yevreevenie* [making Jewish, a rather derisive term for circumcision] among the backward part of the Jewish population. This savage ritual is performed in secret." [24] We can readily surmise the reasons why a religious rite, allowed by law and practiced openly by tens of millions of Moslems and tens of thousands of Jews in the non-European parts of the USSR, is performed in secret in the Bukovina.

At that time a vehement campaign was started in the Bukovina against the *mohel* Schechter, accusing him of afflicting injury to a child he had circumcised. Insight into the circumstances under which the Chernovtsi *mohel* performed the circumcision can be gathered from the interesting description of the case in the book *Bein ha-Patish ve-ha-Magal*, by Ben-Ami. [25] The author had happened to visit Chernovtsi at the time of the *mohel* Schechter affair, and he related the information he gathered in chapter entiled "The Story of the Mohel Schechter." A Jewish couple who had decided to circumcise their newborn son asked Schechter, "one of the secret, active *mohelim* in the community," to perform the operation. A few days later the mother noticed that the baby's wound was bleeding. The father could not find the *mohel,* who was at that time performing a circumcision in a neighboring town, and the alarmed parents called an ambulance. The physician at the clinic bandaged the wound and assured the parents that there was no reason to be worried. They returned home with the baby, and the whole affair would have ended at that point had not the driver of the ambulance brought the case to the attention of the local authorities. The authorities called first the father, interrogated him, and then called the *mohel* Schechter, whom they soon put behind bars. After a two-month "brainwashing" of Schechter large posters appeared in the streets of Chernovtsi announcing a "Jewish atheist cultural evening" in the hall of the Philharmonic. The Jewish public expected that some cultural program of Yiddish songs and recitations would follow the routine atheist lecture and turned out in large numbers. Instead of the expected program, the young father appeared on the stage and told the audience how "under the influence of former prejudices" he had submitted his son to the "barbaric operation" and how, "thanks to the modern techniques of Soviet medicine," his son was saved from imminent death. Then a physician spoke on circumcision and explained why "it violates the requirements of modern science and hygiene," and finally *mohel* Schechter, "a broken man," told the audience that he had performed those "barbaric acts" for many years because it was the only way he could earn a living. He had not understood until now how repulsive his occupation was, but he now knew that the surgery he had performed "is not only unlawful but also contrary to the requirements of the advanced Soviet medicine." Schechter promised the audience that he would no longer engage in these practices and called upon the young parents present not to entrust their young into "the filthy hands of the *mohelim*." The program of the "Jewish atheist-cultural evening" ended with a talk on the "false paradise in the state of Israel" provided by a couple who had returned from Israel. A detailed report of the "cultural evening," with photographs of the father, of the physician and the *mohel*, was then published for the benefit of the entire population in the newspaper *Radianska Bukovina*.

Ben-Ami concluded his story with the remark that "if this is the situation in a town like Chernovtsi where the Jewish population has been divorced from Jewish tradition only since the end of World War II, how much worse is the state of affairs in the central parts of the Soviet Union, where Jews have been estranged from Jewish tradition for three generations. In a Black Sea resort place a grandfather pointed to his two-year old grandson and told me with tears in his eyes: 'Yes, a Jewish child who is not circumcised, but what can we do, there are no *mohelim* in our town and my son did not want to take the risk of traveling with the baby into the big town and search there clandestinely for a *mohel*.' " [26]

Circumcision seems to be quite frequent in the Moldavian SSR, formerly the Rumanian province of Bessarabia, which was incorporated into the Soviet Union in the beginning of World War II, later reoccupied by the Rumanian allies of the Nazis, and in 1944 recaptured by the victorious Soviet army. The subject of circumcision is not treated lightly in the local papers, which gives an indication that the rite must take place often. For example, *Sovetskaia Moldavia* of April 28, 1960, reported in an article called "Under the Synagogue Canopy" by E. Pavlenko that "On January 6, six-month old Lenia Detgar was brought to the district hospital with a serious complication after a ritual operation had been performed by Rabbi Draznin. The child's life was in danger and he was saved, thanks to repeated operations in the hospital." The article reported that a number of similar serious cases were noted by A. Kozin, the head physician of the district hospital. Doctors have "on many occasions given assistance to children who passed through the hands of Rabbi Draznin, a man totally ignorant in the field of human medicine." [27]

The case of little Lenia gave occasion to alter the whole "religious situation" in Falesti. *Moldova Sotsialiste* of May 11, 1960, described the events. The description is characteristic of the manner in which real or alleged medical complications connected with the performance of religious rites are exploited by the Soviet authorities for the purpose of discrediting the ritual and frightening those who take part in it.

In God Yahve's Name

The Falesti district prosecutor, executive committee and the local paper's editorial board received letters from toilers in which they denounced religious officials, who, under the cover of ritual worship and traditions, infringed on Soviet laws. Though the prosecutor could have incriminated S. N. Teper and R. I. Draznin, the heads of the local religious community, by virtue of articles 111 and 112 of the Penal Code, he decided to submit the case to the public tribunal of the district executive committee. Chairman of the Court P. Batniuk and jurymen I. Kishinevsky and Smirnova occupied their seats. Public prosecutors were M. Labunsky and M. Karger, Chairman of the Mezhkolkhozstroy executive committee.

The true face of all those who concealed themselves in the shadow of the synagogue was gradually exposed to the crowded audience of the Falesti cinema hall.

. . . "The child stopped crying. He moaned heavily, his blurred eyes reflecting great suffering. . . ."

. . . "My baby has been taken ill, doctor," the mother said, removing the baby's diaper apprehensively. The physician, a controlled man in general, could not hide his anger.

"What barbarity! How could you have permitted such a thing. Had the child remained at home another two days, he would have been in danger of blood-poisoning!"

The woman kept quiet. While preparations were made for urgent surgery, the surgeon filled out the particulars of the six-month-old patient's disease on medical chart No. 74.

Monia Detgar's life was saved. But who was the one responsible for the infant's sufferings? No lengthy inquiry was necessary to find this out. The culprit had no intentions of going into hiding. Sure of himself, he stood, as usual, near a dirty stall on the market place, slaughtering chickens, plucking them and hastily shoving rubles into his pockets. "Hakham" (slaughterer) Rakhmil Draznin also circumcised new-born boys. He dealt in both trades, as long as he was well-paid. The consequences did not interest him.

Kozin, the hospital's head-physician, continues:

"This is not the first miserable consequence of rituals performed by Draznin in insanitary conditions."

Draznin blames the parents for the heavy losses of blood after his ritual operations, who, he alleges, failed to give their children the necessary antibiotic treatment. The slaughterer, a man ignorant in medicine, does not know, however, that antibiotics are not sprinkled on wounds.

Medical chart No. 74 points to the tortures endured by infants, victims of these cruel rituals—a source of income for synagogue loafers.[28]

The frequency of circumcision is undoubtedly lower in the central parts of the Soviet Union. Joseph Schechtman, who visited the Soviet Union in August 1959, relates that there is a *mohel* at the Odessa synagogue and that in Kiev, the *shohet* (ritual slaughterer) doubles as a *mohel*. Michael Shashar tells about a conversation he had with a new mohel in Leningrad, where there are also few circumcision rites. "It is very difficult here," he said. "There is no Sabbath and no *shehita,* no religious weddings and no bar-mitzvah, and no circumcision. I am jubilant when I perform two circumcisions in one week, instead of ten circumcisions a day according to the number of Jews in town." [29]

The expression that "there is no *shehita,* no Sabbath," etc. is more a matter of speech than an accurate assessment. We know from other sources that people do come to the Leningrad synagogue on the Sabbath, and some come with their fowl to the slaughter house near the synagogue. To be sure, one or two circumcisions a week in Leningrad is very little, but not exactly "nothing." The calculation of the *mohel* that seventy Jewish newborns should be circumcised in Leningrad in a week is not accurate. According to the census of 1959 the Jewish population of Leningrad in that year numbered 165,000. The majority of the Leningrad Jews belong to the higher-than-average income group, with a high proportion of professionals among them. The birth rate for the country as a whole was 2.5 percent in 1956.[30] The yearly birth rate for the urbanized Jewish community of Leningrad would not be higher than 2 percent, or approximately 1 percent for boys, or 1,650 a year, and 30 a week (and not 70). If the Leningrad *mohel* performed between one and two operations a week he performed circumcisions on more than 5 percent of all newborn Jewish boys in Leningrad. But it is dubious that all circumcision operations in Leningrad were performed exclusively by this one *mohel*. Because of the danger and pressures involved in performing circumcision, Soviet Jews tend to take their children out of town to a *mohel,* or to use the services of a person who performs circumcision only occasionally, and unofficially. The number of circumcisions not performed in Leningrad by the town *mohel* cannot be known, but the existence of these unknown and uncounted cases must be considered when the incidence of circumcision in Leningrad, as elsewhere, is discussed.

The *Kommunist* of Saratov, in its issue of November 1961, bemoans the fact that "the good Soviet people, the Komsomol member Boris Katz, and his wife Ada, a person with a higher education and a lecturer at the District Correspondence High School, evidently did not realize what they were doing by subjecting their newborn son to circumcision. The underground clergymen guest artists *(podpolnye gastrolery),* of the type of Zaslavskii, Zinger and others, do their work under the cover of the [Saratov] synagogue. They ask for each operation [circumcision] a fee of 300–500 rubles; they request that their travel expenses and meals be paid for them and their helpers." [31]

Itzhak Fein, who visited the Soviet Union in 1966, reported a private conversation with his relative, a professor:

There is no question about bar-mitzvah. The parents don't want to risk it, and particularly they don't want to cause inconveniences for their son. But circumcision is a different matter. True, it also does not happen too often but he knows about a considerable number of parents who brought their child into the covenant of Abraham. Only two or three persons, the very closest, are invited to the celebration.[32]

An added insight concerning the problem of "religious rites of newborns" is given by an illuminating Soviet sociological study on a subject which is rarely made public. In 1963, the Institute of Sociological Research did a study in the Vyborg Raion of Leningrad of "the causes of the vitality of the ceremony of baptism among various population groups." [33] Vyborg is a large industrial district in Leningrad which also includes the two suburbs of Pargalovo and Levashkovo. There were 472 responses to the study processed, and it was found that "25 percent of the total number of children in the area were baptized," and "it was only in 1962–1963 that a downward trend in the number of baptisms was to be observed." The study showed that the proportion of baptisms was highest in the suburban area of the Vyborg Raion "where most people live in their own small houses" and among non-factory workers. For example, 37 percent of the children of construction workers were baptized. The groups that had the lowest percentage of baptized children were workers in large factories, people with higher education, and those employed in the professions. Parents gave the following reasons for baptizing their children: 1) religiosity (only 8 percent of the total); 2) pressure of grandparents (as high as 33 percent; 3) advice of friends ("it is good to do it—just in case"); 4) emotional and esthetic elements of the ceremony; 5) and, "because it is a Russian custom." [34]

Two aspects should be remembered in discussing the survey. First, it is doubtful whether answers to the interviewers were entirely sincere. Even if we exclude fear of the consequences, the expected disapproval by the interviewer for giving unpopular answers was certainly an important factor. A large proportion of parents, a full one third, who shifted the responsibility for baptism of their children to grandparents shows the discomfort of those who were interviewed in the course of the survey. Second, a survey in highly urbanized Leningrad, where the working class was traditionally more revolutionary and assertedly more anticlerical than in other towns, is by no means typical for the Soviet Union as a whole. The interviewees must have also suspected that the Leningrad survey was not just a scientific investigation—as indeed it was not.

The article in *Voprosy Filosofii* where the survey was discussed that in 1964, only one year after the survey was made, "the number of religious baptisms diminished by more than 35 percent from the 1963 figure." One can surmise that the drastic decrease of 35 percent in one year was the result of a very intensive "campaign" undertaken following the survey. Also, as a result of the survey, a very characteristic innovation was introduced in Leningrad: a ceremonial at the registration of birth, which has since spread to other towns. Recognizing that the ceremony of baptism evolved by the Church, "which has an age-old experience in these matters," is an appealing factor, the old practice of simply registering a newborn in the Civil Registry Office was substituted by a special secular ceremony devised by the state. As a result, the author of the article reports, "the number of baptisms in Church diminished sharply."

Particularly interesting is a passage of the report in which parents asserted that baptism "is not a religious but an old Russian custom" and the report added that "such views are particularly typical of persons of Jewish and Tartar nationality, in whose families the performance of a religious ritual associated with the birth of a child is quite widespread." It is regrettable that figures on "such ceremonies," meaning circumcision, by Jewish and Tartar parents are not given in the study. The term "quite widespread" is undefined in this report where the average figure of religious ceremonies for newborn is 25 percent. Apparently the estimated annual figure of circumcisions of newborn Jewish males in Leningrad arrived at earlier, around 5 percent, should indeed be revised upward.

In Belorussia the territorial concentration of Jews was heavier and the adherence to Jewish traditions stronger than in most other provinces of the Soviet Union. It can be assumed, therefore, that the frequency of the rite of circumcision is higher in Belorussia than it is in Leningrad and in other large Soviet cities where there is a higher proportion of Jews who are estranged from their religion. A visitor to the Soviet Union, Zalmen Yefroikin, recounted in his book the following conversation which took place while he was visiting

Belorussia: "And how about circumcision? 'In this regard it is very bad,' answers one of the women. 'The *mohel* is always in danger. Also those who allow the baby to be circumcised are stamped as obscurants.' " [35]

Gomelskaia Pravda, published in Gomel, Belorussia, tells in its issue of July 24, 1960, of a certain Shmuil Gershon Shmayevich Sorkin "who lives in Gomel, at No. 2, Novo-Vetaranya Street" and who before the war "was the slaughterer of the Jewish community in Novo-Belitsa." On returning to Novo-Belitsa from evacuation in autumn of 1945, Sorkin "devoted all his time to the slaughtering of chickens and to circumcision, which brought him tremendous profits." Because the gains there "seemed too small to this greedy saint" he moved to Gomel, which was a larger town. The slaughtering of chickens "is not the only source of Sorkin's enrichment," reported *Gomelskaia Pravda.*

> This charlatan, who lacks any basic medical knowledge, performs the rite of circumcision on newborn Jewish boys. He travels through the towns of our region and by various ruses, more often than not by threats of "divine punishment," brings the parents to agree to their child's circumcision. This profitable trade—Sorkin takes no less than 150 rubles per circumcision—he practices in Gomel and Zhlobin, Rechitsa and Rogachev, and everywhere trustful men are still to be found.[36]

It is difficult to understand what kind of "ruses" a *mohel* can use to induce parents to agree to have newborn children circumcised. It is even more difficult to understand how "threats of divine punishment" can have any effect on presumably nonreligious parents. Lest the attacks on clergymen be construed as contrary to the professed freedom of religion, *Gomelskaia Pravda* elucidates its position: "It is known that we say we have freedom of religion. This does not mean, however, that we should stand aside upon seeing and knowing how 'saints' of Sorkin's type use God's name to amass money, to promote their personal wealth through all sorts of machinations. We should raise our voices against the corruption and abomination which religion brings into our life." *Gomelskaia Pravda* may have exaggerated the "enrichment" of Sorkin. Nevertheless, it is believable that Sorkin had extensively practiced kosher slaughtering and circumcision in many towns of Belorussia, where "trustful men are still to be found." [37]

Gomelskaia Pravda was behind a series of charges brought against the slaughterer-circumciser Sorkin. "How holy this slaughterer is," says another article in the paper, "is illustrated by the following: he once performed a circumcision on Zaslonaya street, then participated in a drinking bout." He also "tries to deceive trustful people in illegal prayer houses where believers are called not to violate religious laws and rites." The paper named Sorkin's children and gave their places of occupation. A reporter asked his daughter Rakhil Shmuilovna Kanaplanikova, "who works as a doctor in Town Clinic No. 4," and her husband Zalman Moiseevich Kanaplanikov why they were indifferent to their father's occupation; and why Sorkin's second daughter, Mina Chernova, "who was a cashier at the Fotopratsa *artel,* pretended that her father's trade doesn't concern her." [38]

Minsk, the capital of Belorussia, is also a place where *mohelim* apparently had inviting possibilities to practice their profession. *Sovetskaia Belorussia* of February 4, 1960, printed a feuilleton "Under the Synagogue Vaults" in which an imaginary conversation of the "religious activists" in Minsk is recounted: " '. . . And what shall we do with the circumciser? I have Aaron Livshits from Vilnius in mind. He plans to settle down in Minsk and engage in fowl-slaughtering just for appearance's sake. He wants 500 rubles per circumcision. It is true that at present few fools will allow a surgical operation on a healthy child. But I have heard that Livsits has already found some people and this means that there are more. The only thing is that he has had trouble obtaining permission to live here.' " [39] The fact that a man would come from Vilna and expect to earn his living mainly from performing circumcision makes it clear that more than "a few fools" would bring him their sons for his services. As the feuilletons says, "fowl-slaughtering [he will do just] for appearance's sake."

The conversation may be imaginary but the story of the religious Jews of Minsk trying to bring a *mohel* to their city from out of town is not; it is corroborated by a foreign visitor. The late journalist Chaim Shoshkes, who visited Minsk at that time, wrote, "It is true that although there is a synagogue and a shohet in Minsk, circumcision is prohibited and they don't allow a *mohel* to come from another town." [40]

Various sources allow us to make the deduction that there is in the Soviet Union an institution of Jewish "wandering clerics" who go from town to town performing various religious functions, such as of kosher slaughtering or circumcision, act as cantors and readers of the Torah, and who try to religiously stimulate the Jewish communities. It is known from Soviet trials prior to 1939 and from other sources that a number of religious Jews in the Soviet Union, especially followers of the *Lubavicher Rebe,* engaged in this dangerous work and that many of them were sentenced to long prison terms and deportation for their activities. Whether people who adhere to this movement are still active in the Soviet Union is, understandably, not revealed by their compatriots. It can be assumed that some of them are still active in these endeavors. A radio broadcast from Kirovgrad on September 9, 1959 was devoted to "wandering clergymen." "The city's synagogue," said the broadcast, "has become a shelter for all sorts of vagabonds, preachers, and 'prophets,' who come here from Odessa, Siberia, Nikolaiev, Orenburg and other places. They beg money from the till of the Jewish community, spread various superstitions and carry out the rites of circumcision." [41] How many circumcisions are performed by "wandering *mohelim,*" who risk their freedom to a greater extent than the regular *mohelim,* will never be known. Even if complete information about circumcision could be gathered from the "resident *mohelim,*" it would be insufficient for a full account of the number and frequency of circumcisions in a given locality. To the number of known and semisecret operations performed by the local *mohelim* must be added a certain unknown number of "special-secret" circumcisions, executed either out of town or by wandering *mohelim* who perform the operation only on the children of relatives and close friends.

A valuable description of the attitudes toward circumcision of at least part of the older Jewish generation is to be found in the article "Circumcision" by the veteran antireligious writer M. Altshuler in *Nauka i Religiia.*[42] This article is written in the form of a humorous conversation, which may be imaginary or real, between the author and his antagonist—in the style of Sholem Aleichem. The following is an excerpt from the article.

"Is your grandson circumcised?"
"My son-in-law, I should tell you, is a member of the Party, a man

with golden hands and a diamond heart. When he heard that we had performed circumcision on his son and our grandson who is named after my wife's father, he packed his things and left. I am not going to tell you how many tears my daughter shed till we saw him back in our house. Now they are living separately from us, and he, our son-in-law, will not let my wife, his mother-in-law, on the threshold of his home. My wife conducted the operation—I am speaking about the circumcision. The operation was, of course, done by the *mohel,* but the organizer of the whole thing was she, my wife. *I* wouldn't do it. Although, truthfully speaking, if a man is born a Jew he should be circumcised. In the old times, under the Tsars, we had a saying that on the eighth day they cut off the baby's right of residence [*pravozhitelstvo,* in the provinces prohibited to Jews].

"At present, this does not make any legal difference, of course. All nationalities and religions are equal in our country. Still, I wouldn't insist on doing it, but my wife raised hell. I will have to bathe the baby, she said, and I will not bathe an uncircumcised baby. Let me rather become blind, says she, than look at an uncircumcised grandson. And she had her way.

"I have already told you I wouldn't insist. After all, my son-in-law is a member of the Party. But, on the other hand, whom does circumcision harm? Does our government need that little piece? Then what is all the fuss about? I wouldn't speak at all about the whole thing, it is not pleasant for me. But since you had touched this subject, I have told you with all candor how it happened."

Propaganda Against Circumcision

The main arguments used by the Soviet propagandists against circumcision can be divided into four categories:

First, medical considerations purport that circumcision is harmful to health; and special emphasis is added to the charge that the operation is performed by medically untrained men in unsanitary conditions.

Second, its critics call circumcision a "barbaric rite," a remnant of a primitive stage of civilization.

Third, they say it is harmful, just as all religion and all religious observances are harmful to enlightened Soviet citizens.

And fourth, the propagandists call it a chauvinistic Jewish custom that inculcates distinctiveness and a feeling of superiority and even hatred towards other nations.

A few examples will further illustrate the character of the anti-circumcision propaganda. *Voiovnichi Ateist,* the organ of the

Ukranian atheists, criticized circumcision with the following words: "Circumcision is being performed by persons without any medical knowledge. Everybody knows that *mohelim* do not wash their hands and do not clean their fingernails; they perform the operation with unsterilized instruments, stone knives. Medical literature describes many cases of syphilitic epidemics and other illnesses resulting from the ritual of circumcision. Statistical data shows a high percentage of mortality after the operation. In Uman a baby boy died from blood poisoning. In Chernovtsi the operation is performed by an old man who was formerly a slaughterer." [43]

The central organ of the Soviet atheists, *Nauka i Religiia,* which generally tries to keep its antireligious propaganda on a higher level, explains the history and character of circumcision in the following primitive manner:

> This ritual operation has always aimed at establishing the physical difference between the Jewish and non-Jewish worker, the isolation of Jews from people of other creeds, emphasizing that the Jews form a special group of people, surpassing all other nations.
>
> The priests impressed on the believers that in the act of circumcision the Jew acknowledged himself as it were the slave of God, and assumed an ineradicable mark by which God Yahve would immediately distinguish his slave from the rest.
>
> This concept of slavery corresponded to the concept of the chosen Jewish race. The rabbis would consistently preach that although the Jews were the slaves of the God Yahve, they were nevertheless infinitely superior to all other peoples, and had been selected by God in preference to anyone else.
>
> The rabbis say: "All circumcised are the children of God; those who are not circumcised are the children of the devil." This is often mentioned in prayers. Every morning a devout Jew must, in saying his prayers, thank God for the fact that he belongs to the race of Israel.
>
> The rabbis tried to create an atmosphere of reverence before the circumcision ritual. They intimidated the believers by saying that non-fulfilment of this "sacred" ritual spelled death.
>
> Before the Great October Socialist Revolution in Russia the observance of this "sacred" ritual had been the concern not only of the Jewish clergy and the Jewish bourgeoisie but also of the Tsarist Government which was fanning national strife. Strictly seeing to it that all Orthodox peasants had their children christened, and took them regularly to Communion, the Tsarist administration at the same time kept a check on the circumcision of the Jews. The birth certificates issued to Jews had a special column which stated where and when this ritual had taken place.[44]

Several falsehoods are evident in this article. For instance, there is nowhere any mention in the prayers that those who are not circumcised are the children of the devil.

The charge of nationalism is even harsher in *Lvovskaia Pravda*, published in Lvov in the western Ukraine. M. Kuts, "Candidate of Historical Sciences," wrote the following: "The rabbis proclaimed circumcision as a special symbol of the Jewish nation. This custom educates the Jews in the spirit of enmity towards other nations." [45] In the later stages of the vituperative anti-Jewish religious propaganda of the 1950s and 1960s the argument that circumcision educated Jews to hate other people was frequently repeated.

Propaganda against circumcision, like anti-Jewish propaganda in general, was conducted during the years prior to World War II mainly by Jews, was published almost exclusively in Yiddish periodicals and pamphlets, and of course was read by Jews. Jewish antireligious propaganda since World War II, including propaganda against the rite of circumcision, is being conducted almost entirely in languages other than Yiddish, mostly by non-Jews, and is addressed, one may suspect, primarily to a non-Jewish audience, as may be seen by the type of arguments used in the propaganda. Jewish propagandists, when they wrote against circumcision, did not use the accusation that circumcision inculcates enmity and hatred towards non-Jews because these arguments would not have been accepted, even by antireligious Jews. This argument is not put forward with the intention to persuade Jews. It is used both to frighten the Jews and to evoke hatred toward the Jews performing the rite, if not against Jews generally.

The relentless campaign against circumcision and the severe punishments and grave consequences for those involved in the practice of the rite have created among many religious Jews and clergymen a mood of despair and complete resignation regarding the possibility of perpetuating the rite in the Soviet Union. An indication of this mood of resignation concerning the free exercise of the right of circumcision is the fact that even among Jewish clergymen requests for the freedom to perform the rite are very seldom heard. Jewish clergymen venture from time to time to voice a subdued request that students be allowed to come to the Moscow Yeshivah or for prayerbooks to be printed, but not for freedom to circumcise, although circumcision is one of the most fundamental and most deeply rooted Jewish practices.

The writer C. Ayin, in an article "Circumcision in the Soviet Union," calls attention to the fact that even those outside the Soviet Union who demand the restoration of religious rights to the Jews in the Soviet Union do not include in their demands the right to freely perform circumcision. "If the demand will be voiced loudly enough," says the author, "it will be heard also by the Jews in the Soviet Union and will encourage them. The slogan should be, the person who wants to observe the rite of circumcision is not a criminal, but one who is continuing a thousand-year-old national tradition. If the Soviet authorities do not trust the nonqualified *mohelim,* let them allow Jewish physicians to perform the operation." [46]

Conclusions

1. There is a marked difference in the attitude of Soviet authorities to the performance of the rite of circumcision by various groups of Soviet Jews. Circumcision is tolerated, for the members of Oriental Jewish communities of Georgia, the Mountain Jews in the Caucasus, and the Bucharan Jews in Central Asia. It is prosecuted, or persecuted, or subjected to harassment in the European parts of the Soviet Union.

2. The legal position of circumcision, as far as Jews are concerned, is equivocal and paradoxical. While circumcision is not prohibited, most of those who perform the operation are prosecuted or threatened with prosecution. The *mohel* remains criminally responsible for any physical harm or medical complication resulting from the operation. The prosecution is not obligated to prove the *mohel's* negligence as it must do with physicians. A *mohel* is guilty a priori. Methods which clearly violate law and legality, such as intimidation of criminal punishment for an unpunishable act, are used to threaten the *mohel.*

3. Medical discussion on the merits or demerits of circumcision is avoided in the Soviet Union. Foreign research and findings on this subject, and information about the increase of routine circumcision performed in foreign lands by physicians, is consistently withheld. In respect to the problem of circumcision, political and ideological considerations of the Soviet regime take precedence over medical considerations.

4. It is conceivable that the incidence of medical complications after circumcision is higher in the Soviet Union than in other countries for the same reasons that complications after abortions are higher in those countries where they are prohibited. Secretiveness and potential danger are not conducive to sanitary conditions and the availability of competent performers. The possibility of infection is another factor which prevents many parents from subjecting their children to the operation.

5. The ideological propaganda against circumcision, printed and spoken, underscores the following main points: circumcision is a barbaric custom dating back to the primitive beliefs of prehistoric tribes; it exposes the child to great danger, particularly because it is performed by people who have no medical qualifications; it imbues those who undergo the rite with a sense of differentness and separation, and, in the case of Jews, with a sense of superiority and hatred toward non-Jews; and it is not only a Jewish religious rite but it is "nationalistic" in character.

6. The punishment, or harassment, meted out by Soviet authorities through trade and social organizations in the loss of amenities and privileges and in many other ways is more pronounced in case of circumcision than any other religious rite—and the campaign against circumcision is conducted more vehemently than against any other Jewish religious rite.

7. The fight of the Soviet regime against Jewish circumcision has been successful from the regime's point of view. It is impossible to give an estimate of the percentage of Jewish newborn males now being circumcised in the Soviet Union. It appears to be almost universal in Georgia and among the Mountain Jews and Bukharan Jews. The incidence of circumcision is probably lowest in the remote and small Jewish communities of the RSFSR, a little higher in Belorussia and in the Ukraine, and higher still in the Soviet territories acquired in World War II. It is impossible to arrive at an average figure for the whole country, but a *qualified* estimate would be that 10–15 percent of all newborn Jewish males in the Soviet Union were still being circumcised in the 1960s.

8. The mood regarding the possibility of perpetuating the rite of circumcision is one of despair and resignation. The "Black Years" and other anti-Jewish experiences have left behind a feeling of un-

certainty, of a "who knows what might happen again?" apprehension. Many Jewish parents are unwilling to attach to their children a permanent sign (or stigma) of their Jewishness; in case of discovery, in schools, or at summer camps, the children could be subjected to ridicule, or worse. In case of severe persecution, circumcision would be an added risk. Religious Jews consider gaining freedom to perform circumcision as unrealistic, for even the lesser demands, such as the right to be supplied with prayer books and ritual objects, are not being granted. Jews in the Soviet Union have grown accustomed to religious inequality, and they have therefore become resigned to the fact that circumcision will be widely permitted non-Jewish Soviet citizens but not to them.

Notes

1. Genesis, XVII, 10–14, and XXI, 4; Leviticus XII, 3.

2. For a psychoanalytic view of the origins and function of circumcision see Bruno Bettelheim, *Symbolic Wounds* (new rev. ed., Collier Books, 1952).

3. Y. T. Milko. "Ugolovno-pravovaia Borba s Prestupleniami Tserkovnikov i Sektantov" (The Criminal Law Fight Against the Offenses of Clergymen and Sect-Members) (in *Sovetskoe Gosudarstvo i Pravo* (Soviet State and Law), Vol. 7, 1964).

4. In 1944 the author was present at a festive meal rendered by the chairman of a predominantly Moslem kolkhoz in Central Asia, a member of the Communist Party, on the occasion of the circumcision of his son. The festivity was also attended by State officials, Russians and Moslem, including the Secretary of the Raion Party Committee. See also a description of a Moslem circumcision celebration attended by officials from the "Center" in *Literaturnaia Gazeta*, August 8, 1965.

5. Ben-Ami, *Bein ha-Patish ve-ha-Magal* (Between the Hammer and the Sickle), p. 52.

6. Dr. Abraham Ravich, "Circumcision, a Partial Breakthrough Against Cancer?" (in *The National Jewish Monthly*, December 1964).

7. A. Ravich, "The Relationship of Circumcision to Cancer of the Prostate" (in *The Journal of Urology*, Vol. 48, No. 3, September 1942); A. Ravich, M.D., and Robert A. Ravich, M.D., "Prophylaxis of Cancer of the Prostate, Penis and Cervix by Circumcision" (in *New York State Journal of Medicine*, Vol. 51, No. 12, June 15, 1951); Abraham Ravich, M.D., F.A.C.S., "Role of Circumcision in Cancer Prevention" (in *Acto Urologica Japonica*, Vol. 2, No. 2, February 1965).

8. Dr. A. Ravich has supplied us with copies of his works and with the results of his inquiries on circumcision in the Soviet Union. Dr. William Korey, Director of B'nai B'rith International Council, has directed our attention to Dr. Ravich's works.

9. A. L. Shabad (Urological Clinic, Botkin's Hospital, Moscow), "Some Aspects of Etiology and Prevention of Penile Cancer" (in *The Journal of Urology*, December 1964). A copy of the article was sent to us by Dr. Ravich.

10. The method recommended by Dr. Shabad is the "conservative disclosure of the preputial cavity with the aid of the metallic probe" which in his words is "simple and hazardless."

11. A. A. Gershuni, *Yahadut be-Rusiah ha-Sovetit* (Judaism in Soviet Russia) (Jerusalem, 1961), p. 76.

12. *Ibid.*, pp. 76–7.

13. *Ibid.*

14. *Ibid.* p. 75ff.

15. In Kharkov the "religious side" agreed to participate in the "trial." In other cases they refused to take part in the shows, recognizing the futility of it. In Kharkhov the "defendants" were represented by several Jewish scholars who underscored the medical benefits of the circumcision, and by a known *mohel* (Gershuni, *op. cit.*, p. 44).

16. *Emes*, April 20, 1935; Jacob Leshchinsky, *Dos Sovetishe Yidntum*, (New York, 1941, p. 317).

17. L. Zinger, *Dos Banaite Folk* (Moscow 1941, p. 76); I. Sudarski, *Nei-Zlotopoler Raion* (Nei-Zlotopoler County), Moscow, 1933, p. 7; Solomon M. Schwartz, *The Jews in the Soviet Union* (Syracuse 1951, p. 166).

18. According to statistical data in Zinger, *op. cit.* (p. 35 and p. 54). Jews constituted 4 percent of the total number of Party members (125,000 in 1932) in the conutry, whereas the percent of Jews in the total population varied between 1.82 in 1926 and 1.78 in 1939.

19. Deduced from the averages in *SSR v Tsifrakh, v 1964 Godu* (The USSR in Numbers, for the Year 1964), Moscow, 1965, p. 14.

20. Leshchinsky, *ibid.*

21. *Nauka i Religiia*, No. 2, 1960, pp. 43–5; *Jews and Jewish People* (hereafter *JJP*), Vol. 1, No. 1, p. 11.

22. The *New York Times*, August 8, 1956.

23. *Kommunist* (Bruinaksk, Dagestan ASSR), July 30, 1960; *JJP*, Vol. 1, No. 2, p. 1.

24. *JJP*, Vol. 1, No. 2, p. 4.

25. Ben-Ami, *op. cit.*, p. 53.

26. *Ibid.* pp. 53–5.

27. *JJP*, Vol. 1, No. 1, p. 6.

28. *Ibid.*, p. 7. The article was written by a person not familiar with Jewish religion. A *hakham* is not a ritual slaughterer or circumciser. The term is used by Oriental Jews in reference to rabbis.

29. Michael Shashar *Israeli Be-Moskva* (Jerusalem, 1961, p. 44).

30. Robert J. Myers, "Analysis of Mortality and Fertility Data of the Soviet Union" (in *Public Health Reports*, Vol. 74, No. 11, November 1959).

31. *Yevrei i Yevreiski Narod* (hereafter *YYN*), No. 3, p. 4.

32. Itzhak Fine, "Mit Sovetishe Yidn" (in *Yidisher Kemfer*, November 25, 1966).

33. D. M. Aptekman, "Causes of the Ceremony of Baptism under Modern Conditions, on the Basis of the Results of a Concrete Sociological Investigation" (in *Voprosy Filosofii*, No. 3, 1965, translated in *Soviet Sociology*, IASP, White Plains, N. Y., Fall 1965, Vol. 4, No. 2, pp. 10–16).

34. Baptism is the ceremony or sacrament which admits a person into a Christian church by submerging him in water or sprinkling water on him. This ceremony is, of course, much simpler than circumcision.

35. Zalmen Yefroikin. *A Bazuch in Sovet Rusland* (A Visit to Soviet Russia) (New York, 1962), p. 82.

36. *JJP*, Vol. 1, No. 2, pp. 1–2.

37. *Ibid.* Doubling as kosher slaughterer and ritual circumciser is still a common practice in smaller Jewish communities, as it has been in prerevolutionary Russia and as it is at present in the U.S. and in other countries.

38. *Ibid.*

39. *Ibid*

40. Chaim Shoshkes, *Fun Moskve biz Ever Hayarden* (From Moscow to Trans-jordania) (Tel Aviv, 1961, p. 70).

41. *JEE*, No. 4, 1960, p. 40.

42. *Nauka i Religiia*, No. 1, 1962, pp. 52–5.

43. *Voiovnichi Ateist* (The Fighting Atheist), Kiev, No. 8, 1963; photostat of the article in *YYN*, No. 13, 1963, p. 8.

44. S. Gershovich, "Circumcision" (in *Nauka i Religia*, No. 2, 1960, pp. 43–5; English translation in *JJP*, Vol. 1, No. 1, p. 11.

45. M. Kuts, "The Reactionary Essence of the Judaic Religion" (in *Lvovskaia Pravda*, December 19, 1958, quoted in *JEE*, No. 4, 1960, p. 14).

46. *Davar*, Tel Aviv, Nov. 8, 1965.

CHAPTER 7

Religious Education

Of all the oppressive measures taken by the Soviet regime against religious expression, those perpetrated against the religious education of the young were considered by religious Jews to be the most critical. The Jewish religious community was convinced that these measures, more than anything else, threatened the very existence of the Jewish faith. This was also the conviction of the Soviet ideologists.

The Legal Aspect*

Marxist and Soviet theoreticians have insisted that the Soviet regime, by withdrawing the state's support of religion, assures true "neutrality" and genuine religious freedom. However, the right to transmit the tenets of faith from parent to child is one of the basic aspects of religious freedom. Without it, the perpetuation of religious cults is hardly possible. The Soviet regime, in its overall aim to eradicate religious beliefs among its people, has given high priority to opposing the religious education of the young. Yet much confusion and uncertainty exists respecting the legal status of religious education. Is it legal in the Soviet Union to teach religion and to teach the Bible? And if it is, what are the limitations prescribed by Soviet law?

An examination of existing Soviet law can answer these questions.

Early Soviet leaders considered the separation of school from church so important that Lenin incorporated this principle into the title of the basic decree regulating the position of religion in his country ("On the Separation of Church from State and School from Church").[1] The ninth paragraph of the decree deals with schools and religious education. It states briefly that "school is separated from church" and that "instruction of religious doctrines is not allowed in any state or public schools, or in private educational institutions where general subjects are taught. Citizens may teach and

---

* The legal aspect of religious education was treated in greater detail in the author's essay "The Legal Aspect of Religious Education in the Soviet Union," published in *Comparative Education Review*, Vol. 12, No. 1, Feb. 1968.

170

study religion in a private manner." [2] The fundamental Soviet legislative act on religion, still in force, thus establishes two principles: 1) religious subjects may not be taught in institutions of the general school system, and 2) religion may be taught in a private fashion. Whereas the first principle was unequivocal and strictly enforced, the second was variously interpreted, often circumscribed and violated, so much so that in many quarters a false impression has been created that teaching religious doctrines is prohibited by Soviet law.

On August 24, 1918, the People's Commissariat of Justice issued a lengthy "Instruction" for carrying out the Decree of January 23, 1918. The Instruction reiterates the provisions of the Decree on Religious Education and adds that religion may not be taught in any educational establishment "with the exception of special theological institutions." Another provision of the Instruction, seldom remembered, provides that school buildings of the church taken over by the local civil authorities "may be turned over by the local soviet . . . on a rental or other basis, for special educational institutions of all religious faiths." [3] The Instruction interpreting the Decree of January 23, 1918, thus establishes the right for "special religious educational institutions" to function, and the possibility of renting out the former school buildings of the church to these institutions.

The separation of school from church as expounded in the Decree has not, however, insured nonreligious education in the Soviet school system. For one thing, communism, a fundamentally antireligious doctrine, was extensively taught on all levels. Furthermore, after a period of hesitancy the principle of "nonreligious education" accepted at first was finally abandoned and "antireligious education" introduced. A number of official acts of the government and pronouncements of the Communist Party (in practice tantamount to government acts) were issued at various times ordering the introduction of antireligious education and of special atheist courses in the schools. In 1929 the Commissariat of Education issued a directive pertaining to corresponding changes in the methods of instruction to be employed. [4]

The Decree of 1918 leaves open significant possibilities for religious instruction for both young and old. Yet the possibilities have been either thwarted or significantly circumscribed by various "circulars" and "interpretations," often by agencies not empowered to make changes in legislative acts. For instance, a Circular of the Commissariat of Public Education issued on March 3, 1919, flatly contradicts paragraph nine of the Decree of January 23, 1918, by stating that "teaching religious doctrine to persons younger than eighteen years is not permitted."

A later ruling by the same commissariat, issued on April 23, 1921, contradicts its own ruling of March 3, 1919, by ordering officials of the Commissariat to "insure that teaching of religion outside religious institutions to children up to eighteen should not assume the form of establishing regularly functioning educational institutions managed by the clergy." This order indicates that the teaching of religion is permitted, provided it does not assume the character of a regular school under the auspices of the clergy. Undoubtedly this interpretation is closer to the intention of the Decree of January 23, 1918.[5]

The intention of paragraph nine of the Decree of 1918 seems to have been simply to exclude religious instruction from any schools of general instruction. The majority of later Soviet interpretations of the law tended, however, to broaden the prohibition of religious instructions and to include in the ban private instruction which takes the form of school or group instruction. Later, the limitations were arbitrarily broadened still further by banning instruction in small groups and even by prohibiting individual instruction.

On the question of theological schools, the Circular of April 23, 1921, reiterates that "special theological courses may be organized for persons eighteen or over to prepare them for the priesthood." Also separate lessons, discussions, and readings on matters of religious doctrine are permitted, insofar as these do not have the character of systematic school instruction.[6] According to this instruction, study of the Bible, the Koran, the Talmud, and other religious books privately or in a house of prayer is allowed, provided the study is not organized in a school.

A further Instruction was issued on March 16, 1924 (No. 18711) with the important interpretation that teaching religion at home is allowed by law—"at home" meaning either in the home of the child or in the home of the priest or other instructor (who need not have pedagogical training)—and that the number of children receiving religious instruction must be limited to three. They need not, however, be of the same family.

The "Law on Religious Associations" adopted on April 8, 1929, was, after the Decree of January 23, 1918, the second legislative act regulating religious life in the Soviet Union. Concerning religious education, the law provides that "Religious associations may not organize special children's, youth, or women's prayer or other gatherings or general gatherings, groups, circles, sections of biblical, literary . . . , or religious study" (paragraph seventeen). Article eighteen of the law states that "Instruction of religious dogma is prohibited in state, public, and private educational institutions. Such instruction is allowed exclusively in special theological courses by special permission of the Commissariat of Internal Affairs."

In regard to the crucial problem of the previously granted right to teach religious doctrines to children, "in a private manner," the law of 1929 is silent. It does not revoke the right expressed in the Decree of 1918, and it does not give any interpretation as to what "in a private manner" means. With regard to private teaching, therefore, the provision of the Decree of January 23, 1918, remained in force.

In view of the fact that in the years between 1918, when the Decree was issued, and 1929, when this Edict was adopted, many, often contradictory, interpretations were given to the term "in a private manner" and that an authoritative explanation of the term was badly needed, the omission of the subject of private teaching in the new law seems puzzling. It would seem that the omission was deliberate, in order to allow variation of policies, depending on the circumstances of time and place under which the law was to be applied.

After 1929, Soviet policy aimed at the utmost possible curtailment of religious activities. Similarly restrictive policy was applied to the right of religious education. In many cases, the teaching of religious subjects by any person other than a parent was prohibited; in many cases even teaching by a parent was subject to scrutiny and harassment (for the state, it was argued, had the responsibility of preventing the "poisoning of the soul of a Soviet child"). This restrictive policy was especially pronounced in dealing with weak and poorly organized cults. The thaw in state-church relations during and after World War II was marked by a more liberal policy toward religious education.

The interpretations of the rights of religious instruction for children also changed. G. G. Karpov, the head of the newly created

Council for the Affairs of the Russian Orthodox Church, told the Religious News Service in September 1944 that children from any number of homes may gather to receive religious instruction in the homes of priests.[7] This was, however, never issued as an official ruling.

Article 122 of the 1953 Criminal Code of the RSFSR provided that "Any teaching of a religious belief to children or persons under age, done in governmental or private teaching establishments or schools, or in violation of rules issued concerning this matter, shall be punished by compulsory labor." The Criminal Code of the RSFSR of October 27, 1960 (as amended to July 3, 1965) omits this article, and no specific provision of the Code deals with teaching religious beliefs to persons under age. The prohibition of teaching is however implicit in Article 142 of the Code, which establishes punishments for violating laws on separation of church and school. These violations are based on paragraph nine of the Decree of January 23, 1918, in the section on religious teaching. Article 142 of the Criminal Code prescribes penalties in the form of correctional tasks for a term not exceeding one year or a fine not exceeding 50 rubles. An amendment introduced in 1966 increased the penalties for recidivism to a term not exceeding three years of deprivation of freedom.[8]

The authors of an authoritative Soviet source define the criminality of religious education in this manner: "Instruction of any type of religious doctrine given in schools to minors is one of the forms of infringement of the freedom of conscience guaranteed by the USSR Constitution. For commission of criminal action the type of religious thought and the character of the teaching are of no importance."[9] Significantly, and importantly, the definition of criminality pertains only to religious teaching in schools.

Information which the Soviet government submitted to the United Nations states:

> According to the established practice, citizens receive religious instruction in houses of worship in which, in addition to the holding of services of public worship, sermons and homilies are given expounding the tenets of their religious faith; or else they invite ministers of religion to their homes to give them and members of their family private instruction. . . . Instruction in religious dogmas is not per-

mitted in State-administered public educational establishments. Believers may obtain private religious instruction. . . . The existing laws accord to the religious organizations in the Soviet State the right to maintain theological schools for the training of ministers of religion.[10]

Obviously, the Soviet government in presenting this information to the United Nations' study of religious discriminations was eager to portray the Soviet Union as a state in which full religious freedom and freedom to teach religion exist in much the same way as in the capitalist countries where the separation of church and school has been established. However, much detail was omitted in the information submitted.

The statement that citizens receive religious instruction in "houses of worship" contradicts the stated Soviet view that churches are for religious services and prayer only. Close reading reveals the ambiguity of the statement, which could also be interpreted as meaning that the instruction ought to be given in the form of sermons and homilies only.

The problem of teaching religion to children is almost ignored in the information submitted to the United Nations. The right to teach children at home is only indirectly expounded; it is included in the right of parents to invite ministers to their homes to teach religion "to the whole family." This is more than what Soviet practice has often allowed, but less than the law permits and less than what was allowed by one widely recognized interpretation which permitted instruction of groups of three children, not necessarily of one family, in the home of the minister or teacher.

In summary, not only has a clear definition of "freedom of religious teaching in a private manner" as promulgated in paragraph nine of the Decree of January 23, 1918, not been given in any legal act of the Soviet Union, but the failure to give an adequate and binding interpretation is probably *intentional*—its purpose is to help curtail as much as possible the right to teach religion to children.

The basic legal provision regulating the right of religious instruction to children is still centered in paragraph nine of the Decree of January 23, 1918. Neither the law of April 8, 1929, nor any other legislative act has revoked or amended this provision. A literal, nonrestrictive interpretation of paragraph nine would allow for the teaching of religion to groups of any size or in any place, except in schools where general subjects are taught. Accordingly, even Sunday schools or Hebrew religious schools as we know them in the United States would be legal in the Soviet Union. The right to teach religious doctrines to persons eighteen and over and to establish theological seminaries and courses clearly exists; Soviet authorities have nowhere disputed it.

Even the stricter interpretations of the later 1920s concede that religious instruction is allowed in private places "provided it does not take the form of a regular school." The restrictive interpretations adopted in the 1930s and still in force are contrary to both the spirit and the letter of existing Soviet legislation.

The First Twenty-Five Years of Soviet Rule

The traditional Jewish elementary religious school, the *heder,* has remained in existence in the Soviet Union somewhat longer than the religious schools or other cults, with the exception of Moslem schools.

There were a number of reasons for this development. Unlike the schools of the Russian Orthodox Church and the schools of most other cults, the Jewish religious school was, prior to the October Revolution, the most numerous type of school serving Jewish children, particularly the children of the poor, for whom the general schools were inaccessible as a rule.

An entirely new school system had to be established by the Soviet regime for the children whose mother tongue was Yiddish. At that time Soviet policy held that instruction in schools had to be given in the mother tongue of the child, and because of this hundreds of new schools had to be opened.

An additional factor contributing to the delay in the liquidation process of the old *hedorim* was probably the initial reluctance of the new rulers to continue the Tsarist harassment of the Jewish religion. After a short respite, however, action was initiated: the the principal task of fighting the *hedorim* and the yeshivahs (higher schools) was entrusted to the "Jewish sections" (Yevsektsiias). They were aided in their endeavor by the fact that there were many sound reasons to criticize the *hedorim,* for most of them were antiquated, housed in unsuitable quarters, and their curriculum was in most cases limited to religious studies only.

In the years 1922–1923 "Committees for the Liquidation of the *Hedorim*" were organized in towns and hamlets where Jews lived. Religious teachers were forced to give up teaching. Thousands of *hedorim* and yeshivahs were closed. Yet religious education continued to exist for a long time in "underground *hedorim*" and through the legally allowed instruction of individual children. It was estimated that in the city of Minsk about seven hundred children studied in "underground *hedorim*," and a secret Jewish Board of Education existed.

Although teaching in groups of three was legally permitted,[11] Jews complained that they were discriminated against and were not permitted to take advantage of the law. When Lucien Wolf of the British Board of Deputies submitted a memo to Soviet Commissar of Foreign Affairs Rakovsky requesting equal treatment for Jewish religious education, Rakovsky denied that any discrimination against Jewish religion existed.[12] *Hedorim* were liquidated even before the authorities could secure schools for all children. As a result, many Jewish children, some of them orphaned by pogroms and war, remained without schooling.[13]

In the initial period of antireligious propaganda, the institution of "trials" of religion and of specific religious institutions was widely used by the Communists. Public trials of *hedorim* and yeshivahs were arranged in the early 1920s. The "trial of the *heder*" organized in the city of Vitebsk in January 1921 has attracted great attention; it had to be postponed to a later date because of the threatening posture of huge crowds assembled in front of the building where the "trial" had started. The mood at the trial and the posture of the Jewish population, as well as that of the Jewish communist officials, can be best comprehended from the published account of L. Abram, one of the officials in charge of "liquidating Jewish clericalism."

> ... We decided to conduct the trial on January 8 at the Rekord Cinema and invited the Vaad [i.e., quasi-official representation of the synagogues] to send spokesmen for the defense to the trial. We gave them 150 tickets for their people wishing to attend the trial, and the other 250 tickets we divided among the Jewish workers in the factories.
>
> The trial was scheduled for 7 P.M., but when I arrived at 6:30, I saw a crowd of between five and ten thousand people who shouted

that they would not allow the trial of the *heder* to take place, that they would destroy the cinema building, etc.

Delegations who said they spoke in the name of ten thousand Jews approached us three times and demanded to be admitted to the trial or to postpone the trial. When we asked who had sent them they answered that in the Zhorier and Zarecheer houses of prayer thousands who waited for an answer were assembled.

Of course, we were little afraid of the delegations and_ their threats. We knew that this group of tobacco-sniffers [*hevre tabakshmeker*] are not capable of bloody excesses, but we concluded that in view of the obstructions we would not be able to conduct the trial.

When I and comrade Chrapkovsky went out into the street we were greeted by an awful multi-thousand-voice shout "Long live the *Heder,*" and the crowd echoed with *"Hedod"* and "Hurrah," . . . a group of broad-shouldered Jews surrounded us and raising their fists shouted "Aha, Chrapkovsky, you will close the *hedorim?* We will close your eyes, we will break your bones." From the other side I heard several people shouting "Here he is, the Jewish commissar, that tall, dark one, this is Abram, give it to him, don't stay idle [*derlangt, vos shveight yir*]." [14]

Therefore, a new trial, "much better organized" took place at a later date, and sentenced the *heder* to "liquidation."

A well publicized "trial of the yeshivah," lasting eight days, took place in Rostov, in the winter of 1921, when the Lubavicher Rebe and the Lubavicher yeshivah moved to that town. [15]

Yeshivah tried to evade government persecution by moving from one town to another. The most stubborn and prolonged fight for survival was staged by the Lubavicher and Novohorodok yeshivahs, which had established branches in several towns. The faculty and students of the yeshivahs time and again demonstrated extreme devotion and idealism and defied the orders of the Soviet authorities seeking to destroy the underground schools. The most spectacular resistance was displayed by the large Novohorodok yeshivah which finally, after many arrests of its teachers and pupils, decided to close up, on the advice of Chofets Chaim, the great rabbinical authority from Poland; several hundred of its pupils and teachers managed to cross the heavily guarded border and to escape to Poland. [16]

A correspondence from the town of Nevel published in the anti-religious journal *Der Apikoires* as late as January 1, 1933, reported that "some children wear *peios* [sidecurls] and attend both a school and a *heder.*" [17] The American Hebrew writer Daniel Persky, who visited his native town of Minsk in 1928, was present at a teaching session of six children in an "underground *heder.*" [18] The Soviet authorities hinted several times that they would allow the establishment of one legal yeshivah, under the condition that all illegally existing yeshivahs be dissolved, and that the curriculum of the legal yeshivah be restricted to the teaching of religious observances only. Jewish religious leaders rejected the informal proposals, fearing that the authorities' aim was to concentrate all students of the illegal yeshivahs in one place and subsequently to liquidate the one remaining school.

Study of the Torah and of religious literature has continued to be conducted in an informal way in the existing synagogues. In a correspondence from Novozhibkov in the Moscow *Emes,* the reporter complains that secular Yiddish culture is neglected and just (*davke*) the Beth Ha-midrash is always full of people, and there is even a group of young people "who diligently study the mishnah [part of the Talmud]." [19]

Secular Hebrew education was liquidated shortly after the establishment of Soviet rule. The private teaching of the Hebrew language and all cultural activities in Hebrew were prohibited several years later (in the middle and late 1920s). Nonetheless, study of Hebrew persisted illegally many years after Hebrew was outlawed. For instance, the Jewish writer Benjamin West recorded that in Kiev in 1925 "many groups studied Hebrew at home," and that evening courses for adults were in existence. In 1930, "on the outskirts of Moscow, an illegal Hebrew teachers' seminary was organized and existed till the second half of 1931, when all of its students were arrested." [20]

The destruction of the historical centers of Jewish life in the western parts of the Soviet Union by the invading German armies during the war of 1941–1945 brought a final end to the remnants of illegal religious teaching which still existed in areas of the heaviest concentration of the Soviet Jewish population.

The liquidation of the secular Yiddish culture and of all Yiddish publications in 1948 in the wave of the Stalinist anti-Jewish policies of the "Black Years" was also an indirect blow to Jewish religious teaching. Although the publication of Hebrew books was finally prohibited in 1928, Jewish children who studied Yiddish and the Yiddish alphabet were able, with a little additional effort, to read a Hebrew text and a Hebrew prayer book. With the liquidation of Yiddish schools and Yiddish publications and, therefore, the disappearance of the printed Yiddish alphabet, the number of Jewish children able to decipher a Hebrew prayer book was drastically reduced. Teaching Hebrew reading of liturgical books to children who did not know the Yiddish alphabet became immeasurably more difficult. This was, perhaps, one of the motives for the Soviet regime's decision to liquidate Yiddish culture and letters and for its refusal in the post-Stalinist years to reestablish Yiddish schools or even to publish a Yiddish alphabet or textbook for the teaching of the Yiddish language.[21] Yiddish was a likely candidate for ostracism from the Soviet point of view because it contains a substantial Hebraic component; abounds in expressions and terms taken from the religious life of the Jews[22]; and Yiddish literature provides an instructive introduction to Jewish customs and history and to a way of life in which the "religious" and "national" elements of Judaism had merged. If, as it had been reported by many observers, the great majority of the young people who attend religious services in the Soviet synagogues are unable to read the prayer book, it is in some measure due to the liquidation of the Yiddish school system and to the lack of books and teaching aids in Yiddish.

After World War II

Ostensibly, religious education of Jewish children in the Soviet Union was nonexistent in the period following 1945. However, some items in the Soviet press give indirect evidence of the persistent efforts by Jewish parents to impart to their children some knowledge of Hebrew and Jewish religion, although some endeavors, even if done in private, usually provoke repressive actions by local agencies— actions which, we stressed, are contrary to existing Soviet law. Efforts to impart Jewish knowledge to children are usually conducted in secrecy, even in cases when a father teaches his child at his home. Therefore, visiting tourists have a very slight chance to observe or to receive information concerning these proscribed activities. Yet occasionally some glimpses may be had from accounts of tourists.

The most frequent and persistent efforts of teaching Jewish children, at least the rudiments of reading Hebrew prayers, seem to take place in the communities of the non-Western Jews in Georgia, in Central Asia, among the Mountain Jews of the Caucasus, and in the territories acquired after 1939 (particularly in Bessarabia, Bukovina, in the Zacarpathian District and in the Baltic republics). In the Oriental areas the authorities often pretend not to notice the private study of religion, and they do not investigate, for instance, how and where Jewish boys have learned to chant the *Haftorah* at their bar-mitzvah. In the western territories, though, the authorities are on a watchful lookout for possible violations of the allegedly existing laws prohibiting all kinds of religious education of minors; such efforts are swiftly and unquestionably suppressed. In Georgia and in Central Asia the teaching is conducted inconspicuously, probably by parents or other members of the family in their homes, and possibly also by some members of the clergy in small groups. Local Jews are very careful not to divulge or discuss these matters.

An Israeli journalist and diplomat who visited the Georgian Jewish communities reports seeing a group of Jewish children in the synagogue on a Saturday afternoon listening to an old man telling Bible stories and legends from Jewish history. These sessions were made possible through a "gentlemen's agreement" with the official from the local soviet's "religious section" whose responsibility it was to make "surprise visits" to the synagogues and report how many children came to the synagogue. A "scout" standing outside the synagogue was assigned to report whenever the official approached the building, whereupon the children would leave the synagogue and the official would enter. After he left, the children would again return to the synagogue. This arrangement "satisfied both the Jewish community and the official and also the children who found it quite adventurous." [23]

The local newspaper of Suchumi (Abkhazian ASSR, Georgian SSR) attacked one of the leaders of the synagogue "Iliia Botavashvili, or Abai Ilian, as they call him at the synagogue," saying that he told believers, "Your children are excellent students at school but they do not know our Torah. Would it not be better to have it the other way? If you do so, God will make your life longer." Such words, charged the newspaper, "are repeated each day" by the rabbi, the *shohet,* and other members of the religious community.[24]

In western parts of the Soviet Union the Soviet authorities are implacable in their destruction of any attempts to teach Hebrew reading or religion. These attempts seem to be more frequent in the territories that came under Soviet rule later. For instance, *Sovetskaia Moldavia,* a newspaper published in Kishinev, the capital of the Moldavian SSR, reported from the town of Falesti that the local "secondary school's pedagogic council at its meeting of April 1 was compelled to ask the authorities to institute proceedings against the local Jewish community."[25] The proceedings were instituted because a number of boys read prayers at the synagogue. (The newspaper printed their names and the names of their fathers, as well as the names of their teachers who have taught them and other boys and girls to read the prayers.) The newspaper quoted the principal of the secondary school who said: "The synagogue attempts to poison our best pupils with religious venom. It rears liars, bigots, and Pharisees." The local authorities decided to submit the case not to a People's Court but to a "public tribunal." The "show trial" was conducted in the local movie-house and prepared the ground for the closing of the local synagogue and the liquidation of the allegedly lively religious activities in town (circumcision, kosher slaughtering, religious instruction, etc.) and also for the subsequent arrest of Jewish clergymen and their forced renunciation of religious activities. "The witnesses exposed all their ugly activities prohibited by Soviet laws and all their attempts to poison the souls of children with religious venom," said the newspaper.[26]

We do have knowledge of the existence of secret, although completely legal, private teaching of religion in many parts of the Soviet Union—and not only in the western Jewish communities.[27] We have no confirmed knowledge of the existence of illegal Jewish religious schools, but if one can believe the information included in an authoritative reference book for antireligious propagandists, efforts have been made by religious believers for their establishment: "Openly violating the law on separation of school from church, religious fanatics are trying here and there to organize religious schools for children *(hedorim)."* [28]

In Leningrad, the allegedly existing laws were not invoked against the private teaching of religion. Local press reporters who discovered a Jewish boy studying his prayer book instead called for the intervention of "society" and of the Komsomol, as witnessed by this report:

> A certain E. M. Rapaport serves at the synagogue. His son, Isaac, sitting at home at the table puts on a skullcap. He also studies the prayer book. It also happened that on Saturdays he was absent from school. Unseen phylactery straps are holding Isaac and some other young people who visit the synagogue fast. It will not be so easy for them to cut loose those straps, to free themselves from the path of religion, if society and the Komsomol will not intervene.[29]

Few Jewish children know the Hebrew alphabet or know how to read Hebrew in the Latvian republic, which was later incorporated into the Union. A group of children gingerly stood around a visitor from Israel at the Yom Kippur services in the Riga synagogue "and looked into his prayer book; only some were able to distinguish here and there a few Hebrew letters, and only one or two twelve-year-old boys could read a little from the text." [30] One of the boys later approached the visitor and told him: "I don't know how to read Hebrew, but if you will give me your mahzor [prayer book for the High Holidays], I promise that I will learn to read, and I will pray every day in the morning and in the evening.' I gave him the mahzor; the boy kissed the book and kissed me, too." [31]

Adult study of the Torah, if done in an unorganized way and by small groups, is less scrutinized than is the teaching of minors, even if the latter is done in private.

The only synagogue still left in Minsk (capital of the Belorussian republic) is housed in a dilapidated building in the old quarter of the town. A visitor once came there, not in time for the services; he found about two dozen people sitting around a table and "listening to a *shiur* [Talmudic discourse] by one of the oldsters." The unexpected visitor was clearly not welcome.[32]

Informal group study of Talmud, *Shulhan Arukh* (a sixteenth-century code of religious law), and of other religious treatises has been observed by many visitors. One report noted that in the Moscow synagogue "from fifty to sixty people are present at these study sessions held in the weekday mornings and evenings." [33]

The general conclusion which presents itself is that Jewish parents have very few possibilities to teach their children any religious subjects, even the reading of Hebrew, and they are very much afraid to do it when the possibility presents itself even though private teaching to minors is absolutely legal by Soviet law. By contrast, nonregistered adult study in groups, which is not allowed by existing Soviet legislation, is often overlooked and less scrutinized than the legally admissible private teaching of minors.

The Moscow Yeshivah

For forty years, from 1917 to 1957, not a single Jewish theological seminary functioned legally in the Soviet Union. The few promises made in the 1920s to legalize a seminary or yeshivah did not materialize. Illegal yeshivahs existed until the beginning of the 1930s, when mass arrests of teachers and students made their continued existence impossible. The only form of advanced religious study that persisted after the disappearance of the illegal yeshivahs was study by individual adults or small groups of people, done in private.

The detente between the state and organized religion during the "Fatherland War" initiated the establishment of a relatively large number of theological seminaries by the Russian Orthodox Church and other recognized faiths in the Soviet Union. However, the Jewish religion was deprived of this right, a right unequivocally granted by the Soviet legislation on religious cults. In the 1950s it became uncomfortable for the Soviet government to persist in denying to Jews a right granted to other religious cults—differential treatment which could easily be demonstrated to exist by spokesmen of Jewish and non-Jewish public opinion abroad, at that time aroused by the ill-treatment of the Jewish population in the Soviet Union. The wanton liquidation of Jewish culture and of the elite of its creative cadres and the anti-Semitic outbreaks of the "Black Years" of 1948–1953 have become known in foreign countries, and some "concessions" were needed to blunt the harangues of protests. It was evidently considered safer to grant a few "liberties" in the field of Jewish religion than in that of secular Jewish culture. A yeshivah was allowed to be established in 1957, as well as the printing of a *sidur* (prayer book). Both "concessions" were meant to be of passing value. The limited edition of the prayer book was almost immediately sold out and was not able to satisfy the needs of the Jewish religious community for any length of time, and the yeshivah was in a short time "cut to size."

The Moscow Yeshivah opened on January 6, 1957, under the name "Kol Yaakov" (The Voice of Jacob), and was housed in the building of the Moscow synagogue on Arkhipov Street No. 8. Although formally part of the Moscow synagogue, the yeshivah was regarded as a central educational institution, and was supported by religious congregations from all over the country.

The Yeshivah had, at the beginning, 35 students; a large proportion of them came from the Georgian SSR, encouraged by Hakham (Rabbi) Yimanuel of Georgia.

Most of the students were much older than the required minimum age of 18. In 1959, eight of the nineteen students were married. All students were provided with free lodgings, kosher meals, and a stipend of 300 rubles a month. Married students received stipends of 1500 rubles monthly.[34] Rabbi Solomon Schlieffer of the Moscow Synagogue was the organizer and the first head of the Yeshivah; he was indeed the main petitioner who wrested out the Yeshivah from the Soviet authorities. Rabbi Schlieffer died on April 7, 1957, only a few months after the Yeshivah was opened.

Rabbi Judah Leib Levin was then appointed rabbi of the Moscow Central Synagogue and head of the Yeshivah. Rabbi Shimon Trebnik (his name was erroneously misprinted in some foreign sources as Treblink) was named head of the Yeshivah faculty. Rabbi Trebnik died in May of 1961. A curious charge was voiced in the Soviet press before Rabbi Trebnik's death. *Trud,* the central organ of the Soviet Trade Unions, in its issue of December 11, 1960, attacked the *prof-org* (union organizer) of the local union of the Moscow synagogue for issuing membership cards to several persons performing religious functions at the synagogue, among them to the "teacher Sh. Trebnik, who regularly pays his union dues." Trebnik, writes *Trud*, lectures "at a higher Jewish religious school, overburdening the minds of his listeners with quotations from the Talmud, treatises on prayers, etc." [35] and therefore he should not be a member of the Soviet trade union organization.

The teaching staff of the Yeshivah originally numbered eight. Other teachers were Rabbi Chaim Katz and Rabbi Jaakov Kalmanson.[36] Not all students intended to be ordained as rabbis. A number of them, especially those coming from Georgia, studied *shehita,* which would permit them, upon passing the required examination, to function as ritual slaughterers in their communities, where a dire shortage of *shohtim* had existed for a long time.

The premises which house the Yeshivah were considered unsuitable for the purpose, and the Jewish religious community decided to erect a new yeshivah building. The Soviet authorities approved the plans and in a short time 500,000 rubles were contributed by the Moscow Jews for that purpose.[37]

In 1959, it was reported, the Yeshivah had 19 students, and according to another report 16 students, half of them from Central Asia and Georgia.[38] In December 1960, the Yeshivah reportedly had 20 students. The number diminished to 11 in the fall of 1961 and fell to 6 in the fall of 1962.[39] The sharp decrease in the number of students was officially ascribed to a lack of aspirants and to a shortage of housing facilities for those from out of town who were willing to register.

Actually, the situation had been artificially created by the Soviet authorities, with the help of a cunning device. Nine students of the Yeshivah whose place of residence was Georgia were "instructed" to return to Georgia to vote in the elections. (There is no requirement impelling Soviet citizens to return to their place of permanent residence for voting purposes.) When the 9 students later returned to Moscow they were denied permits to reside in town. (A registration permit, *propiska,* is required for residence in the cities of the Soviet Union; in large cities, like Moscow, Leningrad, and Kiev, it is not given freely.) The denial of registration to the out-of-town students, or rather the withdrawal of the already granted registration, of course, prevented the students from further study of the Yeshivah.

The government's action clearly indicated that the Soviet authorities were striving to emaciate the school, leaving only its shell. In addition to engineering the reduction of the number of students by rejecting applications and denying registration to students from out of town, many persons connected with the Yeshivah were, as reported, pressured to resign, among them Judah Leib Lichterov, director of studies, Mordecai Berman, head of the administration committee, and Meir Chanzin, secretary of the Yeshivah.[40]

In 1963, the number of students was already reduced to 5, and these, according to reports by many visitors, were not regular students aiming at graduating from a school with a set course of studies, but older persons who devoted their life to the study of the Torah. At the end of 1963, Soviet Jews feared that the Yeshivah would be closed down.[41]

But at that time, there still remained students at the Yeshivah. The old building urgently needed repairs but the authorities refused permission to use the funds collected in 1957 for that purpose. They also refused to allow the use of the money for the erection of a new building. It was expected that the Yeshivah would soon cease to exist, whether by formal declaration or simply as a matter of fact. However, the Yeshivah continued to exist, at least formally although only 4 or 5 students were enrolled in addition to the several older persons who attended the courses out of their interest in the subjects discussed. Pressure on different levels continued to be used in order to discourage future applicants from registering.

Even Georgyi Leib, chairman of the small Marina Roscha synagogue in Moscow, who was known for his exuberant praises of religious liberty in the Soviet Union, admitted to a visitor from the United States that the problem of registration of out-of-town students "has not been solved."[42]

In 1965 and 1966 a curious situation developed. It became uncertain whether or not the Yeshivah still existed. Foreign visitors were discouraged from entering the classrooms, where supposedly courses were taking place. Some visitors noticed a few persons studying in a small room at the synagogue, but it was hard to determine whether the persons were studying privately or in an organized, although small, class. Rabbi Arthur Schneir, who had visited the Soviet Union in 1966 as a member of the Interfaith Appeal of Conscience Foundation of New York, reported that Rabbi Levin told him "It's not easy to get rabbinical students. I have twelve applications now. They are being processed." Rabbi Schneir remarked in his report: "If the 'processing' is ever completed, I don't know where Rabbi Levin will put the students. The only small classroom in the synagogue was being used to store sacks of flour for Passover matzos."[43]

However, it seems certain that the Yeshivah, as a place for training religious personnel for the needs of the Jewish religious community in the Soviet Union, does not exist anymore. Its present status perfectly fits the needs of the Soviet government. It has no effectiveness for the Jewish religious community, and at the same time provides the Soviet authorities with a propaganda shield, allowing her to include the Yeshivah in the listing of religious facilities in the Soviet Union.

While the yeshivah was reduced to a meaningless status, other religious cults retained most of their higher institutions of religious study. In 1963 the Russian Orthodox Church had two theological academies and eight seminaries and the number of students reached 1500. Four Moslem seminaries (madressahs) having several hundred students functioned regularly; other recognized religious cults also had functioning seminaries.

Questions have been raised as to whether the sorry state of the Moscow Yeshivah is not as much a fault of the Jewish community as of the Soviet government. Why, asked some, was not the Moscow Jewish community able to provide a sufficient number of students for the yeshivah when permission for out-of-town students were revoked? Why has not the Jewish religious community in the Soviet Union displayed a greater measure of zeal and stubbornness in preserving the Moscow institution?

The truth is that, at the time of the Yeshivah's opening in 1957, the late Moscow Rabbi Schlieffer, who was also head of the Yeshivah, said that he had received "enough applications to fill three large schools." Also the American author, Joseph Schechtman, learned on his two visits to the Yeshivah in 1959, from private talks with a few of the students "some young and some over forty, that many more candidates had applied for admission when word spread about the opening of the Yeshivah." [44] (At the time of Schechtman's visit there were 19 pupils at the Yeshivah.) The opening of the Yeshivah was enthusiastically received by the Jewish community of the Soviet Union, which believed at the time that it ushered in a new era, a departure from the Soviet policy of suppressing Jewish religious life. Rabbi Schlieffer thus described the inaugural ceremonies in a letter to Dr. Shimon Federbusch of the World Jewish Congress:

The festivity was attended by hundreds of our pious brethren, headed by rabbis and lay communal leaders. All took part in the great celebration, and with a song in their hearts they joyfully thanked God for His great mercy, for being privileged to open a house for God's Torah where the voice of the students of the Torah, the "voice of Jacob," may resound again.[45]

Jews throughout the Soviet Union eagerly contributed funds to cover the costs necessary for the functioning of the Yeshivah and for stipends for the students. For instance, the Board of the Leningrad synagogue "proudly told" Joseph Schechtman that they were contributing 5000 rubles monthly to the support of the Yeshivah. The Odessa community had sent 33,000 rubles when the Yeshivah was first established. At the time of Schechtman's visit in 1959, the Yeshivah had a balance of 400,000 rubles in the State Bank.[46]

Applications by students of higher religious cults must be checked and accepted not only by the institutions to which they apply, but by the Soviet authorities as well. Without the government's official consent a candidate may not be accepted; the authorities also have a way of "planting" students they want to be enrolled. By this device the State has in its hands the power to regulate the size of the enrollment. Walter Kolarz maintains that the Soviet police infiltrated the seminaries: "Every prospective student of a theological school must present a letter of recommendation from his parish priest. In the Soviet Union it is not beyond the power of police to extort such recommendations when needed." [47]

From the very beginning the Soviet authorities have sought to substantially limit the size of the Yeshivah and to dwarf the expectations of the Jewish religious community. The limitation of the size of religious institutions can be achieved in the Soviet Union by several methods, of which the principal tool is intimidation of the leaders of the institution. A person pressured to resign from leadership will most certainly resign, unless he is prepared to accept all the consequences, including the most dire (which may or may not come, in a sort of "Russian roulette" game). A Jewish community asked to refrain from sending or recommending candidates to a religious school will obey the request, unless it is prepared to suffer governmental reprisals which could be very harsh. Joseph Schechtman reported as a fact that the Riga Jewish community had intended to send several students "but was informed not to do so." [48] No doubt such tactics were not limited to Riga only, but were employed in Moscow as well.

It is very possible that the same methods was also applied in respect to the Georgian students but was not heeded by the defiant Georgian Jews. Therefore, another approach was chosen—that of luring the students out of Moscow and the subsequent refusal to readmit them. If given freedom of choice the Moscow Jewish community would be able to provide a number of students for the Yeshivah. However, it may be assumed that in Moscow their number would be proportionately lower than in Georgia, and also lower than in the later-acquired territories of the Soviet Union where the process of Jewish secularization is much less advanced than in the big cities. In spite of this wretched state of affairs, as long as the Yeshivah is not formally closed it can easily be reactivated, if and when the Soviet government decides it to be in her interest.

Notes

1. "Ob Otdelenii Tserkvi ot Gosudarstva i Shkoly ot Tserkvi" (On the Separation of Church from State and School from Church), Decree of the Council of People's Commissars, January 23, 1918.

2. *Chastnim obrazom,* here translated as "in a private manner," has a slightly different and broader meaning than the term "privately" used in available English translations.

3. N. N. Fioletov, *Tserkov' i Gosudarstvo po Sovetskomu Pravu* (Saratov, 1923, p. 72); *Sobranie Uzakonenii,* 1918, No. 62, st. 685, "Remark" to article 35 of the Instruction.

4. The subject of antireligious education, which is outside the scope of this study, deserves special treatment. The interested reader will find the subject discussed at length in several works dealing with the state of religion in th Soviet Union. *Cf.* J. S. Curtiss, *The Russian Church and the Soviet State* (Boston: Little, Brown, & Co., 1953, pp. 213–23, 271, 279, 285, 321–3); M. Enisherlov, ed., *Voinstvuishchee Bezbozhie v SSSR za 15 Let, 1917–1932* (Militant Atheism in the USSR in the Past 15 Years) (Moscow, 1932, p. 236).

5. As quoted in Curtiss, *op. cit.,* p. 76, and Fioletov, *op. cit.,* p. 73.

However, the Edict (*postanovlenie*) of the All-Union Central Executive Committee of the Soviets (VTsIK) issued June 13, 1921, states that 1) teaching religion to persons under eighteen years is prohibited, 2) special theological courses to prepare for priesthood may be arranged for persons over eighteen, and 3) lectures, discussions, and reading on questions of religious dogma are permitted "insofar as they do not have the character of systematic school instruction" for persons over eighteen. Nevertheless, the Edict also cites the interpretation given by the Commissariat of Justice on June 7, 1919, that the Decree of 1918 does not prohibit the teaching of religion at home. This Edict is not an example of clarity. (Interpretation in *Revolutsiia i Tserkov,* published by the Commissariat of Justice, Nos. 3–5, 1919.)

6. P. V. Gidulianov, ed., *Otdelenie Tserkvi ot Gosudarstva* (The Separation of Church from State) (Moscow, 2nd ed., Izd. NKIu RSFSR, 1924, question no. 18711 [July 16, 1924]; also pp. 27 and 203–5, also quoted in Curtiss, *op. cit.,* p. 77).

7. *Christian Science Monitor,* September 30, 1944; Curtiss, *op. cit.,* p. 294. As a result of, and to implement, the more liberal attitude toward religion and the religious cults, the Soviet government created a special Council for the Affairs of the Russian Orthodox Church in October 1943 and shortly thereafter a similar council for the affairs of all other recognized religious cults.

8. *Ugolovnoe Zakonodatelstvo Soiuza SSR i Soiuznikh Respublik* (Criminal Law of the Soviet Union and Soviet Republics) (Moskva: Gos. Izd. Iuridicheskoi Literatury, 1963), No. 220, p. 108. The amendment is included in an Ukaz of the Presidium of the Supreme Soviet of the RSFSR, March 18, 1966.

9. I. P. Trainin, *et al., Commentaries on the Criminal Code of the RSFSR* (Moscow, 2nd ed., 1964, p. 168).

10. Conference Room Paper No. 35, Commission on Human Rights, United Nations, p. 12.

11. Instruction No. 18711 of March 16, 1924; P. V. Gidulianov, *op. cit.,* p. 373.

12. *Movschowitch Archives* in Yivo Institute for Jewish Research, New York, Files 69 and 71.

13. Jacob Leshchinsky, *Dos Sovetishe Yidntum* (New York, 1941, p. 321).

14. Abram Leib, J. Khinchin, and K. Kaplan. *Der Mishpet Yibern Heider* (The Trial of the Heder) (Vitebsk, 1922, pp. 102, 103).

191

15. Leshchinsky, *op. cit.,* p. 41.

16. See, for instance, the description of this saga in the review of the novel *Bimtzuda Hafrusa* in *Folk un Zion,* No. 9, 1963.

17. Leshchinsky, *op. cit.,* p. 314; see also I. Kantor, *Natsionalnoe Stroitelstvo Sredi Evreev* (National Construction Among the Jews) (Moscow, 1934, p. 26).

18. A. A. Gershuni, *Yahadut be-Rusiah ha-Sovetit* (Judaism in Soviet Russia) (Jerusalem, 1961), p. 55.

19. *Emes,* June 28, 1934, quoted in Leshchinsky, *op. cit.,* p. 270.

20. Gershon West, "Ratnfarband un Hebreish" (in *Folk un Velt,* Nos. 11–12, 1961, pp. 99–102).

21. Joseph B. Saltzberg, a former leader of the Canadian Communist Party reported on his conversations with Khrushchev in 1956, who told him that "it would be bad, even reactionary to foster Jewish separatism by establishing Yiddish schools." (*American Jewish Year Book,* 1958, p. 317.)

22. The Yiddish linguist A. Zaretsky had objected in the Yiddish daily *Shtern* to the use by the Yiddish communist press of religiously tinted expressions like "He is not interested in the Hagadah but in the matzohballs," etc. (*Ktuvim,* Nos. 7–8, 1930).

23. Ben-Ami, *Bein ha-Patish ve-ha-Magal* (Between the Hammer and the Sickle) (Tel Aviv, 1965), p. 167.

24. *Sovetskaia Abkhaziia,* September 22, 1962, photostat in *Yevrei i Yevreiski Narod* (hereafter YYN) No. 17, 1964, pp. 4, 7.

25. "Under the Synagogue Canopy" (in *Sovetskaia Moldavia,* April 28, 1960, reprinted in *Jews and the Jewish People* [hereafter *JJP*], Vol. 1, No. 1).

26. "In God Yahve's Name" (in *Moldavia Sotsialisti,* May 5, 1960, reprinted in *JJP,* Vol. 1, p. 7).

27. For instance, Dr. Chaim Shoshkes reports in his book *Fun Moskve big Ever Hayarden* (From Moscow to Transjordania) (Tel Aviv, 1961, p. 121) that zealous adherents of the Chabad movement "study with small groups of children Hebrew reading, Bible with commentaries. They wander from community to community, remind and do not let forget."

28. I. P. Tsamerian, ed., *Osnovy Nauchnovo Ateizma,* (Fundamentals of Scientific Atheism) Moskva, 1964, p. 156.

29. M. Berman and N. Ioffe, "Pod Seniu Talesa" (Under the Cover of the Prayer-Shawl) (in *Vechernii Leningrad,* October 27, 1962, photostat in YYN, No. 10, p. 4).

30. Michael Shashar, *Israeli be-Moskva* (An Israeli in Moscow) (Jerusalem, 1961, p. 57).

31. *Ibid.,* p. 70.

32. *Ibid.,* p. 71.

33. Joseph Schechtman, *Star in Eclipse* (New York, 1961, p. 121).

34. *Ibid.,* p. 123.

35. *JJP,* Vol. 1, No. 2, p. 5.

36. *American Jewish Year Book* (hereafter *AJYB*), 1958, "Soviet Jewry."

37. *AJYB,* 1959, p. 209.

38. Schechtman, *op. cit.,* reports that he was "Struck by the pitifully small number of pupils—nineteen" (p. 122). The *AJYB* of 1960, on the basis of a report by B. Z. Goldberg in June 1959 in *Der Tog,* has given the number as sixteen.

39. *AJYB,* 1963, "Soviet Union."

40. *Ibid.*

41. *Jewish Chronicle,* November 22, 1963; see *Jews in Eastern Europe,* February 1964, p. 42. (JEE).

42. *JJP,* November 1964, p. 44, *Jewish Currents,* May 1964, in an interview with Bernard Koten.

43. Rabbi Arthur Schneir, "Time Runs Out for Soviet Jews" (in *Look*, November 29, 1966, p. 103).

44. Schechtman, *op. cit.*, p. 122.

45. *Ibid.*

46. *Ibid.*, p. 124.

47. Walter Kolarz, *Religion in the Soviet Union* (New York, 1961, p. 91).

48. Schechtman, *op. cit.*, p. 123.

CHAPTER 8
Burials and Cemeteries

The Jewish Law

From time immemorial Jewish law required that the dead be buried in the soil or in caves instead of being cremated. There are accounts of several burials in the Bible—the burial of Sarah in the *Meorat ha-Makhpelah* in Hebron, the burial of Rachel near Bethlehem, *et al.*

The laws and customs concerning burials and funerals gradually developed until they were almost completely codified in the sixteenth century. Still, the burial ritual which prevails in the Western (Ashkenazic) Jewish communities differs in some details from the burial ritual as it is observed in the Oriental (*Sefardic*) communities.

Burial societies *(Hevra kadishah)* organized mainly on a voluntary basis were always part of the Jewish communal organization. Participation in the burial societies was considered a fulfillment of a religious commandment or *mitzvah,* as it was a *mitzvah* to be in any way helpful with the burial, and to escort the deceased to the cemetery *(levaya).* The burial should take place as soon as possible after the demise, preferably on the following day. A delay which is not due to valid reasons is considered a dishonor to the deceased.

At the burial the prayer for the dead, *Kadish,* is recited by sons or close relatives of the deceased. Jewish law demands that the *Kadish* be said at prayers in the presence of at least ten people *(minyan)* for a whole year, and thereafter on the anniversary of the death *(yarzeit).* Special remembrance prayers for the dead *(Yizkor)* are recited in the synagogues on several holidays.

In Eastern Europe, burial lots were bought either during a person's lifetime, or by relatives after his death. Lots were purchased from the *kehilah* or the agency administering the cemetery. The charge for funeral services, and for the lot, if it was not bought beforehand, was extracted by the *kehilah* or the "burial society" according to the financial situation of the family. Estates of rich people who did not generously contribute to the needs of the community during

194

their lifetime were often taxed heavily; this was a *sui generis* Inheritance Tax exacted for the needs of the community. Heirs, no matter how miserly, could not for long resist the financial demands of the burial society or the *kehilah,* since it was unthinkable for a Jew to be buried in other than a Jewish cemetery. For a Jew the "Jewish burial," carried out according to the prescribed rites *(Kever Israel),* was one of the basic commands of his faith.

Jewish cemeteries reflect a religious and cultural tradition; they are important sources to historians; and the graves of the leading men of the Jewish nation and of recognized religious authorities are places of profound meaning for many Jews.

Soviet Law

The Soviet legislative act concerning cemeteries and burials was issued in 1929 and signed by the People's Commissar for Internal Affairs (NKVD) jointly with the representatives of the Commissariat of Health and the Commissariat of Justice.[1]

The main provisions of the law were as follows: 1) The opening of cemeteries takes place on the basis of a decision made by the local soviet, and the selection of the land and planning of the cemetery is done by the organs administering municipal affairs *(organy komunalnovo khoziaistva).* 2) Cemeteries in urban settlements are administered by the organs of municipal affairs, in rural settlements by the local soviet. The erection of edifices on the cemeteries, and changes to be made at the cemeteries must have prior consent of the local organs of sanitary control, which are also responsible for the sanitary conditions of the cemeteries. 3) Burial plots are allotted free of charge. Fees may be charged for the services performed at funerals, according to a tariff which is accepted by the local soviet and must be commensurate with the financial situation of the deceased and his family and must not be higher than the costs involved in the given service. 4) The burial place cannot be used for a second time before twenty years (on dry grounds) and thirty years (on wet grounds) after the plot was used the first time for burial. 5) After the cemetery has been fully used, and when the grounds cannot be used for secondary burials, the cemetery ought to be closed; cemeteries may also be closed in parts. 6) Grounds of closed cemeteries may be used immediately after closing only for parks, plantations, or meadows under the condition that the topsoil is not removed. These grounds cannot be used under buildings earlier than twenty years (for dry grounds) and thirty years (for wet grounds) after the cemetery was closed for burials.

Of all the provisions of the law cited above, the most relevant for our study are those concerning the closing of cemeteries. Particularly revealing is the possibility under law for use of the same burial plot for another burial after twenty to thirty years, and the prohibition to erect buildings on cemetery grounds twenty to thirty years after they have been closed.

According to indications Soviet practice is to designate an average time limit of twenty-five years for using the cemetery after its closing. Apparently to avoid establishing the humidity of the soil in each case a median of the two time limits (twenty and thirty years) provided by the law has been adopted.

The basic law which regulates religious life, the Law on Religious Associations of April 8, 1929,[2] includes an exception to the general rule that religious ceremonies or rites, or the display of objects of the cult in public buildings and private institutions or enterprises is prohibited. Thus this prohibition does not apply to the performance of religious ceremonies in cemeteries and in crematoria—which are places in public domain (paragraph fifty-eight of the law). The same provision is reiterated in the Instructions of the People's Commissariat of the Interior on Rights and Obligations of Religious Associations issued a few months later in October 1, 1929 (paragraph thirty-three-a).[3]

Article 229 of the Criminal Code pertains directly to burials and funerals; it provides that desecrating a grave or stealing objects in or on a grave shall be punished by deprivation of freedom for a term not exceeding three years or by correctional tasks for a term not exceeding one year.[4]

Other articles of the Criminal Code have *indirect* application. Article 143 deals with obstruction of the performance of religious rites, which is punishable by correctional tasks for a term not exceeding six months or by social censure. This article can be applied in the case of the obstruction of the performance of religious rites at cemeteries and during funerals. Article 143 carries an important qualification of the criminality of the act, however: "insofar as the performances of religious rites do not violate public order and are not accompanied by infringement of the rights of citizens."

Article 142 of the Criminal Code is also liable to find application to various acts and activities connected with cemeteries and burial functions. This article makes punishable any violation of laws concerning the separation of church and state.

Jewish Attitudes and Soviet Policies

For the first two decades of Soviet rule, more exactly until the extinction of the majority of Jewish communities in occupied territories by the German invaders in 1941 and 1942, the prevailing practice was to bury deceased persons of Jewish nationality, whether they were religious believers or not, in Jewish cemeteries. So ingrained was the customary course that even Jewish Communists preferred to have the departed members of their family buried in Jewish cemeteries rather than the general nondenominational ones.

The situation changed considerably after the war. Most Jewish cemeteries were destroyed by the Germans in the areas of their occupation. Communal and neighborly links, still strong in the established Jewish communities, disappeared with the destruction of these communities and the dispersion of most remaining Jews.

When refugees began to return after the end of the war to their old homes, they made attempts to restore the ravaged cemeteries. But this was not an easy task. In small towns the number of returnees was usually not sufficient for such an undertaking. In other places the authorities chose a course of action which would lead to the liquidation of the religious cemetery. This would be a feather in the cap of antireligious achievement, and at the same time would allow the use of the grounds for other needs of the town—for parks, immediately, and for other uses after the lapse of time prescribed by law. Still, abandoned Jewish cemeteries are now a common sight in the Soviet Union. The sorry state of Jewish cemeteries has become known to us not only from visiting tourists, but was confirmed by Soviet sources as well. For instance, *Nauka i Religiia* notes: "In many places, particularly in the western areas of the Soviet Union, Jewish cemeteries are abandoned and in great neglect; they create a depressing aura in the respective localities." [5]

The New York *Day-Morning Journal* (November 15, 1965) noted, in a news item under the title "A Number of Jewish Cemeteries in Communist Countries Confiscated and Plowed Under," that in some localities the bones of the buried were simply thrown out from their resting places. In localities where Jewish cemeteries were not destroyed by the German army, or in cities which were not occupied by the Germans, as in Moscow and Leningrad, Jewish cemeteries were being gradually and systematically confiscated by the local authorities. Strict use is made of the law allowing for the confiscation of burying grounds after they are filled up and not used for twenty to thirty years. In these cases new burial grounds are not provided along religious lines; it becomes then only a matter of time until cemeteries of religious cults will totally disappear.

At present, burials in non-Jewish cemeteries and funerals without religious ceremonies are becoming more and more frequent in the central and eastern parts of the country. The situation in the areas that were incorporated during and after the German-Soviet war of 1941–1945 was somewhat different. In these places, which became part of the Soviet Union much later, many Jewish cemeteries were still open and could not be confiscated because the required period of twenty-five years of nonuse has not yet elapsed.

For that reason, and also because Jews in the later incorporated areas were subjected to Soviet indoctrination and harassment of religion for a considerably shorter time, Jewish burials were much more common there. There was therefore good reason for *Nauka i Religiia* to complain that "Cemeteries along religious lines are still prevalent in these areas, from Estonia in the north to Moldavia in the south. In Riga, only one quarter of all Jewish funerals are performed in nonreligious ceremonies." [6]

In another instance, *Nauka i Religiia* published a long article in which the author tells, in a humorous vein, how he buried his uncle, a religious Jew and a very respected physician, who was a resident of a small Estonian town. [7] The author describes his "ordeal" in trying to convince the members of the family of the departed that they should not insist on a religious funeral.

The Soviet authorities, who have embarked on a policy of liquidation of "Jewish separateness" both in the religious and "national" meaning of the word, are not eager to tolerate separateness in cemeteries. The only remaining places where Jews can meet as Jews are at the synagogue and at a funeral of a relative or friend. A religious ceremony performed in a Jewish cemetery at the burial or at the anniversary of death contributes to the perpetuation of the Jewish religion and is also considered by the authorities to be an important Jewish affair. When burials take place on unconsecrated grounds, where persons of various faiths are buried together, Jewish religious ceremonies may not be performed. Mixed cemeteries would, therefore, have the effect of eradicating another aspect of Jewish religious observance.

Illustrative of the situation of Jewish cemeteries in the Soviet Union is the situation which existed in some large Jewish communities.

The main Jewish cemetery in Kiev, the capital of the Ukrainian SSR, was located in the suburb of Lukianovka, which, symbolically, is near the ravine of Babi Yar, the place that in the first months of German occupation became an instant cemetery for most of Kiev's Jews.

Joseph Schechtman, the American Zionist writer, visited the Lukianovka cemetery in August of 1959. After taxi drivers repeatedly refused to go there (Lukianovka is near Babi Yar, and Babi Yar is very unpopular with the taxi-drivers of Kiev), the author reached his destination in forty-five minutes by trolley and bus, and what he saw at the cemetery was a peculiar sight:

> Lukianovka is divided in three parts, a civilian Christian cemetery, a military section for members of the Soviet armed forces, and a Jewish burial ground. The first two were well-kept. There was an office where one could inquire about the location of a grave. . . . In dismaying contrast, the Jewish cemetery was a site of utter desolation. There was no office at the crumbling gate; registers of burials have vanished. Alleys and pathways were overgrown with weeds and brush. Hundreds of tombstones were dislocated, overturned, broken; so were the railings.[8]

A similar report about the Lukianovka cemetery was given by Michael Shashar, a visitor from Israel. Scores of tombstones, he noted, lie overthrown and broken in the desolated field. The caretaker, an old Ukrainian, explained to the visitors: "This was done by the Germans, in the time of the war." However, one overturned tombstone, the visitor noticed, had the inscription 1948, i.e., it was erected three years after the end of the war.

When the author asked an old man who prayed at the grave of the Makarov Rabbi what the reason for the utter desolation of the place was, he was told: " 'Not many of the former Jewish residents of Kiev remained alive. Those who returned restored the tombstones of their relatives—but who will take care of those where no relative or redeemer remained?' And he whispered in my ear: 'I have heard that soon an airfield will be built on these grounds. . . .' At the Kiev synagogue, which we visited in the evening, we did not succeed in eliciting from the worshipers anything about the cemetery and about Babi Yar, as if they had resolved among themselves to follow a conspiracy of silence." [9]

Shlomo Even-Shushan, who visited the same cemetery in 1963, was told by two non-Jewish attendants that burials had taken place there from 1892 until 1939. The date for the liquidation of the Lukianovka cemetery was set for June 1, 1963 (which was in reality one year before the twenty-five-year limit).

Hearing of the liquidation of the cemetery where many prominent Russian Jews were laid to rest, several Israeli personalities, among them Dr. Zvi Harkavi of the Chief Rabbinate, intervened with the Soviet diplomatic representatives in Israel, and succeeded in having the date postponed for several months (i.e., to the twenty-five-year limit).

Until the date of the formal liquidation of the cemetery, the authorities allowed, for a fee, transfer of the remains of relatives to another burial place. The remains of Ber Borochov, the founder of Zionist Socialism and noted Yiddish linguist, were exhumed and brought from Lukianovka to Israel a few months before the closing of the cemetery.

Many imposing monuments and mausoleums of rich Jews, like that of the Brodsky millionaires who were buried at the Lukianovka cemetery before the October Revolution, were still in good shape when the author (Even-Shushan) visited the cemetery, and it was not known what would happen to these edifices, some of which had high architectural value.

Even-Shushan and a group of his companions were shaken by a scene they observed at the cemetery. "Several people were standing with shovels in their hands. A man, shabbily dressed, kept in his hands a bundle of bones wrapped in a piece of cloth, possibly the bones of his father or his mother, and as he walked with the bundle to a car nearby he did not stop shouting and protesting aloud. When he saw us, foreign tourists, he turned to us with his pleas. We hardly understood him, and could we help him anyway?" [10]

A report in the press in April 1966 informed that the Kiev cemetery was already being plowed and its ground excavated for new buildings to be erected there.[11]

In Moscow, in the largest Jewish community in the country, the Jewish cemetery has been closed. Reportedly, numerous appeals from Rabbi Levin of the Central Synagogue of Moscow to allow a Jewish section of consecrated ground in the municipal cemetery have been denied.[12]

A call from Moscow was received in Canada with pleas for intervention with the Soviet authorities to allow a Jewish cemetery in Moscow. The complaint was that Jews were buried together with non-Jews, and that all local interventions have failed.[13] The impossibility of Jewish religious burials in Moscow has forced a number of Moscow Jews to seek in their desperation devious ways to find interment in consecrated ground. It was reported in the press that persons with the "right connections" were transferring the remains of their relatives from Moskow to the smaller towns where Jewish cemeteries still existed.[14]

When the Israeli writer Shlomo Even-Shushan once came to Minsk, his birthplace, he hastened to visit the cemetery where his father was buried in 1934, and he was struck to see that:

> The cemetery is fenced off but the fence is broken. Only one of the many gates is left, and the Star of David on the gate is without the inscription which has been there. The cemetery is abandoned, with no supervision or care, everyone can enter and do as he pleases. In anticipation of full liquidation, parts of the cemetery are already plowed and trees planted on them. Some monuments and *ohelim* [mausoleums] are intact, but most graves have only an iron stick on them, on which some unclear inscriptions made with white chalk are seen. Three boys sit around a bonfire. "We are playing," they say.

The visitor was not able to find his father's grave. There was no inscription and there was no person whom he could ask.

A Jew he met at the cemetery told him that "ours" have destroyed graves and monuments, and wanted to destroy the whole cemetery, but Khrushchev granted the request of the Minsk Jewish community which based its protest on the law which prohibits the leveling off of cemeteries before twenty-five years have elapsed since its closing; in 1948 burials still took place at the Minsk Jewish cemetery.[15]

A totally different situation was encountered in Riga. The Riga Jewish cemetery had fifteen thousand graves, among them graves of war victims. The nearby synagogue was burned down by the Germans and its fence had been demolished. The fence was later restored and the place is well kept and cared for.

When a visitor asked a man attending a funeral whether all deceased Riga Jews were buried at this cemetery, he was told: "There are many who renegate their people all their life, but in their will they ask to be buried with their ancestors in a Jewish cemetery. They dare to do it because after their death they are not afraid any more." [16]

Reports from the western, later-incorporated parts of Belorussia and the Ukraine, where not many Jews presently reside, indicate that the liquidation of cemeteries proceeded in these localities at a fast pace, in many cases disregarding the twenty-five-year limitation.

In the town of Pinsk, the "Karliner cemetery," one of the two Jewish cemeteries, has been reportedly designated for development as a public park and has been used in the meantime as a refuse dump. Part of the Jewish cemetery in Rovno was requisitioned for development into a park in 1957. The cemeteries in Borislav and Sambor have been closed and Jews were instructed to bury their dead in the town's general cemetery.

In Lida (Belorussian SSR) houses were being erected on the site of the Jewish cemetery, and in Pruzhany the cemetery has been turned over to pasture; tombstones have been used for building purposes.[17]

In some towns, after all the synagogues were closed, Jewish cemeteries and Jewish burial societies were still in existence, for a time at least. A public attack on a burial society would usually mean a forthcoming termination of its existence.

In Chernigov (eastern part of the Ukrainian SSR), the authorities expected that the closing of the synagogue would bring about the termination of Jewish religious observances, at least of those publicly performed, and the disappointment was great when the Jewish burial society continued its existence without the supporting hand of the synagogue. And the local newspaper asked the rhetorical question: "How long will the group of swindlers continue to appear in the name of a nonexistent community and speculate with human grief and superstition? Hasn't the time come to put an end to all this?" [18] *Voiovnichi Ateist,* the central organ of the Ukrainian atheists, assailed "the band of former frauds from Chernigov synagogue which was closed since the Chernigov Jews have become atheists now deal in reforming religious rituals. A Jewish 'burial society' is active in town, and they are paid 50 rubles for a prayer for the dead." [19]

A feuilleton "From the Living and Dead" in the Odessa newspaper attacked those "for whom the third Odessa cemetery is a source of income." There are two groups, asserts the article, which are engaged in chanting the memorial prayers at the graves, one which is recognized by the Jewish religious community, and another "wild group" which competes with the "legal" group. Funerals are also "a source of profit for 38-year-old Cantor Kuperman, a former cultural worker at a vacation resort place. All these prey on the poor and helpless people who come to mourn the departed." [20]

Action Against Religious Funerals

The propaganda against religious funerals is conducted not so much by the usual method of exposing the falsity of religious beliefs, but rather in trying to discredit the people who officiate at the funerals, presenting them as profiteers "who become rich at the expense of citizens under the mask of religion." [21] Evidently, persuasion by "scientific arguments" has had little effect on those requesting the religious rites, and it was found that a more reliable method is to denounce and threaten those who perform the funeral services.

Much in the same way that rabbis and other religious functionaries are put under pressure to submit a letter of resignation because they suddenly "saw that their eyes were blind," members of the burial society and gravediggers find themselves in the same position, although, in fact, these persons are not religious officials and their function is not religious, strictly speaking. Oftentimes they are forced to submit their "resignations," which are published in the press.

Thus a letter by a certain D. Litvak, a pensioner, was published in an Odessa newspaper. The letter, said the editor, "cannot be read without emotion." Litvak, after working two years at the Odessa cemetery had decided "to break away from religious work and religion itself," and he urged the "brigade leader" of the gravediggers and other workers to do the same.[22]

In the Soviet press one can find numerous attacks on cantors who chant the prayers at the funerals. They are accused of making profit from the services they render. For instance, a Tashkent newspaper attacked "Cantor Anatoli Linkovsky [who] sings at weddings and funerals, and after every nuptial and funeral prayer a few hundred rubles find their way into his pocket."[23] The cantor was previously depicted in the newspaper as a swindler and underworld character.

Attacks against the charging of fees for burial lots are frequent in the Soviet press. According to old custom in the East European Jewish communities, funeral expenses, including the price of the burial lot, were paid to the Jewish community council or burial society which provided the lot and established the price for it, according to the size of the deceased's estate, his charitability, and his services to the community. This approach is apparently still in existence in the Soviet Union. When *Sovetskaia Moldavia* scolded Rabbi Teper of Falesti (Moldavian SSR) foor demanding 3000 rubles and finally agreeing to 1500 rubles for a cemetery lot, Rabbi Teper explained that "the man is a stranger from another town, he never gave a single cent to our community."[24]

Desecration of Cemeteries

Desecrations of Jewish cemeteries were not very frequent occurrences in the countries of East Europe, including Russia, either before the October Revolution or after. This was true in spite of the fact that large segments of the population were infested with anti-Semitism. The infractions, if they did occur, were mostly minor. Systematic profanations of Jewish cemeteries were a more typical phenomenon in Germany, even in pre-Hitler times, than in the Slavic countries.

In the 1950s and 1960s several occurrences of profanation of Jewish cemeteries were reported, in Kiev, in Berdichev, and in a few other localities.[25] However, these cases seem to be much less frequent than in contemporary West Germany, and no more frequent than in the United States. They do not constitute a problem of any magnitude in the Soviet Union.

Tombs and Memorials of Famous People

Russia, which was for a rather long period the most important Jewish center in the world, both quantitatively and qualitatively, has produced a galaxy of great figures whose imprint on Jewish life still remains strong. The graves of the great Jews who are buried in the territory of the Soviet Union are the object of reverence for the whole Jewish people and are a place of pilgrimage for their most fervent followers even now.

The grave of Mendele Mokher Sforim, "the grandfather of modern Yiddish literature" as well as of modern Hebrew literature, was considered a shrine in the Odessa Jewish cemetery during the first few decades of Soviet rule, and was under the official care of the Soviet authorities—although it is hardly accorded such reverence now. The burial places of other great Jewish personalities who had been in their views or activities opposed to the communist ideology are, of course, not cared for by the local authorities. The remains of some of these men were permitted to be exhumed and were brought to other lands (as, for instance, the remnants of Ber Borochov.)

The graves of famous rabbis and Talmudic scholars have always been the objects of great reverence and places of pilgrimages for religious believers. Two Jewish religious leaders famous in Jewish history are buried in the soil of the Soviet Union. The grave of *Israel Baal Shem Tov,* the founder of the Hasidic movement, is located in the little town of Medzhibozh (Ukrainian SSR), and the grave of the Vilna Gaon, one of the great rabbinical authorities, is in Vilna. The grave of another great Hasidic rabbi, the Braslaver Rabbi, the founder of "Braslav Hasidism," is in Uman (Ukrainian SSR). These graves are, even at present under the Soviet regime, sites of inconspicuous pilgrimages for their most devoted followers from the Soviet Union and occasionally from foreign countries as well.[26]

It was most revealing to read in the Soviet literary monthly, *Sovetish Heimland,* a description by the Yiddish novelist Shmuel Gordon of his visit to Medzhibozh, where he was told by an old local Jewish woman: "You have not been yet to the Baal Shem? He lies in the old Jewish cemetery, near the water pump. But hurry, Sabbat is nearing. Don't worry, you'll find the way, anyone you'll ask, Jew or non-Jew, will show you the way. Hershele Ostropoler [a famous Jewish folk wit] lies there too, the two graves are next to each other." [27] Gordon found at Baal Shem Tov's grave many notes *(kvitlekh)* in which men and women asked him to intervene with God on their behalf—an old custom the author had thought to be long extinct in the Soviet Union. The Soviet writer was interested to discover what kind of requests people make to God under a socialist regime and he stated approvingly that almost all notes ended with the words: "Let there be peace in the world, amen."

The American rabbinical organization *Geder Avos,* which had as its goal the care of Jewish cemeteries and graves of famous religious personalities in Europe, held a conference in New York, in January 1966. Rabbi Chaim Twersky reported that he "repaired the inscriptions and the monuments of religious scholars and *tsaddikim* [Hasidic rabbis of great sanctity] in the Soviet Union, and the authorities had cooperated and even helped him in many ways.[28]

Rabbi Zvi Bronstein reported on his visit to the Soviet Union, and said that cemeteries and cemetery fences have been repaired by various American "Societies" (organizations of people hailing from the same Soviet towns) and he found the fences undamaged. It was also reported at a previous occasion that Rabbi Bronstein erected a monument at the grave of Aaron Siderski, the son-in-law of the famous rabbinical scholar Israel Salanter.[29]

Exhumation and Transfer of Remains Outside the Soviet Union

The transfer of remains from one cemetery to another and from the Soviet Union to other countries has been allowed by Soviet authorities. The American organization "Maalin ba-Kodesh," which is a branch of *Geder Avos,* announced that its aim is to help transfer to Israel the remains of single persons and those buried in the mass graves of Nazi victims. Rabbi Bronstein, one of the leaders of this organization, reported that he has received assurances from official Soviet authorities that they will not object to these efforts.[30] He also reported that interested persons may arrange the transfer of the remains of their relatives from the "Lukianovka cemetery in Kiev now being liquidated," to another cemetery or to a foreign country. The remains of several rabbis were already transferred from the Soviet

Union to Israel, disclosed Rabbi Bronstein. He has received assurances form "the minister Shavalgin" in Kiev that the Soviet authorities
will help in these endeavors, "just as the minister was helpful two
years ago in the transfer to Israel of the remains of the Novohorodok
Baal Musar, Reb Yosef Yuzl Horovitz." [31]

The Soviet regime's endeavors to liquidate all religious cemeteries
are, of course, part of the antireligious effort. With regard to Jewish
cemeteries there is an additional motive in accelerating their closure.
This is the aim to liquidate Jewish "separateness." In many places
Jewish cemeteries remained the last places for the public manifesta-
tion of Jewishness.

Notes

1. *Ob Ustroistve Kladbishch i o Poriadke Pogrebleniia* (On the Organization of Cemeteries and on the Procedure of Burials) (in *Voprosy Zdravokhronenia* (Problems of Health Organization), Nos. 23–4, 1929, reprinted in N. Orleanskii, *Zakon o Religioznykh Obedineniakh* (The Law on Religious Associations), *op. cit.*, pp. 62–9).

2. Cited frequently in the chapter "The Laws on Religion."

3. *Ibid.*

4. *Ugolovnoe Zakonodatelstvo Soiuza SSR i Soiuznikh Respublic* (Criminal Legislation of the Soviet Union and the Union Republics) (Gos. Izdat. Iuridicheskoi Literatury, Moscow, 1963). English translation in Harold J. Berman, *Soviet Criminal Law and Procedure* (Cambridge, Mass., 1966).

5. *Nauka i Religiia*, No. 4, 1964, p. 48.

6. *Ibid.*

7. Aron Lapidus, "Kak Ia Khoronil Diadiu Natana" (How I Buried Uncle Nathan) (in *Nauka i Religiia*, No. 12, 1962).

8. Joseph Schechtman, *Star in Eclipse* (New York, 1961, pp. 99–100).

9. Michael Shashar, *Israeli be-Moskva* (An Israeli in Moscow) (Jerusalem, 1961, pp. 145–7).

10. *Ibid.*, p. 70. It is interesting to note that Bernard Kohen writing in the pro-communist *Jewish Currents* (May, 1964) reported after his visit to the Soviet Union that he was told in Kiev: "The Jewish old cemetery is being moved and families have been informed that they would be helped to remove the remains to a new cemetery."

11. *The Day-Morning Journal*, New York, April 24, 1966.

12. *Jewish Chronicle*, August 23, 1963; *Jews in Eastern Europe*, (hereafter *JEE*) February, 1964, p. 42; B. Z. Goldberg, *Yidn in Ratn-Farband* (Tel Aviv, 1965, p. 145).

13. *Yalkut Mogen*, June, 1965, p. 18.

14. *The Day-Morning Journal*, October 19, 1965.

15. Shlomo Even Shushan, *Sipuro Shel Masa* (Story of a Trip) (Tel Aviv, 1964, p. 167).

16. Shashar, *op. cit.*, pp. 64–5.

17. *JEE*, November, 1959.

18. *Ibid.*, December 1962, p. 30.

19. *Voiovnichi Ateist*, No. 11, 1965; *JEE*, December 1962, p. 30.

20. I. Mirskii, "S Zhivikh i Mertvykh" (From the Living and the Dead), in *Znamia Kommunizma* [Odessa] October 10, 1963.

21. *Znamia Kommunizma*, January 24, 1964, as quoted in *JEE*, November 1964, p. 24.

22. *Ibid.*

23. *Pravda Vostoka* (Tashkent), December 2, 1960, reprinted in *JJP*, Vol. 1, No. 2, p. 6.

24. *Sovetskaia Moldavia*, April 28, 1960, as reprinted in *JJP*, Vol. 1, No. 1, p. 6.

25. *JEE*, Mid-September 1959, p. 3.

26. A group of thirteen "Braslaver Chasidim" from the United States has made a pilgrimage in 1964 to the reportedly untouched grave of the Rabbi.

27. *Sovetish Heimland*, No. 2, 1966.

28. *Der Tog*, January 18, 1966.

29. *Ibid.*, November 12, 1967.

30. *Ibid.*, November 12, 1965.

31. *Ibid.*, November 5, 1966.

CHAPTER 9

Propaganda Against the Jewish Religion

The Marxist opposition to religion is based on several premises, and the Marxist propaganda against religion was waged on several levels: philosophical, political and sociological.

Friedrich Engels called for total ideological war on religion: "We wish to make a clean sweep of all that presents itself as supernatural and superhuman. . . . We have declared war once and for all on religion and religious concepts." [1]

Lenin set the grounds for Marxist opposition to religion in the following words:

> Marxism is materialism. As such it is mercilessly hostile to religion, as is the materialism of the Encyclopedists of the eighteenth century, or the materialism of Feuerbach. There is no doubt about this. But the dialectical materialism of Marx and Engels goes farther than that of the Encyclopedists and of Feuerbach, because it applies materialist philosophy to the field of history, to the field of social sciences. We must fight against religion. This is the ABC of all materialism, and consequently of Marxism. [2]

In the attempt to explain to the masses the harm of religion in terms that the worker and peasant could understand, several main points were stressed. The most repeated theme was that religion is harmful to the exploited classes because it serves the ruling classes which use religious beliefs and the clergy to subjugate the working class and to perpetuate the capitalist system. Religious doctrines and the ecclesiastical leaders propagate values that are necessary for the perpetuation of the capitalist system. "The social principles of Christianity," wrote Marx, "extoll cowardice, self-contempt, self-humiliation, meekness, submissiveness—all qualities of the rabble." [3]

Another main theme of opposition to religion was that religion is "escapist"; it diverts the poor from their real problems, a proposition which was summed up in Marx's famous dictum that "religion is the opium of the people." Opium was too exotic a substance for the Russians and Lenin translated it into a more familiar idiom: "Religion," he wrote, "is a kind of spiritual cheap booze in which the slaves of capitalism are drowning their human image and their demands for some measure of a dignified human life." [4]

The fight against the clergy is an even more immediate task: "Second—and this is, for Social Democrats, perhaps the most important thing to do—we must explain the class character of the clergy, their support of the ultrareactionary [in the Russian original *chernosotennovo,* a word derived from the name of the infamous "black hundreds" organization] governments and of the bourgeoisie, and their fight against the working class." [5]

Lenin advocated propaganda in his prerevolutionary writings, i.e., persuasion and indoctrination of the individual, as the only really effective method of combating religious beliefs. He exhorted complete freedom of conscience, saying "Every person should be absolutely free to profess any religion he wishes, or not to profess any religion, i.e., to be an atheist, as every socialist usually is. Any differentiation among citizens in their rights because of their religious beliefs is intolerable." [6]

Lenin subtly but effectively shifted his emphasis of "religious freedom" after the October Revolution. Indicative of this change was the correction Lenin made in the title of the important and basic decree on religion of January 23, 1918, which was initially submitted as the "Decree on Freedom of Conscience, Church, and Religions Associations," and was then changed by Lenin to read "Decree on Separation of Church from State and School from Church." Lenin argued that rather than freedom of conscience, the separation of the church from state must be the main principle of the decree. [7]

The Russian Orthodox Church, which had a well-knit organization and exerted strong influence upon millions of Russians, engaged in an active struggle with the new "godless" regime, during the civil war period. The main thrust of Soviet propaganda in those years was aimed against the leadership of the churches and was political in nature. The *ideological* war against religion was postponed for a later, more convenient date.

Propaganda against the Jewish religion and Jewish clergymen was entrusted to the Jewish sections of the Communist Party *(Yevsektsiia)* which could not be accused of anti-Semitism or of adherence to the

Tsarist anti-Jewish policies. The Jewish Communists did not hesitate to indict Jewish religious functionaries for their alleged former collaboration with the Tsarist regime and for their "opposition" to- the new regime. In fact, however, Jewish religious leaders had not made any attempts to actively oppose the new government. It was hardly conceivable that they would have done so by supporting the enemies of the Soviet regime who had instigated or at least tolerated the anti-Jewish pogroms of the civil war.

Yet Jewish clergymen and religious organizations were often penalized, if for no other reason than because action was also being taken against other religious leaders. In addition, Jewish Communists craved "action" and distinction which could best be gained by the discovery and denunciation of the "enemies" in their own midst.

Several methods were used to combat Jewish religion. The most effective method took the form of reprisals and administrative pressures. Another preferred method was to use all kinds of pressures against the obstinate, and incentives for the complaisant, in housing, employment, education for children, and all the other amenities a monopolistic state can provide for its citizens.

However, it was recognized that for long-term goals and as a helpful tool for applying administrative measures, antireligious propaganda was indispensable. The propaganda had to be conducted in various ways: through speeches, lectures, discussions, street demonstrations and masquerades, antireligious exhibitions, and printed material of many varieties.

A peculiar form of propaganda which the Yevsektsiia employed in the first years of the Soviet regime was the "community trials." The trials were highly publicized, supposedly impartial, and allowed the accused the right of self-defense.

The trials were not always successful, and those who dared to take up the defense of the accused often had the sympathies of the audience. The number of trials consequently decreased with each year as administrative enforcement increased. The latest known trial, which was on circumcision, took place in Kharkov in 1928.

Spoken and written propaganda was mostly in Yiddish, the language of the "Jewish masses." Less than twenty Russian titles published since 1917 are in the category of Jewish antireligious literature, around one fourth of the number published in Yiddish. The material published in Yiddish reflects best the themes and tenor of Soviet antireligious propaganda in the Jewish milieu.

Antireligious diatribes are found in every kind of Soviet Yiddish publications, be it a newspaper or a scholarly discourse. But there was an extensive category of publications devoted exclusively to antireligious propaganda, a so-called "antireligious literature."

Seventy-four titles of Yiddish antireligious literature, a good part of them pamphlets, are listed in the authoritative bibliography of Soviet Yiddish (and for a short time also Hebrew) publications.[8]

The first antireligious publications came out in 1922. From October 1917, when the Bolsheviks took over the government, until 1922, no publication is noted in the bibliography. These were the years of civil war when the Soviet regime tried not to antagonize the millions of religious observers, during the government's life and death struggle for survival.

The number of publications in the respective years reflects the intensity of the antireligious campaigns in the particular periods of Soviet rule. In 1922, three titles; in 1923, three titles; in 1924, two; in 1925, three; in 1926, one; in 1927, four; in 1928, three; in 1929, thirteen; in 1930, seventeen; in 1931, six; in 1932, five; in 1933, two; in 1934, three; in 1935, none; in 1936, two; in 1937, two; in 1938, two; in 1939, three.

In addition to the enumerated books and pamphlets, four one-time local antireligious leaflets are noted, and a periodical *Der Apikoires* (The Nonbeliever) was published in Moscow from 1931 to 1935 by the League of Militant Nonbelievers.[9]

The most intensive period of publishing was from 1927 to 1935, when 53 of the 75 titles and the only exclusively antireligious periodical appeared. This parallels the Soviet government's intensified administrative campaign against religion which started in 1927–1928. There was a considerable letdown in the antireligious campaign after 1934. In 1940, only one Yiddish antireligious publication appeared and none were printed in the war years of 1941–1946, when the *entente* between the state and religion set in. There appeared again one Yiddish antireligious publication after the war, in 1947, and nothing more was noted as a separate title after 1947. In 1948, all Yiddish publications were closed down. A few Yiddish books have appeared again since 1959, but none has been of an antireligious nature.

Jewish antireligious propaganda can be divided into several categories according to its principal themes. The frequency of the subjects reflects the respective degrees of importance accorded by the Soviet authorities to the particular holidays, religious rites, or ceremonies. Some publications treat not one but several themes and topics. The majority (16 of the 76 titles) addresses itself to the Jewish religion generally, its rites, beliefs, and tenets. The second largest group, 14 books, is devoted to an exploration of the nature and the misdeeds of the clergy, their role as former supporters of the Tsarist regime and as enemies of the Soviet ideology and regime. Thirteen books and pamphlets explain and advise how to study and to teach atheism, and what materials to use in private study, in the classroom, and for adult courses and lectures.

Very characteristic is the large number of titles, 11 in all, which are devoted exclusively to the holiday of Passover. This quantity surpasses the literature devoted to any other Jewish holiday, including even the High Holidays to which only 9 titles are devoted. The amount of literature on Passover and on the seder celebration is an indication of how widespread the observance of the holiday remained among the Jewish population and, one may suspect, among some Jewish Communists. (For many Jews Passover was a holiday of national liberation and the seder not so much a religious rite as a national custom and ceremony.)

Seven publications are anthologies and fictional material to be used mostly for readings at "antireligious evenings." Three pamphlets were aimed at discrediting the Jewish religious school *(heder)* and three pamphlets had the rite of circumcision and kosher slaughtering as their theme.

The non-printed antireligious propaganda also began in earnest only after 1921. For instance, *Der Emes* of January 10, 1922 reported under the heading "Party life; anticlerical campaign" the following activities form various towns. In Gomel (Belorussia) "materials for a trial of the yeshivahs were assembled and Comrade Slavin of Moscow was called by telegraph to conduct the trial." In Kiev a two-day trial of the *heder* took place; in Katerinoslav a "dispute about God was organized, attended mostly by the youth." Also in Kiev, a

trial was staged by the Yevsektsiia on Rosh Hashonah. All partici-
pants, both "believers" and "nonbelievers," were members of the
Yevsektsiia, who appeared in appropriate costumes and read the parts
prepared for them. The "prosecutor" demanded a "death sentence
for the Jewish religion." The Hebrew teacher and former civic leader
Moshe Rosenblat who was present at the trial was given the right
to dispute; he audaciously accused the "Red judges" of following in
the footsteps of the organizers of the Beilis trial, besmirching the
Jewish religion and doing the work of the anti-Semites. Rosenblat's
words were greeted, to the dismay of the organizers of the "trial," by
applause from the audience.[10] Occurrences of applause for the de-
fenders of the Jewish religion at the "trials" were not rare. Many
nonreligious Jews and even some Communists felt that an overly
offensive, biased campaign, operating with overblown accusations,
could prove useful for the anti-Semites.

Under the heading "antireligious propaganda," *Emes* of February
18, 1923, reported several antireligious meetings held in the localities
the Klintz *uyezd* (county), Gomel *gubernia* (district). "In some
instances," reported the newspaper, "the question whether a God
existed was submitted to vote and the majority's verdict was that there
is no God." [11]

Besides the public trials against religion and particular religious
observances, "political trials" against workers committing antireligious
transgressions were also organized. The workers were accused of
having ties with religious superstitions, notwithstanding their membership in the avant-garde of the Revolution. *Der Emes* reported
(October 6, 1922) the holding of a "political trial against two workers
who still had ties with the synagogue." "As a result of this trial,"
boasted the newspaper, "a large number of workers worked on the
High Holidays." In another issue of the newspaper (September 29,
1922) it was reported theses had been worked out for a campaign
against the religious holidays and an "exemplary trial of a young
worker who attends the prayer house" had taken place.

The antireligious propaganda, both in the initial period of Soviet
rule and in later years, affected the Jewish believers very little. It had,
however, an effect on younger people who were the recipients of
intensive propaganda both in school and in the very active youth
organization (Pioneers and Komsomol). The communist Yiddish

press often complained about the tenacity of the believers. For instance, we read a complaint (*Der Emes,* August 19, 1923) that in the Crimea "The Jewish masses are even more backward than the Tartars. The Moslem mullahs complain that the mosques are empty but our clergymen trade with their heavenly merchandise before the High Holidays *oif vos di velt shteit* [full blast]."

There are indications that many years after the October Revolution some workers of the older generation paid no more than lip-service to the "fight against religion." A rather humorous fact was related concerning a certain Gershon Metlitz who, after saying the Kol Nidre prayers in the synagogue, rushed to an antireligious meeting in the club. He put his prayer shawl under his coat, and being an "activist" he was elected to the presidium of the meeting. In the course of his speech he "butchered religion." When on the next day Metlitz was again seen at the synagogue "leisurely chanting along with the cantor," and someone pointed out to him this "small contradiction in his activities," he murmured that "one has to be an activist both to God and to man." [12]

The Jewish Communists were proud of the organizational talents they displayed in antireligious propaganda activities. Madame Frumkin, one of the leaders of the Yevsektsiia, known by her pseudonym Esther, wrote in her Russian brochure "Down With the Rabbis,"

> Our Russian comrades will see from this brochure that the antireligious propaganda and the fight against the influence of the clergy is being conducted in the Jewish milieu with no less vigor, and with greater determination and stubbornness, and particularly in a more methodical way, than in the non-Jewish milieu. [13]

In the late twenties, along with the harsh administrative measures against the ministers of the cults in the form of arrests and deportations, the emphasis of antireligious propaganda was put not so much on the harm of religious beliefs as on the evils of the clergy and clericalism. For instance, the Second All-Union Conference of the Jewish Culture Workers which was held in Kharkov April 9–15, 1928, adopted resolutions (nos. 36 and 37) in which it was said (and the reader must bear with the peculiar jargon of the "politprose" of that period):

The struggle against clericalism must become one of the main tasks of the whole polit-enlightening work of all types of polit-enlightening institutions—clubs, reading rooms, libraries, evening schools.

In order to combat clericalism, a temporary one-time campaign is not sufficient any more. A systematic endeavor is necessary, through the organization of atheist [apikorsim] circles, through a systematic antireligious propaganda in depth, influencing not only through lectures but also by other means such as organizations of trials, recitations, shows, etc. It is necessary to link antireligious propaganda with the dissemination of natural sciences and with exposing the counter-revolutionary character of the Jewish clerical groups, of their parasitic life, etc. It is necessary for this work to mobilize all cultural forces in the shtetl and in the Jewish village, to involve the youth.

In order to combat the attacks of clericalism it is necessary to provide our mass polit-enlight-institutions with the proper antireligious literature. It is necessary to increase the antireligious publications, prepare cadres of antireligious propagandists at special courses, conduct antireligious propaganda in the Jewish sections of the Party schools, etc.[14]

After the war of 1941–1945 Jewish antireligious propaganda, conducted before almost exclusively in Yiddish, was now conducted in Russian, and extensively also in the Ukrainian and Moldavian languages read by only a very small number of Jews. According to the census of 1959, only 3 percent of the Jewish population in the Ukraine declared Ukrainian to be their native language, and only 2 percent in the Moldavian republic claimed the Moldavian language as their native tongue. The overwhelming majority of Jews in the Soviet Union speak and read Russian and/or Yiddish.

The inescapable conclusion must therefore be that the antireligious Jewish propaganda conducted in languages other than Yiddish and Russian was aimed not at Jews but at their non-Jewish neighbors. Characteristically, Jewish antireligious items which sometimes appeared in the Yiddish-language journals Sovetish Heimland and Biro-Bidzhaner Shtern were much milder in form and devoid of the specific charges raised exclusively against the Jewish religion.

The character and calibre of Soviet anti-Jewish propaganda have become familiar to the west through the book Yudaism Bes Prikras (Judaism Without Embelishment) by Trofim Kichko, published in Kiev in 1963. Yet Kichko's book was but a compilation of the arguments and charges against Judaism to which previous Soviet publications had given repeated expression. The furor aroused by the book outside Russia was probably due to the concentration in one volume of so many groundless accusations and falsifications, to the inclusion of Nazi-type caricatures, and to the publication of the book by a scholarly institution, the Ukrainian Academy of Science. Contrary to popular belief the book was, in its essence, not repudiated by the Communist Party, which only pointed out some "mistakes" in presentation. Following the barrage of protests from abroad, including petitions from most communist parties of the west, the book was however silently withdrawn from circulation.

Toward the end of the 1950s, Jewish antireligious propaganda become more intensive and more vitriolic. It also differed in tenor from the propaganda directed against other religious cults. The following arguments were used frequently against the Jewish religion:

1. The tenets of the Jewish religion are of a particularly immoral character; money is the god of the Jewish faith. 2. The Jewish religion promulgates the idea that the Jewish people is a chosen people, a notion that breeds Jewish hatred of other peoples. 3. The Jewish religion promotes allegiance to another state, the State of Israel, and to a reactionary, proimperialist movement—namely, Zionism.[15]

In the 1960s two streams of anti-Judaic propaganda existed. One followed the classic line that all religions "including the Jewish" are harmful, being contrary to science, the materialistic world outlook, etc. The other theme was that the Jewish religion is different from other religions, being a· peculiarly harmful and dangerous religious doctrine.

These two themes can be found concurrently in Soviet publications. The first variation, with its old-fashioned strain of antireligious abuse, follows the line of the defunct League of the Militant Godless. The second variation seems to come not from the heirs of the Militant Godless, but rather originates with Soviet political groups having a particular target in mind—apparently the KGB (Kommissariat Gosudarstvennoi Bezopasnosti—the all-powerful Ministry of Internal Security). This theme was in no uncertain words exposed in the introduction printed on the cover of Kichko's *Judaism Without Embellishment*. The publishers of the book (not the author) declared: "Judaism, one of the oldest religions of the world, has incorporated and condensed everything that is most reactionary and most antihumane in the writings of contemporary religions."

All members of the Jewish faith are, with very few exceptions, Jews by nationality, but there is no way of ascertaining which members of the Jewish nationality are also "Judaists," adherents of the Jewish faith. The propaganda against "Judaism" must, therefore, affect all Soviet Jews, both religious and nonreligious. The anti-Judaic propaganda impugning the ethics and historical past of the Jewish people charts a distorted and maligned picture of the Jew. The negative assumption applies to every Jew and the onus of disproving the assumption lies on each Jewish individual.

One can find books, treatises, and scholarly research projects on any Soviet nationality and ethnic group except the Jews. The published material in the areas of Jewish history, sociology, and philosophy is almost exclusively confined to propagandistic and pseudo-scholarly treatises against Zionism, Israel, and the Jewish religion. Soviet Jews are repeatedly reminded that they belong to a people which created the worst type of religion and one of the most repulsive states, the State of Israel, and that there are no positive Jewish achievements to counterbalance the negative Jewish creations so frequently written about in Soviet publications.

The sense of hurt Jewish dignity, which the Jewish antireligious propaganda constantly feeds and exacerbates, is a result of the cultural and spiritual genocide of the Jewish ethnic group attempted in the Soviet Union. The cultural annihilation is perpetrated on several levels and has become a paramount component of the "Jewish problem" in the Soviet Union. This has become a problem not only for the Jews but for the Soviet Union as well, a problem which the Soviet leadership will not be able to solve so easily on *their* terms. We are reminded that spiritual oppression so often provokes spiritual opposition which even a dictatorship cannot control.

Notes

1. Quoted from *Deutsch-Französische Jahrbücher* in J. Curtiss, *The Russian Church and the Soviet State, 1917–1950* (Boston, 1951, p. 44).

2. Vladimir I. Lenin, *Sochineniia* (Works) (Izd. 4, Moscow, 1941, Vol. 10, pp. 65–6).

3. Karl Marx and Friedrich Engels, *Sochineniia* (Works) (Izd. 2, Moscow, 1955, Vol. 4. pp. 204–5).

4. Lenin, *op. cit.* Vol. 10, pp. 65–9.

5. F. Garkovenko, ed., *O Religii i Tserkvi: Sbornik Dokumentov* (Moscow, 1965, p. 31).

6. *Ibid.,* p. 18.

7. *Voprosy Istorii Religii i Ateizma.* Moscow, 1958, p. 16.

8. Y. Cohen, *Pirsumim Yehudiim be-Verit ha-Moatzot 1917–1960.* (Jerusalem, 1961, pp. 45–52, 410).

9. *Der Apikoires,* organ of the Central Board of the League of Militant Non-believers, responsible editor M. Altshuler, Moscow 1931–1935. The periodical appeared irregularly—in 1931, ten issues were published, in 1932, twelve. There were frequent changes in the editorial board of the periodical.

10. A. Tsherikover, ed., *Yin der Tkufe fun Revolutsie* (Berlin, 1924, pp. 385–9).

11. *Der Emes,* February 18, 1923.

12. *Ibid.,* October 1935, as reported in Joseph Leshchinsky in *Dos Sovetishe Yidntum* (New York, 1941, p. 318).

13. A. A. Gershuni, *Yahadut be-Rusiah ha-Sovetit* (Judaism in Soviet Russia) (Jerusalem, 1961), p. 103.

14. *Fun Tsveitn Alfarbandishen Tsusamenfor fun di Yidishe Kultur-Tuer, 9–15 April 1928* (From the Second All-Union Conference of the Jewish Culture Workers, April 9–15, 1928) (Kharkov, Tsentzfarlag, 1928, p. 39).

15. Characteristic of the caliber of anti-Jewish Soviet propaganda of that period was the highly critical attitude taken even by the pro-Soviet communist parties of the west. For instance, the official organ of the Italian communist party, *L'Unità,* criticized on December 15, 1964, the booklet *Contemporary Judaism and Zionism,* by F. Mayatsky, under the unequivocal heading "An Antisemitic Libel"; the article rebukes the author for asserting that "Judaism is the worst of all religions: pessimistic, nationalistic, antifeminist and antipopular. . . . Born from such principles, the State of Israel could only become the worst of all States" (in *Jews in Eastern Europe,* May 1965, p. 16).

Appendix

I

Legal Acts of the Soviet Government and Resolutions and Pronouncements of the Communist Party Pertaining to Religious Matters

1. Declaration of Rights of the Peoples of Russia (*Deklaratsia prav narodov Rosii*), of November 2, 1917
2. Ordinance (*Postanovlenie*) of the Government Ordering Religious Organizations to Transfer Their Schools to the People's Commissariat of Education, of December 11, 1917
3. Decree Nationalizing All Land, Including the Land of the Church and the Monasteries of December 4, 1917
4. Decree of the Council of People's Commissars on Civil Marriages, Children and Civil Acts Registry, of December 18, 1917
5. Order (*Prikaz*) of the People's Commissar of Social Welfare (*Gosudarstvennovo Prizrenia*) Withholding State Funds for Churches, Clergy, etc., of January 20, 1918
6. Decree of the Council of People's Commissars "On Separation of Church from State and School from Church" (*Ob Otdelenii Tserkvi ot Gosudarstva i Shkoly ot Tserkvi*), of January 23, 1918 (basic law on religious matters)
7. Constitution of RSFSR Adopted by the Fifth Congress of the Soviets, of July 10, 1918 (paragraph thirteen)
8. Ordinance "For Carrying Out the Decree on Separation of Church from State and School from State (Instruction)," by the People's Commissariat of Justice, of August 24, 1918
9. Circular on the Problem of Separation of the Church from the State, by the VIII Department of the People's Commissariat of Justice, of January 3, 1919
10. Circular of the People's Commissariat of Public Education on Teaching Religious Doctrines to Persons Below the Age of Eighteen, of March 3, 1919
11. Explanation of the People's Commissariat of Education on Teaching Religious Subjects, of April 23, 1921
12. Edict of the People's Commissariat of Justice "On the Liquidation of Mummies" (*O Likvidatsii Moshchei*), of August 27, 1920

13. Program of the Russian Communist Party (RKP b) adopted at the Eighth Congress of the Party (paragraph thirteen), of March 1919

14. Resolution of the Eighth Congress of the Communist Party "About Political Propaganda and Cultural-Educational Work in Villages" ("O Politicheskoi Propagande i Kulturno-Prosvetilelnoi Rabote v Derevne"), of March 1919

15. Resolution of the Tenth Congress of the Communist Party on Political Education and Tasks of the Party in Agitation and Propaganda (*O Glavpolitprosviete i Agitatsionno-Propagandicheskikh Zadachakh Partii*), of March 1921

16. Ordinance of the Central Committee of the Communist Party "On the Organization of Antireligious Propaganda and on the Violation of Paragraph Thirteen of the Program" (*O Postanovke Antireligioznoi Propagandy i o Narushenii Punkta 13 Programmy*), of 1921

17. "Directives of the Central Committee of the Party to the Soviet and Party Organs on the Question of the Attitude to Sects and to Policy in Relation to Religious Groups Generally" (*Direktivy TsK RKP (b) Sovietskim i Partiinym Organam po Voprosu ob Otnoshenii k Sektam i Politiki v Otnoshenii Religioznikh Grup Vobshche*), of 1922

18. Resolution of the Twelfth Congress of the Communist Party, "On Propaganda, the Press, and Agitation" (*O Propagande, Pechati, i Agitatsii*), of April 1923

19. Resolution of the Twelfth Congress of the Communist Party "On the Organization of Antireligious Propaganda and Agitation (*O Postanovke Antireligioznoi Agitatsii i Propagandy*), of April 1923

20. Resolution of the Thirteenth Congress of the Communist Party on "Work in the Villages" (*O Rabote v Derevne*), of May 1924

21. Circular of the People's Commissariat of Internal Affairs "On the Performance of Religious Ceremonies Within the Homes of Believers," of 1925

22. Law "On Religious Associations" (*O Religioznykh Obiedinieniakh*), of April 8, 1929. Edict of the All-Russian Central Executive Committee and Council of People's Commissars (Basic law).

23. "Instructions on Rights and Obligations of Religious Associations" (*O Pravakh i Obiazannostiakh Religioznykh Obedinienii*), of the People's Commissariat of Interior, October 1, 1929 (basic law)

24. Decree of the Presidium of the Central Executive Committee of the Soviets Establishing a Standing Commission on Matters of Cults, of April 8, 1929

25. Decree of the Presidium of the Central Executive Committee of the Soviets Ordering "the unconditional elimination of additional restrictions upon the disenfranchised and their families," of March 1930

26. Decree of the Council of People's Commissars of the USSR introducing the continuous work week
27. Resolution of the Sixteenth Congress of the Communist Party "On the Struggle Against Distortions of the Party Line in the Kolkhoz Movement" (*O Borbe c Iskrivleniiami Partlinni v Kolkhoznom Dvizhenii*), (section 6), of 1930
28. The statutes on secondary schools of 1934
29. Amendment of Article Four of the Constitution of RSFSR by the Fourteenth Congress of Soviets, of May 1929
30. The "Stalin Constitution" of 1936 (Article 124, Article 135 etc.)
31. Ordinance of the Central Committee of the Communist Party "On the Organization of Scientific-Enlightment Propaganda" (*Ob Organizatsii Nauchno-Prosvetitelnoi Propagandy*), of 1944
32. Ordinance of the Central Committee of the Communist Party "On the Huge Deficiencies in the Scientific-Atheist Propaganda and the Means of Improving Them (*O Krupnykh Nedostatkakh v Nauchno-Ateisticheskoi Propagande i Merakh Ei Uluchsheniia*), Postanovlenie TsK KPSS, of July 7, 1954
33. Ordinance of the Central Committee of the Communist Party "On the Mistakes in Conducting Scientific-Atheist Propaganda Among the Population" (*Ob Oshibkakh v Provedenii Nauchno-Ateisticheskoi Propagandy Sredi Naselenia*). Postanovlenie TsK KPSS, November 10, 1954
34. Ordinance of the Central Committee of the Communist Party "On the Tasks of Party Propaganda in Present-Day Conditions" (*Postanovlenie TsK KPSS 'O Zadachakh Partiinoi Propagandy v Sovremennykh Usloviakh"*), of January 9, 1960
35. Program of the Communist Party of the Soviet Union, adopted at the Twenty-second Congress, of 1961
36. Criminal Code of RSFSR, articles 70, 142, 143, 227 (and comparable articles in the Criminal Codes of other republics), of 1960, amended in 1962
37. Edict of the Presidium of the Supreme Soviet of the RSFSR on "Strengthening the Fight Against Persons Avoiding Socially Useful Work," (*Ob Usilenii Borby s Litsami Uklaniashchiuisiia od Obshchestvennovo Poleznovo Truda*), of May 4, 1961 (identical laws issued in other Soviet Republics)
38. Ordinance of the Plenum of the Central Committee of the Communist Party of the Soviet Union "On Present Tasks of the Ideological Work of the Party" (*Ob Ocherednikh Zadachakh Ideologicheskoi Raboty Partii*), of June 18–21, 1963

39. "On Measures to Strengthen Atheist Education of the People" (*O Meropriiatiakh po Usileniiu Ateisticheskovo Vospitaniia Naseleniia*), Instructions of the Ideological Commission at the Central Committee of Communist Party, approved by the Central Committee of the Party, 1964.

II

Administration and Supervision
of Religious Associations*

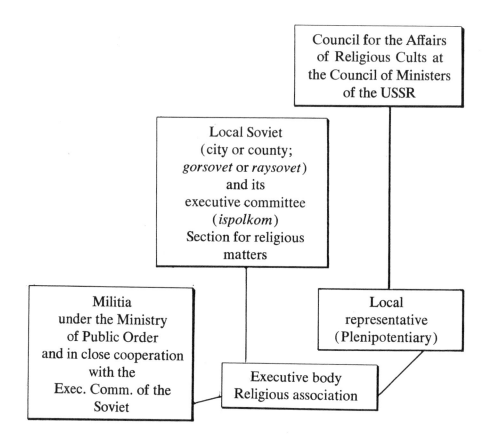

* Supervision is also exercised by the *Communist Party Committees*, by the *State security agencies* (KGB) and the *Prokurators*.

III

*Composition of Religious Societies
and Groups of Believers*
(According to the laws in force)*

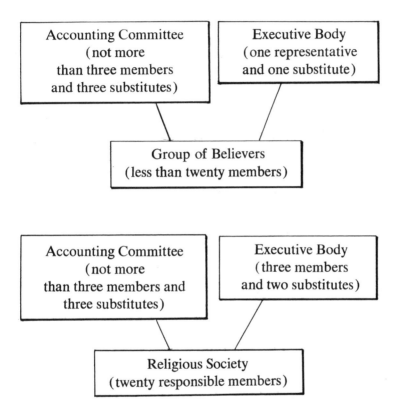

Accounting Committee
(not more
than three members
and three substitutes)

Executive Body
(one representative
and one substitute)

Group of Believers
(less than twenty members)

Accounting Committee
(not more
than three members and
three substitutes)

Executive Body
(three members
and two substitutes)

Religious Society
(twenty responsible members)

* Executive Committees and Accounting Committees are elected at the general
assembly of the "religious society" or "group of believers."

Groups of believers, while provided for in the law, do not seem to be able to
function freely.

Religious societies *must not have more than twenty registered members* responsible
to the authorities.

INDEX

Abram, L., 177-178
Abramski, Yehezkel, 129, 139n
Ahad Ha'am (Ginzberg, Asher), 2, 69
Alaiev, I. H., Rabbi, 107
Alexandrov, Shmuel, 130
Alma-Ata, *Bet Shehita* in, 106
Alter, Victor, 147
Altshuler, M., 99n, 161, 219n
America, (Jesuit Weekly), 134
American Jewish Year Book (AJYB), 67n, 68n, 99n, 100n, 125n, 139n, 192n
Antireligious campaign, "Battle against God," 131; in 1927-28, 42; confiscation of religious articles, 131; against calendar writers, 134; against circumcision, 147-150, 152; to liquidate *hedorim,* 177; to liquidate religious cemeteries, 194-207; confiscation of religious articles, 131; *see* Holidays and Observances. Anti-Saturday campaign, Anti-Holidays campaign, Sabbath
Antireligious education, 171, 191n
Antiparasite laws, amendment of, 21-22, 64
Antireligious literature, 9-10, 211-213; against High Holidays and Passover, 83, 213; against Jewish calendar, 136; against circumcision, 152, 154-155, 156, 159, 161; against religious education, 182; Marxist, 209-210; Soviet Yiddish, 211-212; intensive publication of, (1927-1935), 212; against clergy, 216; *Yudaism Bes Prikras,* 216-218
Antireligious propaganda, 9-10, 209-219; among national minorities, 10; party pronouncements on, 18-19; in schools, 6, 18-19, 213; and Jewish holidays, 82, 93; by Jewish Communists, 83, 164, 177, 210-212; against Jewish calendar, 136; against circumcision, 147-150, 152, 159-160, 162-165, 166; against *hedorim,* 176-179, 182; against Jewish burials and cemeteries, 203-204; in terms of Marxist ideology, 209-210; against clergy, 210-211, 215-216; "community trials," 211-212, 214; anti-religious literature, 212; categories of, 213, 217; "political trials", 214; effect on young and old Jews, 214-215; aimed at non-Jews, 216; intensification of, toward end of 1950's, 217, 219n; in the 1960's, 217-218.
Anti-Soviet propaganda, 51, 63, 64, 136
Apikoires, 75, 98n, 109, 125n, 178, 212, 219n
Aptekman, D. M., 169n
Armenian Church, 137
Aronov, Zalman Y., 29-32
Artels, 71-72, 75, 160
Asch, Sholem, 146-147
Auerbach, Efraim, 67n
Ayin, C., 165

INDEX

108-111; and religious weddings, 111-120; and bar-mitzvah rites, 120-124; and circumcision, 102, 106, 108, 110, 118, 122, 123; and burials, 194-208; antireligious propaganda against, 213
Religious Societies, 10-14, 27-35, 66, 223-224; and collection and expenditures of funds, 11, 30-33; executive bodies of, 11-12; vs. groups of believers 13-14; legal status of, 14-15; liquidation of, 13-14; meetings and conventions of, 12; registration of, 11, 14-15; reporting of, 12; surveillance of, 12-13, 22-27; and use of buildings, 15, 29-33; legal and illegal, 45-46; dissolution of, 66; burial societies (Hevra Kadishah), 194, 202-203, 206
"Religious" vs. "national" identity, 1-2, 6, 148, 163-164, 198, 213
Religious weddings, 111-120; legal status of, 111, 119; restrictions against, 111; legal decisions and circulars concerning, 111; hupah, 113, 114, 115, 117; rate of Jewish intermarriage, 113-114; hapuh zal, 114-115; in Ukraine and Belorussia, 115; matchmakers (shadhanim), 117; differences between Western and Oriental Jewish communities in, 117; response of Soviet rabbis concerning, 118; in Leningrad, 155-156
Responsa, 118, 137
Riabushin, Vladimir, 73
Riga: matzoh baking in, 88; mikvah in, 110; Yom Kippur services in, 183; Jewish community of, 190; cemetery in, 202
Ritual bathhouses (mikvahs), 108-111; use of among Jewish population, 108, 109; attempts to close, 108-109, 110; after 1945, 109-110
Rogachev, 159
Roman Catholics, 87
Rosenberg, E., Rabbi, 45, 130, 134
Rosenblat, Moshe, 214
Rosh Hashonah, 69, 74, 76, 78, 214. See also High Holidays
Rostov: "trial of the yeshiva" in, 178
Rovno (Ukrainian SSR), 202
RSFSR (Russian Soviet Federated Socialist Republic), 150; constitution of, 7-8; anti-parasite law of, 21-22; criminal code of, 19-21, 174, 196-197
Rubinstein, Yosef, 99n
Rumanian armies, 60
Russian Orthodox Church: World War II revival of, 17; religious articles removed from, 131; Moscow Patriarchate of, 137; schools of, 176, 184, 188; antireligious propaganda against, 210
Russokovska, Hanna, 52, 53
Sabbath, 69-74, 97, 135, 206; status before October Revolution, 69-70; "anti-Saturday campaign," and Jewish protest against, 70-74; protest of Poltava Jewish Community Council, 70-71; and Jewish employment, 69-70, 72-73; synagogue attendance on, 73-74, 81; in Leningrad, 155-156
Salanter, Israel, 206
Saltzberg, Joseph B., 192n
Samarkand (Uzbek SSR): antireligious campaign against Jews in, 106, 107; alleged Kosher cattle slaughtering in, 107; attacking ritual bathing, 110; see also Oriental Jews, Bukhara
Sambor (Ukrainian SSR), 202
Saratov, 156, 191n